7

For Kevin,
  a Penn Stater
though and through!
Hope you enjoy
the book.
    Best regards,
      Ken Rappoport

Playing for JoePa

Jordan Hyman and Ken Rappoport

Foreword by Jay Paterno

SP

SPORTS
PUBLISHING
L.L.C.

SportsPublishingLLC.com

ISBN-10: 1-59670-176-5
ISBN-13: 978-1-59670-176-2

Publishers: Peter L. Bannon and Joseph J. Bannon Sr.
Senior managing editor: Susan M. Moyer
Editor: Doug Hoepker
Art director: K. Jeffrey Higgerson
Cover design: Joseph Brumleve
Project manager: Kathryn R. Holleman
Photo editor: Erin Linden-Levy

Sports Publishing L.L.C.
804 North Neil Street
Champaign, IL 61820
Phone: 1-877-424-2665
Fax: 217-363-2073
www.SportsPublishingLLC.com

Printed in the United States of America

Library of Congress Cataloging-in-Publication Data

Hyman, Jordan, 1977-
Playing for Joe Pa / Jordan Hyman and Ken Rappoport ; foreword by Jay Paterno.
    p. cm.
Includes index.
   ISBN-13: 978-1-59670-176-2 (hard cover : alk. paper)
   ISBN-10: 1-59670-176-5 (hard cover : alk. paper)
   1. Paterno, Joe, 1926- 2. Football coaches--United States. 3. Pennsylvania State University--Football--History. 4. Penn State Nittany Lions (Football team) --History. 5. Football--Coaching. I. Rappoport, Ken. II. Title.
GV939.P37H88 2007
796.332092--dc22
                              2007013429

To the Paternos and the extended family that is Penn State.

CONTENTS

FOREWORD

ANOTHER YEAR HAS COME AND GONE in Happy Valley. On the last afternoon of 2006, a day before we finished our season with a 20-10 victory over Tennessee in the Outback Bowl, I stood near a stage in the Tampa Convention Center awaiting the start of a pep rally. More than 1,000 miles from campus, 8,000 fans had gathered to celebrate Penn State and all that the University means to them.

The Blue Band marched in to the familiar drumbeats of its grand entrance into Beaver Stadium. Hearing the roar of the crowd as the first few notes of "Hail to The Lion" blasted through that vast hall, chills shot up my spine and tears welled in my eyes. Witnessing the immense pride of so many fellow alumni, I knew they shared my emotions.

Why does Penn State stir such passion in so many? Because it is home, it is family; it is a place that always welcomes us back with open arms. It is a place where we arrived unsure of the future, or as the Alma Mater says, "Shapeless in the Hands of Fate. . . ." It is a place that prepared us, sent us on our way, and it instills fierce pride in nearly all of us.

The Penn State experience is similar for most students, but for the people in this book, their participation in Penn State football gave them a new family element. It brought them together with young men from all over the country and from diverse cultural and socioeconomic backgrounds. Football at Penn State is a family—not in a clichéd, campaign-slogan-type way. It is the great American experience of the melting pot. In the huddle you see black and white, rich and poor, Christians, Jews, and Muslims holding hands bound in a common purpose. Some of that, however, exists at other universities and other football programs across the country. Which begs the question, what makes Penn State different? What makes recruits and their parents year after year say they were impressed by the family atmosphere at Penn State? What makes our student-athletes say—often after just one year of school—that this is home?

Perhaps it can best be summed up by today's news. With the announcement of Nick Saban's contract with Alabama, there are now five head coaches earning more than $3 million a year to coach college football; 11 head coaches are making more than $2 million a year. Coaches jump ship for the next big contract or hold their own school hostage using the NFL or another university as leverage.

At the student-athlete level, Penn State's program has never been about business. The coaches have remained loyal to the university and to the student-athlete. Coaches make decisions with the best interests of the student-athlete in mind. Sometimes wins are sacrificed for the academic well being of an individual or a group of individual students. How many administrations would stand by that today?

From Bob Higgins to Rip Engle to Joe Paterno, we've had great leadership by visionary men who never lost sight of one fact: Every student-athlete at Penn State is someone's child. That child was raised by a mother, a father, or maybe both, or perhaps by a grandparent or an uncle or aunt. The adults in the child's life made sacrifices and put countless hours of effort into that young man. Nearing the end of the high school years, they prepared to hand their loved one to a university and its coach.

The head coaches at Penn State have never forgotten their enormous responsibility, nor have they neglected the bond of trust the parents or guardians of student-athletes have with our school. The people at this university are constantly reminded by Joe Paterno that, "We are not selling used cars when we recruit. We are dealing with people. Treat these young men as you would want your own children treated." That is what it has always been about—treating these young men as though they were our own children. As I write this, it has been nearly seven years since I became a parent, and in seeing my own children grow, the words of our head coach have rung truer than ever.

It is that welcoming atmosphere, that "adoption" of these young men as children of our own, that has created a family at Penn State. It has been the education they have been encouraged—in some cases prodded—to attain that has made these student-athletes proud. These things and more are what make one family member encourage other members to attend Penn State as well.

Nearing the end of the 2004 season, we stood alone at the bottom of the Big Ten. The program seemed lost; the ideals and values of our program seemed quaint and outdated in the 21st century. During those dark days I thought about Penn State and the responsibility I had as one of our coaches. On my early morning walks with my dog, I imagined the eyes of those before us looking down on me. Many were people long since passed—Ridge Riley, Rip Engle, Steve Suhey. Some were people still living. I could see the black and white photos of so many All-Americans, from "Mother" Dunn to the photo of John Cappelletti I keep in my office.

Displaying our trademark loyalty, our football family rallied together and helped us push through the tough times. Since that down period, we have won 22 of 27 games including two New Year's Day bowl games. Most important, we have returned Penn State and our family values back to the national consciousness.

Here are the stories of so many outstanding families. The Higgins/Suhey family, the Jacksons, the Hamiltons, the Conlins. The Harrises and the Gumans, the Ganters, the Sanduskys, and many more. They all came from different places and different backgrounds, but all were welcomed and given a place at the table at Penn State.

Every family member also came with his own dreams and lofty aspirations. Many realized those dreams. Others fell short, but all left Penn State better prepared for life than when they arrived. Penn State, too, was made a better place for having had them here.

As we move toward the future, more Penn State family members will join us. When we welcome our 2007 recruiting class, we will be welcoming our 20th and 21st father-son combinations to have played for Joe Paterno. Can a grandfather-grandson combination be far behind? With the continued pride and loyalty of the Penn State family, don't bet against it.

For the Glory of Old State,
Jay Paterno
football letterman 1989

January 4, 2007

one

THE BRADLEYS

JOE PATERNO IS TOM BRADLEY'S FATHER. Well, not really. But if you listen long enough to Bradley—Penn State's affable defensive coordinator—speak of Paterno, then you'll understand. Part of it is how deftly he bounces between memories of his father, Sam, who passed away a few years ago, and Paterno, who's been part of his life for the last 32 years. Much of it is how closely aligned Sam Bradley's values and philosophies on life were with the values and philosophies Paterno has held close to heart through six decades of coaching football.

"Both were strong disciplinarians," says Tom, the longest-tenured (in consecutive years) assistant on the Penn State football coaching staff. "I never had any trouble with that. I understood rules and regulations. That was old hat for me."

That was Sam Bradley. He loved his seven children, four girls and three boys. But if one of his kids got busted dunking another kid's body part in the school urinal, then that child would meet Dad's wrath—and occasionally that of his belt. Sam's children watched the curse words when Dad was around. They respected his authority. And when the 11 p.m. horn blew signaling a shift change at one of Johnstown's steel mills, Sam's kids double-timed it home.

Playing for JoePa

"When I first left for college, my buddy took me, and my dad didn't get up from the table," says Tom, a lightly recruited defensive back who arrived in University Park, Pennsylvania, in 1975. Sam was never much for long speeches or tearful goodbyes. He'd write one-word notes, telling his kids to "Study" or "Focus." Brief were his messages, but the point was never hard to miss.

As a freshman entering college, Tom was following in the footsteps—and by then, the legacy—of older brother Jimmy. That made his parting words for Tom all the clearer. His dad asked him, "You know the difference between right and wrong?"

"Sure do, Dad," Tom answered.

"Well Goddamn don't ever forget it!" Sam barked. "See ya later. When's the first game?"

By the time Tom left for Penn State, Sam had already witnessed Jimmy's four-year career, both the realization of on-field success and the fulfillment of off-field promises made by Paterno and his staff. Perhaps that's where Sam and Joe truly meshed. At home in Johnstown, Sam was boss. At home in University Park, Joe was boss. For Tom and his brothers, determining where one man's influence ended and the other's began is the beauty of their story.

✳ ✳ ✳

Sam and wife Cass raised three future Penn State football players in a house in Johnstown's eighth ward, four or five blocks from the office where Sam worked as a cardiologist. The office was located in a house next to Memorial Hospital, so Sam often read EKGs for hospital patients. In fact, for nearly two decades Sam, a University of Pittsburgh basketball player who'd graduated from Georgetown med school, read EKGs for the whole city. Cass worked as a secretary in the office while also running the household.

At home it was two kids to a room. Jim and Tom bunked together for 10 or 11 years. When Jim departed for college, youngest brother Matt moved into the room. Tom would drive Jim nuts when he'd keep them both up late listening to Pittsburgh Pirates games by radio. "I'd be yelling at him, 'Turn that damn thing off!' says Jim, chuckling.

The Bradleys

"But Tom knew all the plays. He was really into statistics. It was a premonition towards coaching, I guess."

As parents, Sam and Cass never discouraged their kids' athletic pursuits. It would have been hard to do so in Johnstown, where no matter the time, kids were always up for a game. There was a playground behind the family house, and on weekends, there could be as many as three football games going at once: oldest, middle, and youngest kids. If you were talented enough, you'd get promoted to a game with the older kids. When one guy got called to dinner, another took his place.

The playground's "fields" were asphalt, the games "semi-contact." Matt, the brash, athletically gifted youngest son, once dove to catch a touchdown pass and broke his arm and ankle upon landing on the pavement. "I caught the pass, though," he told his father.

The Bradleys had a tiny backyard, but one year, says Jim, Tom asked for a basketball hoop for his birthday. Sam, recognizing an opportunity to keep the kids active yet close to home, paved the entire yard, creating a court fully enclosed by house, garage, cement wall, and fence. Sam, who'd been an electrician while stationed in Guam with the Army, rigged a homemade lighting system to illuminate the court, which made the Bradleys' home the main neighborhood gathering ground all summer long. "It was lit up like Yankee Stadium," recalls Tom.

True to form, though, there were rules, Sam's rules: Games had to end by midnight and no swearing was allowed. Sam, whose bedroom overlooked the hoop, heard everything. Between heated games—"There was no out of bounds," Tom says, "so guys would fly into the house, the window would get busted. . ."—kids would discuss bogus plans for the evening to throw Sam off their scent. "We'd make stuff up, like I'm going over to church tonight, or going over to the library," Tom says, chuckling. "Every once in a while my dad would yell out, 'You think I'm falling for that S-H-I-T?' We had a lot of fun."

And they played a lot of sports. The Bradleys all played football, basketball, baseball, and ran track well into high school. Before Paterno, the boys learned their football basics from Fran Zima, who coached their first organized teams and remains the athletic director at

Playing for JoePa

Bishop McCort High School—Jim, Tom, and Matt's alma mater. Zima arranged for his youth football teams to use the high school's equipment and facilities. The youth teams all had nice uniforms and pads, and Zima drilled his young players on fundamentals the same way he'd coached older boys.

Zima had the support of parents in working their kids overtime, and it paid off for the Bradleys. In a mill town loaded with football talent, Jim rose to the fore first, receiving more than 80 Division I college scholarship offers in football and basketball. Cass wanted Jim to consider the Naval Academy, but Jim, who used to go on the occasional medical rounds with his dad, was already thinking med school, which Navy did not offer. The University of Miami, another favorite, was too far away for a kid who hadn't traveled much beyond the 80-mile radius surrounding Johnstown—Pittsburgh to the west and State College to the east.

Jerry Sandusky, then a Penn State assistant, came to Johnstown first. Then Jim and his parents drove to State College, including a stop at Joe and Sue Paterno's house for dinner, a recruiting-weekend tradition that lives on today. Joe was blunt. He confirmed the four-year scholarship offer, telling Sam and Cass that their son would be required to attend class and study hall and to earn good marks. He would have to graduate. And Joe said the magic words: "We're gonna take care of him."

Cass, who'd been conflicted, was now on board. Inside, Sam was nodding the whole time. Jim could have played sports pretty much anywhere that met his liking, from coast to coast. But clearly Penn State was the place where Jim's upbringing would continue in a similar path to the one Sam had molded for his first son. That made the choice easy for Sam, and subsequently, for Jim.

Tom remembers it this way: "They were talking, and my brother said to Joe, 'Coach, you haven't told me what position I'm going to be playing.' My dad said, 'I'll answer that question, Coach: Whatever damn position you tell him to play! And if he doesn't like it, kick him in the you know where and send him home.' Joe said, 'Boy, that's a good answer.'

"The one thing that was always amazing about my father was that he never asked much about football," Tom continues. "It was always

The Bradleys

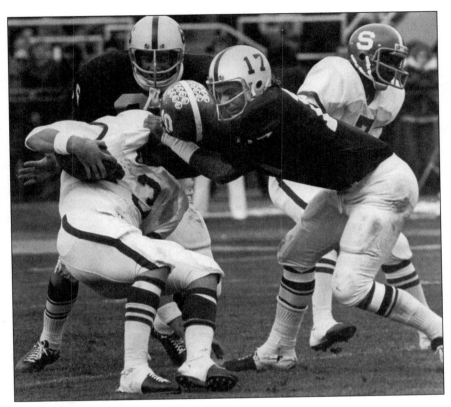

Jim Bradley, No. 17.

about school. And in my house, believe me, Joe was always right. No ifs, ands, or buts. He was the boss and that was it, period."

✳ ✳ ✳

Jim Bradley was a terrific athlete who thrived in Penn State's system. He led the undefeated 1973 team in interceptions with four and in 1974, the senior was named a co-captain for the 10-2 Nittany Lions. But Jim's play isn't what drew Tom in 1975 and later Matt in '78 to Happy Valley. His positive experience off the field did. Jim told his blood brothers about his Blue and White brothers, the bond they'd learned to share. He discovered truth in Paterno's system, especially when it came to stressing academics above football.

Playing for JoePa

In the spring of 1978, Jim needed to take an organic chemistry lab that was only being offered that semester. The class conflicted with spring football practice, but it wasn't a conflict for Paterno. When Jim told him about the class, Paterno told him to take it, even though it meant missing one, sometimes two practices per week. "Here I am his starting cornerback," Jim says, "and he's saying, 'No, you gotta do that now.'"

A year later Jim decided to make the Bradley name a legacy at Georgetown, too, by applying to the same med school his father had attended. Jim asked Paterno for a letter of recommendation, and Paterno responded by asking Jim who else would be writing a letter for him. Jim said he planned to approach the dean of his science school, but Paterno nixed the idea. Instead the coach called John Oswald, University president at the time, on Jim's behalf.

"I get an interview at Georgetown and I'm nervous—very nervous," says Jim, who has been the Pittsburgh Steelers team doctor since 1991. "I'm thinking, 'Here's this dumb football player with all these smart kids.' I walk in the room and there's this big German guy. He looks at me over these tiny wire-rimmed glasses and goes, 'Who the heck do you know? Look at these letters!' Soon as he said that I became really relaxed.

"I later went back up to Joe's office. I said, 'Coach, I never knew you liked me this much.' He said, 'Well, sometimes you have to stretch the truth a little bit.' I mean, he would stand behind me and literally scream at the top of his lungs about how bad I was, and then he'd write a letter like that. But that's just the way he was."

At least most of the time. With Jim and then Tom, who lettered in 1977 and '78, it took a kick in the butt to spark anger that in turn produced their best play on the gridiron. With Matt, a sometimes troublemaker with a deep compassionate side, motivation was equal to positive reinforcement. Matt could get down on himself. Sam knew it, and he handled his youngest son differently in that regard. Tom might drop 22 points in a basketball game only to have Sam rail on him about not using his left hand enough. Matt, on the other hand, would instantly hang his head, so Dad would build him back up. Joe took a similar approach. Like he has hundreds of times, Paterno recognized

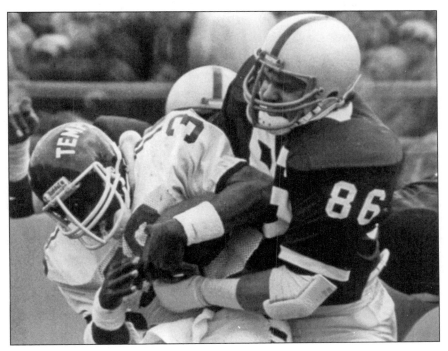

Matt Bradley, No. 86.

the differences in the Bradley kids and handled each in unique fashion without, of course, abandoning the system and the rules that defined his program then and now.

Talent-wise, Tom will readily admit he lagged behind his brothers. But he worked hard, deciding early on, in part because of Fran Zima's influence, that he wanted to enter the coaching profession. So he worked like every day was a job interview. At Penn State, that's essentially how it happened. In 1978 Tom received a call from Joe's secretary, informing him that Joe wanted to see him. Tom was miffed. He and his buddies were all for a solid practical joke from time to time, but maybe they'd gone too far this time. Or maybe Tom really was in for a tongue-lashing from Coach.

It was no prank. Paterno was as blunt as a nail head, but his message was unexpected.

"You want to coach here?" he asked Tom. "J.T. White is retiring."

Bradley was speechless. "Uh . . . okay," was all he could muster.

"Alright, don't know what I can tell you," Paterno said, "but I'll let you know."

Bradley nodded, blew out of the office, and immediately sought his buddies. He couldn't contain himself: "Hey, guess who Joe hired?"

✳ ✳ ✳

Tom Bradley has spent more than 30 years now earning every promotion given to him by Paterno, but he's as grateful now for the opportunity as he was as a fresh-faced graduate assistant with the 1979 squad. Just as Sam knew what was best for his kids, Joe's known what's been best for his coaches. For example, before he was named Sandusky's replacement as defensive coordinator in 2000, Bradley had coached Penn State receivers, defensive backs, defensive ends, linebackers, special teams, and even served as recruiting coordinator. Paterno made sure Bradley built a multidimensional rèsumè.

"The one time I didn't want to switch," Tom says, "his line was, 'A coach is a coach is a coach. If you can coach here, you can coach there.' Some guys coach the same position their whole lives. They never realize what someone has to go through when the shoe's on the other foot. I really appreciate that he gave me those opportunities."

Tom's career has served different purposes. Personally, it's allowed him to grow as a coach, to use his own experiences to help others. He's endeared himself to generations of Penn State players because he was once one of them. A little comedy doesn't hurt, either: Tom can impersonate Paterno's high-pitched gesticulations with the best of them. He knows all the stories, to the point where Paterno will sometimes preface his anecdotes with, "Everyone's interested except Tommy. He's heard this one 20 times." He's even been chewed out for showing up late to meetings, which in Paterno Time is five to 10 minutes early.

"Guys will say, 'Coach, you ever been in the doghouse?'" Tom says. "I say, 'Oh yeah. The water was warm, it was crowded, jump right in.' They're always amazed."

The Bradleys

Tom Bradley.

For Tom's family, his sustained presence in Happy Valley has connected the Bradleys even closer to the Penn State and Paterno families. For years before he passed away, Sam would regularly make the two-hour, 86-mile trek from Johnstown to State College to watch the Lions play at Beaver Stadium. The faces in the car might change, but two remained the same—Sam and his grandson, Jim Kanuch.

Since about the time he could pronounce JoePa, Kanuch—his mother, Kitty, is Tom's older sister—had blue and white stars in his eyes. He didn't miss a home game for nearly 10 years. On those glorious football Saturdays, Tom would sneak his nephew into Penn State's locker room, introduce him to players, and send him off beaming with a stash of free swag in his hand—hats, jackets, shorts, shoes, whatever.

"It was good being young and taking your friends up there," Kanuch says. "They're like, 'Ohhhhh, we went into Penn State's locker room!' By that point I was like, 'Yeah, I've been in there a couple hundred times.' It was fun. I was a fan favorite in middle school because of that."

Playing for JoePa

It came as no surprise that before Kanuch graduated Johnstown's Westmont Hilltop High in 2002, he chose to play college ball at Penn State. For a kid who'd idolized wide receiver O.J. McDuffie, who remembers watching one of his grandmother's old tapes showing his uncle Matt intercept Pitt quarterback Dan Marino, who shared countless "We Are" shouting matches with Grandpa Sam, this was destiny realized.

Kanuch redshirted in 2002, played three seasons as a reserve in the secondary, then passed up his final year of eligibility in '06 to pursue a public relations career. In his last season, Penn State went 11-1, won the Big Ten title, beat Florida State in the Orange Bowl, and finished No. 3 in every major poll. Not a bad way to go out.

Yet Kanuch's college career spanned sad occasions, too. Sam, the patriarch, passed away in October 2001. Less than two years later, Tom showed up at Matt's house. He'd been unable to reach his brother on the phone. Matt was sitting in his La-Z-Boy recliner with a crossword puzzle when Tom stepped through the glass sliding door. "Why aren't you working today?" Tom asked his brother, before walking up to him and realizing he was dead. At 42 years old, he'd suffered an aneurysm.

"I love my brother and miss him every day; hard to believe almost three years for him," Tom says of his brother's 2003 passing. "That was a tough time for my family."

A few seconds later Tom laughs. There are too many good memories to dwell on that last day. "You get together with the guys and they'll be telling stories about my brother Matt, and I'll go, 'Oh boy, yeah, I remember when he did that,'" he says. "It's always amazing. People go, 'Oh, I knew your brother.' I go, 'Which one? My brother Jimmy's like a saint. My brother Matt was like the devil. Just so I know where I'm starting from, let me know which one you're talking about.'"

When Cass passed away not long after Matt's death, it was the close of a sad chapter in the family's lineage. The toll of losing a husband and son so close together had weighed heavily on Tom's mother.

"It's hard to believe," Tom says, almost to himself, "but I'm sure they're up there complaining [about my coaching decisions]: 'What'd

The Bradleys

Jim Kanuch.

you do that for?' I can hear them. As long as you keep them in the vision of your heart, you never lose them."

It's helped that he's had other family to lean on in the past five years. "I called Joe right away [after Matt died]," he continues. "And you know, Coach, he's a lot more emotional than most people would think. When my father died, the first guy in the church was Joe Paterno. He had to come to [Matt's] funeral and then to my mother's. . . . He's so loyal to our family. He talks about family and he means it."

＊ ＊ ＊

Jim Bradley's steady hands have performed surgery on multimillionaire athletes. When the Steelers play, he's a sea of calm, assessing injury, making quick decisions. But when Penn State's on TV, no med school training can settle his nerves.

"Oh my gosh," he says, "I can't take it. I'm telling you, I get nervous, I get up, move around. If we're at home watching on TV, my wife leaves the room because I throw things."

Playing for JoePa

A lot of the anxiety is due to his close friendship with Tom, with whom he speaks nearly every day. But Jim's also yelling because of Joe, the team's figure of stability since 1966, when he took over for Rip Engle as head coach. Jim paces for the program, because of who and what the Penn State name represents to him. Paterno, self-effacing as he is generous, loves to paint himself as a caretaker of someone else's program. He'll say he's a guy lucky enough to have followed Engle, just as someone, Tom Bradley perhaps, will be lucky enough to one day follow him. But you don't spend 40 years as head coach at one school without carving out, even unintentionally, a legacy of your own. To the Bradleys, that legacy is people—the players and coaches and parents and grandkids and friends who benefited from Penn State football; the players and coaches and parents and grandkids and friends who benefited from one another.

"Great organizations start at the top and trickle down," says Jim, a dual nod to both Penn State and his current employer, the Steelers. "It's like your house. You had the mother, the father, then the kids. It was the same way [at Penn State]. There was Joe and it kind of went down from there. Everyone knew where they were in the pecking order.

"With the players, it's like a brotherhood. Once you've gone through it, it's kind of like going to war with somebody. There's a bond you can't break. I get calls from all over the country from old teammates or [their] younger brothers or something. 'Should I get surgery here? Who's the best guy to do it?' I haven't talked to them for like a year, but they'll call and it's like I talked to them yesterday. There's a familiarity with the program."

Tom has seen the legacy grow with Paterno's nurturing, or more specifically, his acute memory. Paterno might be a step slower jogging out of the tunnel, but his mind can spit out names and places like a digital college football encyclopedia. He recalls friends who retired 30 years ago from Pennsylvania high school coaching jobs. He can tell you where Wilmerding, Pennsylvania, is, sans Mapquest. He knows the kids he's recruited from Monaca, Pennsylvania, kids whose own kids have long since graduated State. Joe even knows where the library used to be at Duquesne High School. Or the delicatessen to hit next time you're in Ambridge, Pennsylvania.

The Bradleys

It's the same with Nittany Lions past. Kanuch recalls stories Paterno would tell in which he'd drop the names of guys who played 40, 50 years ago. He alludes to Jack Ham and Franco Harris even though those legends retired from the game before today's Penn Staters were born. That's his history. That's program history. That's family history.

Tom has watched Joe open doors with phone calls one day and break up meetings the next because someone, somewhere needs a favor. He never forgets.

"When you're in a car with Coach and there's no one around, there's no one buggin' him, and you're just driving," says Tom, pausing to picture the scene in the car, "and he brings up stuff about yourself, and you're thinking, 'How did he know that? I never thought he knew that.'

"A lot of people just see him on stage," he says, continuing. "They don't get to see him in these moments of one on one. Even sportswriters don't get him one on one. There's a trust factor. He's telling you different things. And I always find it interesting—the car rides, recruiting—they're amazing. I love when you take Joe in the car, because you've made the trip to the school at least 100 times, but you'll be driving with him going, 'Oh boy, I hope I'm going the right way.'"

Of course, for Tom, there's only ever been one right way. And time and time again, it's led him back to Joe Paterno's house.

two

THE BUZINS

RICH BUZIN'S HECTIC DAY at the office was interrupted by a phone call. "Hey, Rich—Joe Paterno's on the phone!"

It had been nearly 30 years since Buzin had played on Paterno's first team in 1966, so his colleague had to forgive Rich for adopting a skeptical look. "I figured somebody was pulling my leg," Rich recalls.

Nope. It was actually Paterno, calling with concern about Rich's son, Mike, then a defensive player himself for the Nittany Lions. This is the message Rich remembers Coach Paterno imparting: "I know you're worried about Michael not playing a lot. He's smart enough to play any position, and sometimes we need somebody to fill a spot. He's not getting as much playing time as we'd like, but in terms of his versatility, we have to move him around. It doesn't give him the opportunity to work on one position."

Rich thanked Paterno for calling, grateful that the busy coach cared enough to take the time to call and provide an honest response. "He was nice enough to do it," he says.

When Rich reflects back on the choices he made as a teenager, he considers himself lucky to have ever received that telephone call from Paterno. Things might have been different for both father and son had Rich chosen another school, say Michigan or Ohio State. Both schools were in his sights growing up in Youngstown, Ohio. Mike could have wound up at either of those schools as well. But like his dad, Mike favored Penn State too, even if he wasn't so sure he wanted to endure the comparisons to his father that would likely follow.

Weighing his options one day, Mike asked his father, "Dad, if I go to Michigan, will you root against me?"

Rich's reply: "Of course not, son."

* * *

Rich's summer days were spent in typical fashion for a young boy: In the morning, he'd hop on his bike, grab his baseball glove, and peddle to the ballpark to join in a game. He'd peddle back home for lunch, refuel, and head out to the basketball court or the swimming pool. "We'd play all day," Rich says.

In Youngstown's public school system, he was a natural—an athlete for all seasons. He lettered in football, basketball, and baseball, and was a shot-putter for the track team. Even though his personal focus was on the gridiron, some suggested that Rich's athleticism may be better suited on the basketball court. In his senior year, his Woodrow Wilson High basketball team faced a daunting challenge from Cleveland East Tech in the state quarterfinals. The game went down to the wire, but Woodrow Wilson High lost by a few points. Cleveland East's coach had some kind words for his rival coach about Rich's abilities: "Jeez, we scouted you guys and we thought you had nothing but a football tackle playing center. We were really surprised that he scored 28 points against us."

Rich's size was impressive. Playing on the offensive line during his sophomore year, he already stood 6-foot-3 and weighed 240 pounds. "That was a pretty good size for 1961," Rich says.

Rich Buzin credits his genes for his build. He calls his grandfather, John, "a huge guy for the time, about 6-foot-5, 250 pounds. He had a big handlebar mustache, and he used to work down at the steel mills. And the story was, he would take a bucket of soup for his lunch."

Rich himself later worked at the steel mills for a while. "Guys would come up to me. 'Boy, your grandfather, he was a huge man, he used to lift up those big, steel pipes.' I never got to know him, but those were the stories, that he was this big, old Lithuanian that came over from the old country. That was his history, with his bucket of soup."

Both Rich's father, Lawrence, and uncle, Alex, worked in the steel mills and played in the sandlot football leagues there. But there would be no sandlot football league for Rich—he was going to college.

"I pretty much had the choice of wherever I wanted to go," recalls Rich.

That was the problem; he couldn't make up his mind. Rich visited a number of schools. Ara Parseghian was in his first season as head coach at Notre Dame, and Parseghian wasted no time in making his point upon meeting Rich. The teenager was startled when the coach handed him a scholarship right off the bat. Rich recalls, "He just signed it and said, 'It's yours if you want it. Just send it back.'"

Ohio State's Woody Hayes was equally interested, as was Bump Elliott at Michigan. Among others, Rich also visited Purdue, Michigan State, and Pitt.

Enter Rip Engle and a fellow named Skip Rowland, whose father at the time was the president of the board of trustees at Penn State. Football recruiting was a different beast in the 1960s. There were no regulations then concerning how many times a coach could visit a recruit.

"Rip and Skip would come over once a month or so, and my mother would make them stuffed cabbage, which they really loved," says Rich. "My mother really liked Rip Engle. It was so funny, because she didn't particularly like Woody Hayes. Rip was more of a father [figure]—gray hair and a smooth talker. He wasn't high pressure, whereas Woody was a little more pushy."

To Rich, Penn State simply meshed with his preference for a small-town vibe. "I'd always envisioned a college with a campus within a small town," he says. "That was just my imagination, and then when I saw Penn State, it really fit my idea of what a college campus should be."

But after choosing Penn State, Buzin had second thoughts. "I started reading these magazines and hearing things about how good the other football teams were, and I started to doubt myself. Did I go to the right school? Should I have gone to Michigan? Notre Dame? It's part of life: 'Did you make the right decision?'"

It took a game against Ohio State during the 1964 season to reassure Rich. Even though Penn State had beaten Hayes-coached powerhouses in 1956 and 1963, the '64 game seemed to be an impossible mission for the Nittany Lions. Ohio State was unbeaten and ranked No. 2 in the country, while Penn State was struggling with a 3-4 record. Worse yet: the game was being played in the hostile environment of Ohio Stadium.

Paterno, the quarterbacks coach, was under fire for his choice of Gary Wydman as the Penn State quarterback. But he stubbornly stuck to his man despite a series of mistakes that previously cost the Lions some victories. There was plenty of reason to fret about Wydman's performance against a powerhouse like Ohio State. But as it turned out, the worrying was for naught. Wydman drove the Lions to touchdowns in each of the first three quarters, scoring once himself, before handing the ball over to the second-stringers in a 27-0 rout. The game was one of the most important victories in Penn State history, as the Nittany Lions served notice that much-maligned Eastern football was not as weak as most everyone thought.

"At that point," Rich says, "I felt I had made the right choice."

The transition from high school to a major college program, however, was a wakeup call. Rich had been among the elite high school players in the state of Ohio, but at Penn State he was scrimmaging against other players who were also the best from their respective states. And the biggest.

"When I first went up to Penn State, I thought I was a big shot. I had made All-State, All-America—all that stuff," he says. "I walked in there and there were six, eight guys as big as I was. The running backs were like 210, 215 [pounds]. I was thinking they were guards. This guy says, 'No, I'm a halfback.' I was sort of taken aback. I thought, 'Holy cow, what did I get myself into?'"

Actually, Buzin need not have worried. He eventually became a force on Penn State's offensive line. By that time, he was playing for Paterno's first team in 1966. Engle had stepped down after the '65 season, handing the coaching reins to Paterno. Rich could see it coming.

The Buzins

Rich Buzin.

"When I was a sophomore in '65, Joe sort of ran the meetings and ran the practices, and Rip was just more of a figurehead. Rip would speak a little at the meetings, but then Joe would get up and talk most of the time," recalls Rich. "So you had the sense that although Rip was the head coach, Joe was monitoring the whole program. . . . So it was not a big surprise."

Rich was more surprised when Paterno told him he needed to lose weight for his junior year. Rich weighed in at around 280, not large by today's standards, but fairly hefty for that era. Paterno instructed him to drop 20 pounds in the off-season and return for his junior season at 260 pounds. Instead of turning to the gymnasium, Rich worked his connections to land a summer job at a steel mill in his hometown.

Rich remembers those sweaty days well: "I worked at the open hearth, and worked and worked and worked." And shed pounds, many more than Paterno expected. When Rich returned to Penn State at the end of the summer, he had dropped his weight to 238, shocking his head coach not only with his svelte body, but with his gains in speed and stamina.

"We had to run something like 12 minutes," Rich says, "and I almost did two miles in 12 minutes." The dedication and desire that Rich displayed earned him a lot of points with Paterno. "To lose almost 50 pounds, to come back in that kind of shape, showed him how badly I wanted to play."

Buzin's first starting assignment of the '66 season came at offensive guard against Michigan State. "I played against Bubba Smith," says Rich. "I guess the reason was I was probably one of the biggest guys on the offensive line. Joe put me at guard because Bubba was playing nose guard at that point. We got killed (42-8), but that was my first game starting."

Paterno then made some changes. For one thing, he moved Rich to offensive tackle. As Rich improved, so too did his team. After going 5-5 in his junior season, the Nittany Lions improved to 8-2-1 in 1967, including a 17-17 tie with Florida State in the Gator Bowl—Paterno's first bowl game as a head coach.

The Nittany Lions actually had the opportunity to put the game out of reach, but failed to do so as the result of one of Paterno's well-known gambles. The Lions were leading 17-0 and had the ball on Florida State's 15-yard line in the second half. On fourth down with six inches to go, Paterno chose to go for it with a quarterback sneak by Tom Sherman rather than kick a field goal. The play failed, and Florida State came back to tie the game with a late rally.

"Joe still says they gave him a bad spot, but I don't know," says Rich. "I told him, 'If you had run behind me, I would have gotten you that first down.'"

Despite the failure of the play, the decision to strive for that half-yard best expressed an aggressive philosophy and style that would follow Paterno throughout his entire career at Penn State. Paterno himself points to that decision as a turning point for the program. The following two years, the reborn Nittany Lions put together back-to-back 11-0 seasons, part of a school-record 31-game unbeaten streak.

The Buzins

The 1967 season launched Buzin into the NFL, where he played for five seasons with the New York Giants, Los Angeles Rams, and Chicago Bears. He also had a brief fling with Orlando in the ill-fated World Football League. Even though he was making "pretty good money" at the time thanks to a three-year contract with the Giants worth a total of $100,000, Rich found a job on Wall Street during the off-season selling institutional bonds to corporations, banks, insurance companies, and the like.

"When I was [playing football], for six months I really had no income, other than living off what I made in football," he says. "I wanted to start some kind of career doing something different."

The salaries weren't the only discrepancy between the NFL then and now. "We played 14 games, and once the season was over, everybody came in, packed up their stuff, and went back to their hometowns," Rich says. "And then you'd never see anybody until July. Nowadays, you generally live in the town you play in and work out all year round."

In three years with the Giants, Rich didn't miss a game and became one of the stalwarts on the offensive line. One of his proudest achievements: clearing the way for team record-breaking running back Ron Johnson. In 1970, Johnson ran for 1,027 yards, a team record he later broke himself. With that total in the '70 season, Johnson became the first 1,000-yard rusher in the Giants' 39-year history.

Rich was considered an equally good pass blocker. Playing one day against the Rams' Deacon Jones, one of the star defensive linemen of the time, Buzin kept Jones away from Giants quarterback Fran Tarkenton. Surprisingly, that success caused his days as a Giant to come to a close. "It got me traded," Rich says. "Tommy Prothro had just taken over as head coach of the Rams. Dick Vermeil was an assistant coach then. He saw the tape of the game and recommended that Prothro trade for me because I had done really well against Deacon Jones."

During his professional career, Buzin caught up with some of his boyhood heroes, including Gary Collins, who caught two touchdown passes to help the Cleveland Browns beat the Baltimore Colts in the 1964 NFL championship game. By the time Rich joined Orlando in the WFL, Collins was an assistant coach there.

Playing for JoePa

Today, Buzin, who has retired from his job as a bond investor, has one defining memory of his days as a pro: "I played with a lot of really good ballplayers that never won Super Bowls." Among the players on Rich's list: Tarkenton, Ernie Koy, Jim Katcavage, Tucker Frederickson, Roman Gabriel, Jack Snow, Deacon Jones, Merlin Olsen, Gale Sayers, and Dick Butkus. "Today you see these second stringers going to Super Bowls and getting Super Bowl rings, and they never played much. You hardly know their names," Rich says. "But some of these great players never have gone [to the Super Bowl], which I thought was an irony."

* * *

By the time Rich Buzin was out of football, he had already moved his family to Cleveland. There he coached his son at every opportunity. "Peewee, Little League . . . fifth, sixth, seventh, eighth grades. . . . I coached Michael through all those years," Rich says. "He got in the car, all muddy and dirty, and we wiped off the seats. It was two, three hours we would spend together every day during the football season."

Mike especially loved football, and he and his father would take road trips to watch college football games in Columbus or State College. At Penn State, Rich would take his son inside the locker room. "He idolized the players," Rich says of Mike. "He saw where Shane Conlan's locker was, Blair Thomas. All that had an influence on him."

Years later, Rich took his teenage son to Penn State to watch a team practice. As they walked around Holuba Hall, the indoor practice facility at Penn State, casually minding their own business, a familiar voice shouted at them from a distance.

"Mike, come here!" yelled Paterno.

Mike ran over to Joe, who led him into the huddle. The team called a play as a wide-eyed Mike took it all in.

"He was like, 'Holy cow, this is pretty neat,'" his dad remembers. "It was something really nice that Joe did. It made Michael feel really good."

The Buzins

The gesture made quite the impression on Mike Buzin, the teenager; later, it would pay dividends with Mike Buzin, the football player. Mike's career at St. Ignatius High School in Cleveland, where he helped his team win three straight state championships as a defensive lineman, would eventually earn him the same sort of recognition that benefited his father. When it came time to pick a college, Mike knew that his father preferred for Mike to attend his alma mater; but Mike was feeling a bit rebellious.

"At the age when I was getting recruited, that's the age when you rebel from your parents," Mike says. "I was like, 'I'm not going to Penn State, Dad—I'm going to Notre Dame or Michigan.'"

Mike knew all about his father's exploits at Penn State—after all, it had been ingrained in him since boyhood. He wanted a chance to carve out his own identity as a football player. So Mike continued to shop around—to no avail. Like his father, he had an idea about the kind of school he wanted: big campus situated in a small town. Having attended a high school in downtown Cleveland, Mike wanted to flee the metropolis. That ruled out Ohio State; even Michigan felt too big for him. He considered Notre Dame for a while, but he felt there was more to do in State College than in South Bend.

"Penn State was just perfect for me," Mike says now. Like father, like son.

Mike walked into a football program already in high gear. In his freshman season, the 1994 Nittany Lions went 12-0 and captured a Rose Bowl victory over Oregon. That made it four straight unbeaten seasons for Mike, dating back to high school. That put a smile on Paterno's face. "We'd like to keep that streak going," the coach told Mike's father.

The Lions gave that goal the old college try during Mike's time at State College. Over a five-year period, Penn State compiled a 50-11 record. Paterno was fielding a winning team in the classroom, too. "I remember, it must have been my second or third year, [Paterno] really started getting on us about going to class," Mike recalls. "He'd say, 'Make sure you go to breakfast, and make sure you go to class.' So Paterno would make us go to breakfast, and generally what that translated to is, 'Well, I'm going to go to class.'"

Playing for JoePa

The 1996 season was Mike's personal favorite. He was not a starter that season, but he did see a lot of action, including playing time in a 38-15 Fiesta Bowl victory over Texas. With two years of eligibility still remaining following that season, Buzin was starting to turn the corner. He was the winner of the Jim O'Hora Award, given to the team's most improved defensive player, and earned himself a starting job at defensive tackle for the 1997 season. That's when he hit one sturdy roadblock.

"Things were really good," he remembers of the days leading up to his fourth year at Penn State in 1997. "For the first time in my career, I'm wearing the blue jersey, which means I'm the starter. I've been wearing it all preseason and we were a week and a half away from our first game.

"I was in the best physical shape of my life—probably 6-foot-4, 276, 277 pounds. I was lean, feeling really comfortable with what I was doing."

Then, just before the season opener, the team was completing a double-team drill during practice. As an offensive lineman, Mike was learning the proper technique to break a double team.

"I go against these two guys in a drill and I hit in, and I'm straining against them, pushing back against them, and all of a sudden, my patella tendon and my hamstring both popped at the same time," Mike recalls.

The result was a partial tear in his patella, and a serious tear in his hamstring. Buzin went through four weeks of rehab and by the time he returned to the field, practically half the season was gone and he was left competing in a bulky knee brace.

"Frankly, I wasn't running the same," he says. "You could look on video and you could see I was kind of favoring the other leg."

Mike had lost his starting job, but not his value to Paterno. The Penn State coach regarded him as a "super sub" of sorts, using him to fill in everywhere he was needed. To acknowledge Mike's contribution to the Penn State football program, Paterno named him captain when the Nittany Lions played Ohio State in his senior year. Mike played multiple positions—from tackle and nose guard to defensive end on occasion—and just rotated around when people needed a break.

The Buzins

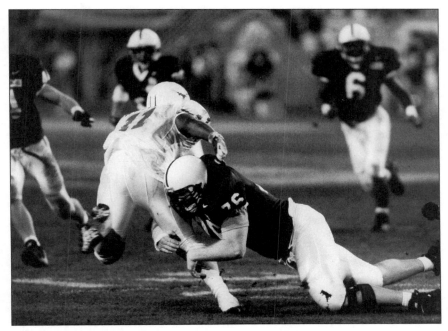

Mike Buzin makes the tackle.

Then, in the spring of 1998, he ripped his patella tendon again. The team doctor advised him to take better care of his knees, or he was going to have problems.

"What do you want to do?" the doctor asked.

"I want to continue playing, there's no question about that," Mike replied.

So Mike ended up playing, injury and all, on the blocking side.

"I played a little tight end on blocking situations, field goals, extra points, short yardage. That was a perfect fit for me, because nobody tries to cut you when you're a tight end. They don't go after your legs."

A visit to his fifth postseason game, a 26-14 victory over Kentucky in the Outback Bowl, rounded out Mike Buzin's football career at Penn State. It wasn't the end of his Penn State story, though. During the fall semester, Mike knew he would be running out of scholarship time. He had already graduated with a degree in business management, and needed just one more semester to finish his master's degree. But he didn't have the money for it. So Mike turned to his coach, who had been so good at finding him a place on the team year after year.

"I know I'm not a superstar," Buzin said to Paterno, "but I'm hoping you'll hear me out. I think it would be a good idea if you keep me on scholarship for my spring semester."

Scholarships were not typically given for the final semester of the player's fifth year. Yet Paterno knew that Buzin would do anything he asked of him in order to get that scholarship money. Buzin made his pitch.

"I looked at [Paterno] and said, 'For every kid that's in my shoes, kind of a decent football player, but just not the greatest, the parents are going to be asking you, "What are you going to do to make sure my son graduates?'

"You can always tell them [about me]. . . . 'I kept him on scholarship for that final semester, and he not only graduated, he graduated with his masters in five years.'"

Paterno had a big smile on his face. "Yeah, that doesn't sound so bad," he told Mike, who left Paterno's office that day with the understanding that if he performed well in his fall classes, he could be rewarded. Later in the year, Buzin walked back into Paterno's office with a glowing report card. "This was right about bowl time," he recalls. "I walked into his office with a 12-credit load, which is four classes, and I had a straight 4-point average."

Paterno granted Mike the scholarship. In turn, Mike gave Paterno some of his time in the weight room, helping to train other players. Mike got his wish and made good on it, a point of pride for both he and his father. It's easy to see why: There aren't many football players wandering around with master's degrees earned so swiftly.

"Anytime I've interviewed for a job, given my résumé out, people always ask me about that sort of thing: 'Wow, you got your master's degree, and you were playing football," says Mike, who is now employed as a plant manager for Corning Glass in Lexington, Kentucky. "That always goes back to Joe. And then they say, 'How was it playing for Paterno?' And I say, 'Well, he was tough but fair, and he ended up doing me a great many favors in terms of the stuff he did for me on the academic side.'

The Buzins

"I think it really [gets at] the whole point of what Joe Paterno stands for."

three

THE SHULERS

MICKEY SHULER HAS TAUGHT his only son a lot of things. He's taught him about football and the tight end position, pass-catching techniques, agility drills, and blocking. He's given Mickey Jr. confidence in his ability to compete at any level, and preached patience when the opportunity to compete has remained out of grasp. But if Mickey Sr. had to select just one lesson to impress upon Mickey Jr., it would come in the form of a poem.

It's the poem that's inscribed on a poster hanging on Mickey Jr.'s bedroom wall in his apartment at Penn State. Its words are flanked on all sides by images and text that neatly summarize the football career and life of Mickey Sr. The Shulers had the original poster artwork created when the elder Mickey was still playing football with the New York Jets in the 1980s. It was made initially for charitable purposes, but Mickey Sr. says it has since served as an example of what can be accomplished through hard work and dedication to one's goals.

"We had a drawing of me kneeling in reflection after a game . . . kind of sweaty and dirty," Mickey Sr. says, describing the artwork. "We took that and made a collage of accomplishments and goals I'd had in my life. Anything that was achieved and actually happened was in color. Anything that was a goal and wasn't achieved was in black and white or gray. It shows my whole life. Shows me as a little kid, shows me in Little League, shows me in high school, shows me in college, shows me playing pro football. . . ."

Mickey Sr. continues to tick off layers of his impressive résumé and the stages of his life, both personal and professional, that are portrayed in the poster. "Then," he finally says, "in the back, behind it all, is that poem." It's called the *Man in the Glass*. Its author, at least for the version the Shulers used in the poster, remains anonymous, though certain stanzas stem from Peter "Dale" Wimbrow Sr.'s 1934 poem titled *Guy in the Glass*.

Mickey Sr. can recite the words from memory:

"When you reach your goal in the world of sports, and you have worked the big game that day, just go to the mirror and look at yourself and see what the man has to say. For it isn't your family or friends or the coaches whose judgment upon you must pass; the fellow whose verdict counts in your life is the one staring at you from the glass. You may fool all of the world down the avenue of years and get pats on the back as you pass, but your only reward will be remorse and regret, if you have cheated the man in the glass."

Mickey Sr. was first given the poem by a guy named George "Speed" Ebersole, a family friend and high school athletic trainer in the Harrisburg area when Shuler was growing up. (Penn State later approached Ebersole about coming to work there as a trainer with the football team.) He isn't sure how Ebersole came upon the poem. But when Mickey Sr. first read it, everything clicked.

"You have to see my poster to understand me," he says. "I was pretty disciplined in workouts and work habits when I grew up. I always had good people around me and in front of me. I had people talk to me about hard work and dedication and sacrifice, and to whom much is given, much is expected. And I had faith."

Faith is a funny thing. It means different things to different people, and it can pulse stronger in one man than in another. For

The Shulers

Mickey Shuler Sr., faith was a belief in himself and his abilities that made him into a three-year starter at Penn State. It was faith that carried him to become a third-round NFL draft pick in 1978 and later to a pair of Pro Bowl appearances as a Jet. It's why he talks about God having fingerprints on his life, and why he's always signed everything—from his poster to old football cards—with the same line, "Keep the faith." And now, a generation later, it's the faith embodied in *Man in the Glass* that Shuler hopes his son will embrace in his own football pursuits.

✳ ✳ ✳

Enola is off Route 81 in Central Pennsylvania, just across the Susquehanna River from Harrisburg. Mickey Shuler was actually born in Harrisburg in 1956, but his family—he eventually became the oldest of four, a brother and two sisters—lived in Enola throughout his childhood.

Mickey's father, Robert, was an industrial arts teacher in the East Pennsboro school district. He also coached football and basketball at East Pennsboro High right up until the time Mickey got there. Robert quit football responsibilities and stuck with basketball only for a time, until he walked away from that as well so as not to create any controversies should he someday coach his son, who had helped his dad on the court in several capacities since he was in elementary school.

"I was lucky," Mickey says, "because I [grew] up as a coach's kid." But that doesn't mean he had it easy. His father made sure of that. "It was a privilege for me to go to a game," he continues. "If I wanted to be the waterboy, I had to do certain things and act a certain way, behave a certain way. It was a privilege."

While he never formally coached Mickey in football or basketball at East Pennsboro, Robert was hands on with his son off the field and court. He coached him at home and "from the stands," is how Mickey remembers it. "If I did anything stupid, cursed or anything, it got back to him," Mickey says.

Robert built his son's confidence, showing him the skills necessary to excel in both basketball and football. Robert used his coaching connections to acquire the best supplies a kid could want. Shoes, gloves, cleats, you name it. Mickey says much of it was pro-quality equipment that had slight blemishes, but nothing a lanky teen couldn't overlook.

Robert also took his oldest son to summer camps, where he not only could hone his skills, but where he could learn while surrounded by athletic role models. Mickey went to a basketball camp in the Poconos, where he met the likes of Hal Greer, an NBA All-Star who would someday earn induction into the Naismith Basketball Hall of Fame, and Dave Cowens, the future Celtics star who was Mickey's counselor for a summer. Mickey credits Cowens with first turning him on to lifting weights.

The Shulers returned to that Poconos hoops camp for several summers. It was run by Harry Litwack, the former Temple head coach and a Hall of Famer in his own right, and Bill Foster, then the head coach at Rutgers (which is how former Rutgers point guard Jim Valvano also wound up as a counselor at the camp). Litwack and Foster would bring in younger coaches from around the country to run drills. When Mickey was a camper, two of those coaches were Bob Knight and Dean Smith, both then early in their illustrious careers.

"If you didn't have skinned knees," Mickey says with a chuckle, "[Knight] wouldn't even talk to you."

Mickey must have made Knight proud on at least one occasion, when he dove into a wall to save a ball in a camp All-Star game and sliced open his hand. With no hospital nearby, Smith and Knight drove Shuler out of town to get help, Knight holding his arm and Smith at the wheel.

Shuler went to football camp too. For three summers he drove up to New Hampshire to a camp run by then-Boston College coach Joe Yukica—a friend of Speed Ebersole's—and the coaches of several other colleges in the Northeast. On weekends during those summers Mickey would sometimes head to the B.C. campus to hang out with Yukica and Barry Gallup, a former Eagles player and B.C. assistant coach at the time. Mickey says his parents could only afford the cost of one of the camp's two weeks, but Ebersole landed him a job to cover the cost of week two. (In actuality, Mickey says he thinks the job was just a front so that Ebersole, his friend, could pay the remainder of the camp bill guilt-free.)

With all that training, Mickey was a well-rounded athlete by the time he reached East Pennsboro High. There he played football, basketball, and ran track, and he might have steered toward basketball primarily if not for heeding the advice of his father, who told him that playing football would improve his footwork and aggressiveness for basketball. Thing is, as time came to start thinking about playing sports in college, Shuler realized that at 6-foot-3, 185 pounds, he would likely have to play guard at the next level. And his dribbling skills simply weren't there. As a standout wide receiver, he started receiving a lot more attention from football programs than basketball programs, though one of those who showed interest in Shuler for hoops was Smith, the head coach at North Carolina.

Once committed to football, Shuler needed to decide how committed he was to Boston College, a bond he'd formed through his friendship with Yukika and Gallup in those summers at football camp. "I looked at Miami, Kentucky, North Carolina, South Carolina, Temple, Pitt, Boston College, Syracuse," Mickey says, "but I was really headed toward Boston College by the time it was all said and done."

Penn State also was in the mix mostly because it was close to home. Despite having grown up two hours east of State College, Shuler was not a Penn State fan. He liked the Miami Dolphins in the NFL, and if he had to watch college ball, it was usually Oklahoma. Still, proximity became an increasingly important issue, especially after Shuler had a candid conversation with Gallup in the heat of the recruiting scrum for his services.

"He said, 'You're a lot like me. You're close to your family,'" Shuler recalls Gallup telling him. "At that time it would have been difficult for my family to see me play somewhere else. Physically and financially, to be able to travel and go see things, they just wouldn't have been able to do it. So Barry said, 'I think you feel obligated to come to Boston College because of me and Joe Yukika, but you know what? You need to do what's best for your family. We understand.'"

Next thing he knew, Mickey was on his official visit to Penn State, while Robert and his wife, Frances, were at the Paternos' house in State

College, enjoying Sue's home cooking and Joe's equally delectable spin on what the Penn State football program could do for Mickey. The Shulers left town feeling like they'd just met two long-lost family members.

"They knew I was going to be taken care of more than just as a football player," Mickey says.

They were right.

✳ ✳ ✳

If the "Man in the Glass" needed to mature any further when he left Enola for State College in the summer of 1974, then he had ample opportunity to do so in the ensuing four years. Shuler says his inclination to work hard and his ability to focus—and to have faith—was present when he showed up as a bright-eyed freshman. Still, all good players endure a period of doubt, and Shuler admits he was overwhelmed by the pool of talented athletes that Paterno had amassed in Happy Valley. "Seemed like everybody was bigger, faster, and stronger than I was," he says. "I was just worried I wasn't going to be able to compete."

So he did what he'd always done best. He worked. He worked and worked and worked, so much so that he nearly won the Red Worrell Award in his first spring practice in 1975, just losing out to Dave Stutts, a rising senior whom Mickey admired for his own work ethic. The award is named for Robert T. "Red" Worrell, a Penn State freshman fullback who was electrocuted in his home in 1957. It's given annually to the Penn State player who demonstrates "exemplary conduct, loyalty, interest, attitude, and improvement" during spring practice, and in 1975, it was the only award handed out at the end of spring ball.

It was a big deal.

In the spring of 1976, Shuler left no further doubts about his abilities, winning the Worrell Award and never looking back. A former wide receiver who converted to tight end after his freshman year to fill a void left in part by Randy Sidler's move from tight end to defense, Shuler grabbed the starting tight end job during the 1976 season and finished tied for second on the team in catches.

The Shulers

Mickey Shuler, Sr.

In his junior and senior seasons, he emerged into Penn State's top pass-catching threat, leading the Lions in receptions both years, including 33 catches for 600 yards in 1977 to earn second-team All-America honors for the 11-1 Lions. Shuler finished his Penn State career with 66 catches for 1,016 yards, still among the top 20 in school history for career receiving yardage. It's more impressive when you consider how conservative Paterno was with his offensive play-calling in the mid-1970s.

"I wondered every year why Joe didn't throw the ball more," Shuler says with a hint of a smile. "I'm serious about it. I think we'd have been national champions if he'd have thrown the ball. But who knows? That's just hindsight."

Hindsight, however, can confirm that what Joe and Sue Paterno fed Robert and Frances Shuler that night in the early '70s was more than just a hot meal with a side of hot air. Mickey's makeup might have been a snug fit with the selfless, all-for-the-program approach that's been Penn State's hallmark for more than 50 years, but he was also taken care of both on and off the field.

Mickey matured. Given time to study and the option of whether to goof off or actually open his books, Mickey chose wisely. "We were given carte blanche to do pretty much what we wanted whenever we wanted to do it with some time constraints," Mickey says. "I know when I got to the pros, I was a lot more mature as far as taking care of myself and doing things for myself than the guys who came in and were my peers. I was a lot more prepared to be a professional athlete than they were.

"There's something that they do up there [at Penn State]. It's almost like a cookie cutter. You come out with an awful lot of the same thought patterns and values, and it's because of the example that Joe sets. No matter what you say about him, he's consistent. He does what he thinks is the best thing for the school, the athletic program, and the kids."

It should come as little surprise then that more than two decades after playing his last game in a Penn State uniform, Mickey and wife, Sue, a Penn Stater herself, began sending the first of their four children to Penn State. Part of their reasoning was an ongoing love for the school; the Shulers had bought the season tickets once owned by Mickey's in-laws, who'd first attended games back when Beaver Stadium was casting shadows on Rec Hall. The school's proximity to their home played a role as well; Mickey and Sue are very close with (in age order) Nicole, Karah, Brooke, and Mickey Jr.

Part of it too, at least for Mickey Sr., was Joe Paterno and the knowledge that what he'd promised and delivered for Mickey Sr. could be available for Mickey Jr. That's what made the night so surreal when, in 2004, Mickey Sr. and Sue found themselves in Joe and Sue Paterno's living room with the parents of other recruits nearly 30 years after Robert and Frances had been there for the same purpose.

"Joe is a family guy, he lives in a modest house, he is the coach of Penn State University, he's gonna make sure you get an education, and you're gonna be a better man for having been through his program," Mickey Sr. says. "I think that's what sold my parents."

Mickey Jr., however, was another matter. On the one hand, he'd grown up fully absorbed by his father's football legacy at East

The Shulers

The Shulers.

Pennsboro, at Penn State, and in the pros. Mickey Jr.'s first football memories are of his father reaching over the railing at the conclusion of Jets and Eagles games, lifting his little son in the air and carrying him into the locker room. Later, with his father retired from the NFL, Mickey Jr. would join his family on road trips to Penn State on football Saturdays, tailgating out of the trunk and making sure to catch pregame pep rallies in the Bryce Jordan Center.

Father and son were tight. Mickey Sr. made a commitment to his family and to himself that once football was over, while his kids were still young, he would not take another job that would fully consume him the way the NFL had for 14 years. For Mickey Jr. it meant that when he reached East Pennsboro High and found himself as the next-to-last guy off the bench for the jayvee hoops team—and hearing low rumblings that he'd never be half the athlete his father was—Dad was there to help spark his growth.

It started in November 2002. Mickey Jr. realized then that he wanted to become a Division I athlete, and that to get there, he'd have to make sacrifices as his father once had. So he gave up much of his social life and began a focused training regimen, many hours of which he spent with Mickey Sr. looking over his shoulder. In one comical memory, Mickey Jr. recalls his father taping a basketball to a lat pull-down machine that they had in their garage, where they'd often work out. Mickey Sr. would tap his son, and Mickey Jr. would have to reach up and grab the ball, then pull it down rapidly. Reach up, grab the ball, pull it down. Over and over.

Many nights the two would work on pass-catching and shooting drills under the glow of a 400-watt floodlight Mickey Sr. had rigged up to illuminate the hoop in their driveway. Mickey Sr. made his son run track, too, in the off-season—some hurdles, a few relays, the 400. When the track season started, Mickey Jr.'s coach at East Pennsboro was mom Sue, who resigned those responsibilities in January 2007.

Everything began to pay off for Mickey Jr. around Christmastime of that same sophomore year, 2002. He was asked by Steve Naticha, then the East Pennsboro varsity basketball coach, if he'd fill a bench spot on varsity in place of a regular who had a conflict for an upcoming holiday tournament. Mickey Jr. jumped at the chance, not knowing whether he'd see any action. But when Naticha did get him into one of the tournament games, Mickey Jr. had an immediate impact and helped his team to victory. From that point forward, he never sniffed jayvee again, earning a starting spot on varsity that he held onto for the remainder of his prep career.

Two years before Mickey Jr. began playing football at East Pennsboro, Mickey Sr. began volunteering as an assistant coach at his alma mater. He did it in the beginning as a favor to head football coach Todd Studer, who'd coached two of Mickey's daughters in track. But the reward for the Shulers came two years later when Mickey Sr. began to tutor his son the same way he'd learned from his own father.

When he wasn't practicing under his father's watchful eye, Mickey Jr. would spend summers attending Penn State's football camps, which allowed coaches there to see the progress the kid was making as a year-round student of his All-Pro father. "I think people started to believe that he wasn't me, that he was his own guy and that he was going to be something special, too," Mickey Sr. says. "Some people believed it and some people seemed to be hoping against it, but it worked out."

Once he decided he wanted to play football in college—and once he began approaching the size of a Division I-A player—recruiters started to show interest from Ivy League schools on up. The Shulers took a long road trip with stops at West Virginia, Virginia, Duke, North Carolina, and North Carolina State, just to see the schools. Mickey Sr. did most of the driving on that trip, installing a mattress in the back of the family's Chevy Suburban so Mickey Jr. could sleep while they were on the highway and be fresh for workouts at each campus.

Most recruiters, though, assumed Mickey Jr. would wind up at Penn State. It helped that Mickey Jr. had been quoted in a newspaper story his junior year saying that if Penn State offered him a scholarship, he was going there. "To possibly get to play in Beaver Stadium in front of 110,000 people . . . why not?" Mickey Jr. says now.

He only hesitated momentarily to consider his father's legacy. It isn't that he was in awe of his dad and his fame. Never. Mickey Jr. saved that for his friends who would come to the Shuler house in Enola to watch highlight tapes of Mickey Sr. in the pros. No, Mickey Jr. feared what others might say about a son following in the footsteps of such an accomplished father.

"I just didn't want people saying, 'He's going there because his dad went there,'" Mickey Jr. says. "I wanted to prove people wrong and go to another school and play. But then I figured I could do the same thing and play at Penn State."

✳ ✳ ✳

It's a strange thing, being someone famous and wondering when—if ever—is the right time to say something on behalf of one of your kids. Mickey Shuler can attest to that.

Mickey Jr. committed to Penn State in 2004. The 6-foot-4, 220-pound tight end redshirted in 2005, then entered the 2006 season (by then he was up to 240 pounds), figuring to see at least some playing time at a wide-open tight end position. It didn't work out that way.

Playing for JoePa

While Andrew Quarless was developing into Penn State's surprisingly most consistent pass receiver, Mickey Jr. found himself switched temporarily to fullback, then back to tight end for a season spent primarily on the scout team.

"It's hard to go in and say something," says Mickey Sr., who adds that Quarless' success story was the exact tale he'd envisioned his son leading in 2006. "I think as long as you get a chance to compete, all things are fair and equal."

Mickey Sr. never spoke to Paterno or any of the Penn State assistants on behalf of his son. He and Sue wanted their only son to stand on his own, something they still believe in firmly today. Mickey Sr. has, however, had discussions with Paterno about his own aspirations. In fact, twice in the last 10 years Mickey Sr. expressed interest in coming onboard as a Penn State assistant. The first time, when Kenny Jackson left Penn State to coach with the Pittsburgh Steelers, Mickey Sr. only casually mentioned the possibility to Paterno. Some time later, after Shuler had told Paterno that he was serious about coaching, Paterno asked that he come see him when he was ready.

Two years ago, when another assistant's job came open in the wake of Kenny Carter's departure, Shuler was told about the opening from two players on the team. Shuler, who had previously worked with some of Penn State's tight ends and receivers from the greater Harrisburg area, put together a formal résumé and cover letter and delivered one copy to Joe's office and to his home, handing the latter to Sue Paterno. Penn State, though, wound up shifting around some responsibilities and decided to bring in Galen Hall to run the offense and to give Mike McQueary responsibilities that included coaching the wide receivers.

"[Paterno] said he really didn't know what was going on and he didn't want to be unfair to me or unfair to the people around him," says Mickey Sr., who remains fourth in all-time career receiving yards in New York Jets history. "He's very loyal and he's very family-oriented. He doesn't want to disrupt families. So I don't know. I still would like to do it.

"I think I'd have a good rapport with the players, because today's players, they want to know that [making it to the NFL] can be accomplished. In my letter to Joe, I tried to tell him, I am your experiment. I'm the guy who came in, worked hard, played there, earned my degree, left there, played in the NFL, had a family, raised a family, ran a business, got my kids through college—they all went to Penn State—and now I'm ready to coach. Tell me what kid and his parent doesn't want their kid to have opportunities like that?"

Further endorsement is the person Mickey Jr.'s become while waiting to become the player he and his father know he can be. Here's a kid who hardly ever brings up on-field comparisons between himself and his father because he's learned that faith in himself is all that matters. Here's a kid who could have gone to another school and maybe be starting already; instead he's playing for coaches who can look at him on the practice field and see Mickey Sr. staring back at them. Mickey Jr.'s waiting for his shot to leave the jayvee in the dust.

"I'm going to live up to my own expectations," Mickey Jr. says. "I really don't feel too much pressure about it."

Spoken like a young man who's embraced his own "Man in the Glass." That has to make Dad proud.

four

THE GARRITYS

IN A SEA OF BLUE AND GOLD, there dwelled a lone Blue and White dot. The Garritys, always different, tough out the fierce crowd with a resolve that could only be called "true blue"—Penn State all the way.

Gregg Garrity grew up in Pittsburgh, rooting for the right team in the wrong town. "No one ever mentioned Pitt around the house," says Gregg. "It was almost like a swear word." No wonder: Gregg's father, Jim, played football for the Nittany Lions in the early '50s, when Joe Paterno was just a guy named Joe. And Gregg's mother, Gail, met Jim Garrity when both were college students at Penn State. For the couple, they balanced the roar of the crowd in Beaver Stadium with quiet walks across the campus.

So, you see, it was inevitable that all five Garrity kids remained Blue and White through and through while growing up in Pittsburgh. Just as it seemed inevitable that Gregg was destined to be a Nittany Lion like his dad. The most important catch in Penn State's football history, on the other hand, was a bit of a surprise.

Playing for JoePa

✳ ✳ ✳

Jim Garrity prides himself on being Joe Paterno's first official recruit, back when JoePa was an assistant coach under Rip Engle. But while Garrity was Paterno's first choice, Penn State was not at the top of Jim's list. Garrity had committed to play for Kentucky, at that time coached by Paul "Bear" Bryant.

Paterno and a fellow assistant coach, Earl Bruce, tag-teamed on Garrity, refusing to take "No" for an answer. After being told of Jim's decision to attend Kentucky, Paterno and Bruce traveled to watch Garrity play at an all-star game. After the game, Paterno again talked to Garrity about the advantages of attending Penn State. He didn't stop there; he visited Jim's parents, too. Eventually, Paterno's aggressiveness paid off. Three weeks before Garrity was supposed to leave for Kentucky, he suddenly changed directions.

In an era when there was no national letter of intent or signing day, recruits could change their minds at any point. Which is exactly what happened. Garrity says he developed a gut feeling about Penn State, noting a personal connection he had developed with Paterno, who wasn't much older than Jim. Plus, Garrity admired Bruce. It also helped that State College was an easy drive from his parents' home, so they could watch him play. With that, the recruiting class of 1951 had its first Paterno-earned addition. And what a class it was: joining Garrity were Roosevelt Grier, Jesse Arnelle, Don Shank, and Buddy Rowell, who would all quickly make their presence felt on the Lions' team.

Despite being part of a highly regarded class, Garrity's first taste of Penn State football wasn't exactly glamorous. While the varsity dressed in the comfort of the locker room, freshmen had to dress in the campus water tower near Rec Hall. At that time, Beaver Stadium had a horseshoe formation, which is now the base of the new stadium, and was less than half the size it is today.

"We all had to go there, climb up the stairs, [get dressed], climb down, and go to the stadium with the varsity," Garrity recalls.

When Jim Garrity started to play in 1952, sports were being broadcast on TV only in black and white, and Paterno was a youthful, little-known quarterbacks coach. Joe also had another title—resident

The Garritys

Jim Garrity.

counselor. Paterno was put in charge of the dormitory that housed only the football players. Not the easiest job in the world.

"He lived in our dorm the first year," Garrity recalls of Paterno. "It was absolutely bonkers, a wild time, and Joe tried to control us."

As the head coach in later years, Paterno would not segregate football players. He believed they should be part of the general student population and not singled out as something special. As a young coach, Paterno walked the line between disciplinarian and friend. "I spent a lot of time with Joe," Garrity recalls. "We played basketball together. We played handball together. He was just one of the guys."

Garrity developed into a top-flight receiver on those early Engle teams at Penn State in an era where the running game moved the chains on offense. He led the Lions in receptions in 1953 with 30 catches for 349 yards, an average of 11.6 yards. In 1954, he co-captained the team and tied for the Lions' lead with Jack Sherry, making 11 catches for 131 yards.

"My parents came for all the games, no matter where I went," Jim says. "They even came out to the East-West Shrine Game in California to see me play. I did the same with Gregg. Wherever he was, we would be there for the whole weekend. It goes back to the family atmosphere I experienced in my college career."

Due to a limited number of bowl games in Garrity's era, the Nittany Lions were shut out of postseason appearances despite records of 7-2-1, 6-3, and 7-2. A generation later, Gregg would make up for his father's lack of postseason activity by playing on four bowl-winning teams at Penn State.

✳ ✳ ✳

When Gregg Garrity was a tyke, he wondered why his Pittsburgh home was decorated with so many items bearing the letters "PSU." "At first I didn't understand what PSU was," he says. "I thought it stood for some dirty name."

Possibly, to neighbors of the Garritys who rooted for Pitt, PSU did represent a dirty name. But to the Garritys, those three letters were like the gospel. When Penn State was on television in the '70s, it was a special event in the Garrity household. Gregg, who grew to learn precisely what PSU stood for, loved to watch those games with his dad and his older brother, Duke. Jim explained the football tactics to his young sons, who were star-struck by black-and-white images of John Cappelletti, Franco Harris, and Lydell Mitchell.

When the game wasn't on, Jim, one of the founders of the Midget Football League in North Allegheny, made sure his sons had a place to play organized football. As soon as his sons were able to tie on cleats, he signed them up. Gregg was about eight when he played in his first organized football game. Jim coached his sons, teaching them in practice the fundamentals that he preached to them during State games.

Gregg can't remember a time in his youth when he wasn't playing football. The Garritys even participated in an annual "Turkey Bowl"

The Garritys

with another nearby family—one clan versus the other. "They had a really nice field, and it had these pine trees they used as goal posts," Gregg recalls. "I was very, very little, probably five at the most. At the halftime, they'd let me play. They'd say, 'Do a buttonhook around the pine tree,' and that made me feel great. It made me feel like I was actually playing with the adults, and that was really fun."

As he was growing up, Gregg enjoyed other sports, including ice hockey. His neighbors had a huge, spring-fed pond on their lot that served as an ideal outdoor ice rink. "They'd cut holes in the ice and if you were thirsty, you'd stuff your face in it and get a fresh drink of water," Gregg remembers. But he's quick to point out that football ruled supreme at the Garritys.

Even though Jim never pushed his son to follow in his footsteps at Penn State, he did hope he would go to State College. To introduce the youngster to the Penn State campus, Garrity sent his son there for a week-long summer camp. "He got the feel of the stadium and the coaches," Jim says. "He was pretty impressed with the facilities." But a key question remained: Would Penn State be impressed with him?

During his high school years, Gregg was a speedy running back and defensive back for North Allegheny High. Despite obvious strengths in his game, he was deemed too small by the general consensus. At 5-foot-10, 140 pounds, Gregg wasn't receiving interest from any big-time programs, Penn State included. From West Virginia to Syracuse, all Gregg heard was, "no thanks." Even Kent State turned him down.

Choosing a smaller program would not be a first for the Garrity family. Duke, two years Gregg's senior, was already playing ball at Slippery Rock. But there were some people, including Gregg's father, who believed that Gregg could play at the major college level. Finally, Jim suggested that he and his son speak to Paterno face to face. Father and son headed for Penn State, where Jim ran interference for his son, introducing him to Joe. Paterno took them around on a tour of the facilities. While checking out the weight room, Gregg was astonished at the size of players Matt Millen and Bruce Clark. It was his first look at the kind of players who suited up for Penn State.

Playing for JoePa

"Here I am, a 140-pound kid, and these guys are houses. I thought, 'You've got to be kidding me.' Bruce Clark's thighs were bigger than me. He was a specimen. . . . You can see them on TV, but when you're standing next to them and they're that big, it kind of makes you doubt yourself a little bit."

Paterno extended an offer for Gregg to walk-on at Penn State. There would be no scholarship—just an opportunity to prove himself worthy of being a Lion. Jim and Gregg jumped at the chance, knowing that Gregg would be given a fair shot to make the squad. In the summer of 1979, Gregg headed to the Lions' training camp.

"We were there by ourselves, two weeks before the students got there," Gregg recalls. "We'd stay at East Halls, which is right up from where the practice facility was. [Our rooms] looked like little army barracks. There was no air conditioning . . . no nothing. The windows opened a little bit, but it was hot."

After a rough night trying to catch some shut-eye, the players would be roused out of bed by team managers tooting on horns. "It was a brutal thing," Gregg says. "You'd have to get up around seven and eat breakfast, and walk down to the facility. They'd open up the gates for the chicken coops, and it stunk so badly. It was gross, and stinky, and you're tired and you had to walk through that place in the heat of summer."

Hard work, for certain, but Gregg says the point of such trials wasn't lost on the team: unity. That's how a 140-pound walk-on freshman found a home for himself amongst the Millens and Clarks of the team.

"The way practice was set up, the offense was on one field, and right beside it was the defense," Gregg remembers. "If you did something wrong and Joe was on the other field, he would run 100 yards, yelling as he was running toward you. He'd get right in your face, he'd yell at you, and he'd take a step away. Then he'd turn around and get right back in your face. *And another thing!*'

"It was ruthless, but you know what? I think he knew who he could do that to and who he couldn't. I know it got me going. I was the kind of guy that if someone told me that I can't do it, I'm going to try five times as hard just to prove him wrong."

The Garritys

Gregg Garrity.

That's precisely what Gregg Garrity did in making the team. Flash forward two seasons, and Gregg was ready to make his mark at Penn State. In 1981, Gregg led the Lions with an average of 18 yards a catch as Penn State went 10-2 and whipped Southern Cal in the Fiesta Bowl. Then came the memorable 1982 season and Gregg's signature catch in the Sugar Bowl against the Herschel Walker-led Georgia Bulldogs. Penn State was leading 20-16 in the fourth quarter when quarterback Todd Blackledge called a familiar play in the huddle.

"We ran the play a lot that year," Gregg recalls. "Basically, it was four guys (going out as receivers). The running back and tight end, Curt Warner and Mike McCloskey, ran down the hashes, and Kenny Jackson on one side and me on the other just ran fly routes on the outside. Four people, all seams, and someone should be open.

"During the year, sometimes I was open and sometimes I wasn't, but I never really got the ball [when we ran that play]. But Georgia happened to be in the right defense on that play, and when we called it, fortunately I was open."

Garrity fully extended his body in the end zone to make a spectacular grab of Blackledge's pass, completing a 47-yard play. It turned out to be the winning score as the Nittany Lions held on for a 27-23 victory and Paterno's first national championship. Garrity also made another important catch on third down later in the game to keep a drive going. But it was his sensational TD catch that made headlines, including the front cover of *Sports Illustrated*.

A special moment, for sure, and forever remembered in Penn State lore as "The Catch." It was ironic that the son of Paterno's first recruit had a hand in delivering the coach his first championship after so many close calls. The ball Gregg caught might as well have been thrown by Jim, whose gut feeling on Paterno and Penn State so many years earlier had helped to bring this family legacy—and national glory—to Happy Valley.

Watching Gregg play was almost as much fun for Jim Garrity as playing himself. Sometimes even more. Saturday mornings on game day were as much a social event for the proud father as they were a football game.

"There were a number of parents that got to know each other over the years," Jim recalls. "We would get there very early every Saturday morning on game day." While the kids dressed, the parents waited in the parking lot and socialized. After the game, the same parents would take their sons out for dinner. "My experience was always pretty family oriented with the Penn State football team," Jim says.

If Jim enjoyed watching his son carry on the family legacy at Penn State, then he doubly enjoyed witnessing his son start a new legacy for the family in the National Football League. The player regarded as too small to play major college ball would go on to play in the NFL for seven seasons with the Pittsburgh Steelers and Philadelphia Eagles.

The Garritys

✳ ✳ ✳

Gregg Garrity is now a construction contractor in Bradford Woods, Pennsylvania. Just like his dad, Gregg coaches his own son in the Midget League that his father founded. Since Gregg Garrity played there, the North Allegheny Pride has grown into a huge league with its own football field—a grass stadium, fenced in with lights, and a big parking lot.

Jim Garrity is now a grandfather of eight, maintaining two residences—one in California, the other in upper New York state—after a successful career in private business. Whether traveling to Texas or coming back to Pennsylvania, he makes it a priority to watch his grandsons play football, just as he did when his own sons were growing up.

He has relived the same scene in the North Allegheny Pride league on many occasions:

It's a dry, cool, day—perfect for football. The field is fast, the footing especially good for long pass plays. Wide receiver Gregg Garrity, Jr., known within family circles as "Pookey," gets set to spring downfield.

The ball is snapped, and he's off!

"Go Pookey!" Jim yells from the stands through cupped hands.

Gregg Jr. has outraced the secondary. He catches the ball on the fly without missing a step, just as his dad used to do.

Six points.

"If they throw him the ball, he's gone," a prideful Jim Garrity says of his grandson. "And he's done this for a couple of years. I think it's great, because it's reminiscent of Gregg."

You can tell the elder Garrity is excited by the prospects of doing it all over again.

five

TERRY SMITH & JUSTIN KING

JUSTIN KING HAD A DECISION TO MAKE. There were no life or death implications, but his answer was important nonetheless, because it would be so telling about his character, so revealing of his future successes and failures. He was still in middle school at the time, just coming into his own as a young football player, learning the game at the same speed with which he'd blow past teammates in practice.

It was simple, really a yes or no question. It came posed to him by his stepfather, Terry Smith, who asked it once and then several other times in ensuing months, but who never once applied pressure to prompt one response or the other.

"Justin," Terry said flatly, "do you want to be great, or do you want to be like everyone else?"

Justin paused for parts of a second, then responded with five words that tell a father his kid will be special someday: "I want to be great."

"So I'd say, 'Then let's go,'" says Terry today, reflecting on that memory. "If he said he wanted to be like everyone else, we wouldn't go."

Go, of course, meant go practice football at a nearby field. And once Justin announced his commitment to reaping the full rewards of his God-given talents, Terry, a former Penn State wide receiver, knew just what to do with his adolescent stepson: Drive him. Push him. Ignite him.

"In the beginning it wasn't really fun," says Justin of those practices with his stepdad, "because I didn't know why I was doing it, and then I would complain. So whenever I didn't want to do something, [Terry] would always ask me, 'Do you want to be good or do you want to be great?' He said, 'I'll let you answer that yourself.' And we'd get up and go work out.

"It was one of his sayings. He kept saying, 'Never be satisfied with what you have. Always work hard. You're already good, but to be great, you have to do the extra things.'"

It helped that the harder he worked, the more success King began to realize, both on the football field and the track, where as an eighth-grader, the Pittsburgh native finished third in his age group in the 100-meter dash at nationals.

For Smith's part, the experience of challenging his stepson and witnessing such a mature, focused response in return was highly rewarding. It strengthened his relationship with Justin, whom Terry had met a few years earlier after he'd started dating Justin's mom, Alison. But it also took Terry back to his childhood and his own relationship with his father, who used to drill Terry one-on-one, sharpening the kid's tools and cementing a lifetime love affair with football.

✳ ✳ ✳

Somewhere along the line, college football morphed into a game of physical numbers: Six-foot-what? What does he bench? What's his 40 time? Terry Smith didn't have numbers that draw recruiters to your front stoop. He wasn't 6-foot-what; he was 5-foot-8, give or take an inch depending who you ask and which media guide you're thumbing through. Call him 133 pounds—after a meat-and-potatoes Sunday dinner. Worse still, he played quarterback, a position traditionally reserved for 6-foot-4, 220-pound gunslingers.

You can't teach size, and Terry's dad, Harvey, knew that well. Skills, however, were another story. Field smarts? Same deal. A hunger for greatness, that too could be concocted within. So when Terry, the youngest of three kids, reached high school, Harvey began to work with him and his older brother Harvey Jr., pounding home a work ethic that years later Terry would pass on to his stepson.

"He always took us to the field and gave us that extra workout we needed to get a little bit ahead of our competition," says Terry, who was born in Aliquippa, Pennsylvania, and moved to nearby Monroeville when he was five years old. "My brother and I were both undersized players, so we had to work a little bit harder so the coach would overlook our size."

It worked. By the time he finished quarterbacking the Gateway Gators to the 1986 WPIAL Class 4-A championship, more than 15 Division I schools had offered him scholarships, Pitt and Penn State among them. Penn State already held a special place in Smith's family. Dad Harvey was a PSU alum, and Terry's cousin, Marques Henderson, started at safety (known at Penn State as the Hero position) for the Nittany Lions squad that won the 1986 national title. Smith and his family drove to State College several times between 1985 and '87 to watch Henderson, three years older than Smith, play for the Lions.

By that point, Smith knew better than to picture himself at quarterback past high school. Recruiters instead saw him as a wide receiver, where his speed and sure hands could help make up for questions about height and frame. Thus when Smith came to see Henderson play in the fall of 1987, he waited until his cousin and the rest of the defense were off the field so he could focus on Penn State's offense, particularly receivers Mike Alexander, Ray Roundtree, and Michael Timpson. All three were wideouts Smith looked up to, a trio he says he studied and stole moves from to implement in his own growing arsenal.

In the end, Smith's decision to pick Penn State over Pitt hinged on three key factors. One, Dad made his preference known. When recruiting attention warmed, Harvey let his son take visits to Wisconsin, Missouri, West Virginia—Terry's brother Harvey Jr. was a three-year starter for the Mountaineers—and Pitt. But "everything was always compared to Penn State," Terry says. "Not, 'How does it compare to Pitt?' but Penn State."

Playing for JoePa

Two, when Smith asked Tom Bradley, the Penn State assistant who was recruiting him—ironically, Bradley was the same assistant who would court Justin King 18 years later—whether head coach Joe Paterno would come out to Monroeville, he received his answer the next day. Like a prophet, Paterno showed up at Gateway High, then drove to the Smiths' house for dinner that night. "That made me feel real special," Smith says.

Three, call it a gut feeling. Smith may have grown up 15 miles from the Pitt campus, but as he was pondering his choice of schools, all he heard from locals was how Penn State was the greatest place in the world. And when he asked Henderson to second those rave reviews, he received the inside story of a close-knit program where football was just the start of a much longer-lasting tie.

"The tradition, the loyalty, what they have to offer beyond football—that Penn State bond is just something that's irreplaceable," Smith says. "Even now I'm reaping the benefits of the network aspect of it."

When he said yes to Bradley and Paterno, Smith opened the door to a happy four-year period in his life, a time when he learned a lot about himself and what it means to work hard in a tight team setting, a theme he'd carry forward in life. Oh yeah, and he played some darn good football, too.

At a school that forever had emphasized run over pass, Smith became a glaring anomaly. In the 20 seasons before his 1988 freshman year at Penn State, only one Nittany Lion wide receiver had caught more than 40 passes in a season (Kenny Jackson had 41 receptions in 1982.) Smith changed all that. He averaged better than 18 yards a grab in each of his first three years. In 1991, the senior co-captain cemented his leadership status with a 10-catch, 165-yard, one-touchdown game against Southern California. At that time, only one Lion had ever caught more than 10 balls in a game. In his senior season, Smith reeled in 55 total passes, more than Penn State's previous leading receiver, Dave Daniels, had amassed in 1989 and '90 combined. Those 55 catches set a single-season school record, at least until the next year when O.J. McDuffie snagged 63 receptions.

Terry Smith & Justin King

Terry Smith hauls in a pass.

"When I first went," says Smith, who racked up 846 yards and eight touchdowns in 1991, "the receivers at Penn State were pretty much an extension of the running game. They didn't really throw the ball a lot. By the time I became a senior, Joe really started to throw the ball. . . . So it really developed into a great experience.

"You know, when you go off to college, it's a change in lifestyle, and for the average student, they don't know who their roommate is. With the football team, we have a built-in fraternity from Day 1. So we bond with each other, we eat and we sleep together, we practice and sweat together. And there's a bond when we go out on that field. You're playing with your brothers."

Speaking of family, Smith's parents were in the stands at nearly every game from 1988 to '91, watching his impressive career unfold. He ticks off two road games that his parents could not make, pauses, then shrugs. Nope, just those two. "It's one of those family traits," he says. "Like [in 2005], we didn't miss any of [Justin's] games."

Playing for JoePa

Smith departed Penn State with 108 career receptions (now sixth all time in Penn State history) for 1,825 yards (seventh all time), an average of 16.9 yards per catch. He left town with a group of close friends including Daniels, Sam Gash, and Leroy Thompson, not to mention a degree in business management. He planned to give pro football a try, but the Washington Redskins cut him not long after selecting him in the 11th round of the 1992 draft. It didn't help that they'd taken Michigan's Desmond Howard several rounds earlier. Smith later tore a hamstring trying to catch on with the Atlanta Falcons.

After sitting out a full season while rehabbing, Smith hung on for two years in the Canadian Football League, followed by a season in the Arena Football League, after which, he says, "I just decided it was time to move on with my life." And just like that, he retired from the game and returned to Western Pennsylvania, where he took a job in sales in order to moonlight as an assistant football coach at Greensburg's Hempfield High.

That year Smith married the woman he'd been dating for several years. At the altar that day in 1996, Smith's bride-to-be, Alison, was given away by her nine-year-old son, Justin Thomas King.

A new family was born.

✳ ✳ ✳

Believe or not, Justin King hated sports as a kid—just weren't his thing. When he thinks back to his first encounter with Smith, King recalls his future stepfather as being "real nice and genuine," he says, "but the only thing was, he was really, really involved in sports."

King was only five years old when he met Smith, who then was just a year removed from his Penn State playing days. "I knew he played football and everything, and I knew he always talked about how good he was and stuff like that," says King with a smirk. "I just knew he was a big sports fan. It wasn't a secret. We would get into arguments over the TV, like whether to watch football or Nickelodeon."

As King soon learned, cartoons were no match for touchdowns in the Smith clan, especially because that passion for all things sports wasn't coming from Terry alone. In the months during which Terry and Alison grew closer, Justin spent more and more time with Terry's family: his father, his brother, and Smith's nephew Aaron, a year younger than Justin and already a budding sports enthusiast himself. King laughs that despite his notion about football being boring, he really never had a choice but to give it a shot.

That's exactly what happened January 2, 1995. Justin was seven then, and like any other night, he planned to commandeer the TV for some more of that good ol' Nickelodeon programming. But the Rose Bowl was on, Penn State-Oregon from Pasadena. King's options were limited.

"It was one of the first arguments he won over the TV," King says of his stepfather. "He's like, 'You're gonna watch it.' I just remember Ki-Jana Carter breaking a run and me being real interested in it. . . . That Rose Bowl was the first football game I watched all the way through. It was just a coincidence that it was Penn State."

Coincidence or not, something magical happened as Terry and Justin sat side by side, just two guys rooting on the Nittany Lions to a 38-20 victory. Justin got hooked. Soon after, Alison signed up eight-year-old Justin for his first football team. Justin, who'd been enthused by the football he'd seen on TV, wasn't as thrilled about his own early playing experiences. He was big for his age, and as is custom for big kids in Pop Warner, he was put on the offensive and defensive lines. No glory, no action.

King stuck with it, partly because of pride, partly because Smith urged him to trudge on. There was a race held one day in Pop Warner practice, and King, the lineman, smoked everyone by 10 yards. Heads turned. Why not give the kid a shot carrying the ball? Another time, while running bases in a local baseball tournament, King flashed more of that blistering speed. Next thing he knew, he was invited to join a middle school rec football team in the Woodland Hills school district, the same place that had bred names like Jason Taylor (now of the Miami Dolphins) and University of Michigan standouts Steve Breaston and Ryan Mundy.

"He was always naturally talented, always a little bit faster than everybody else," Smith says of King. And what the kid may have lacked in game knowledge, he could attain through sound coaching.

Playing for JoePa

"I did with him what my dad did with me," says Smith, who coached King in track and baseball in middle school while serving as an assistant at Duquesne to former Nittany Lion Greg Gattuso, then the Dukes' head coach. Smith left Duquesne in 2001 to become an assistant at Gateway High, where King was starting his freshman year. "I'd take him to the field on off days and work with his skills and backpedaling and form running and drills—just trying to teach him the game so he understood football."

King certainly understood success. With Smith's help and those quick feet, he soon blossomed into a two-way speedster at Gateway, where Smith became head coach in 2002 (he added the title of athletic director a year later). There were glimpses of star power early on, like the game in 2002 when Justin and his cousin Aaron combined for all the scoring to clinch the Gators' first section title in more than a decade. Aaron—he's now at Pitt on scholarship—was the quarterback, Justin the running back. Or how about the time a year earlier when King, then still a frosh, broke an 85-yard touchdown run late in the game to upset Penn Hills, quarterbacked at the time by current Penn State signal-caller Anthony Morelli?

Even as King enjoyed some success and colleges began to woo him, Smith felt his stepson needed additional motivation—monetary motivation. Smith remembers starting their deal at $50 per touchdown, back when King was still in sixth or seventh grade. King says the rate was half that. "It was $25 a touchdown, two touchdowns would be $50, and if you scored three, it was a bonus, like $100," he says. "My first year it was so-so. I would be happy to get a touchdown. But when I started to get the ball, it was like clockwork.

"I think it was a way to install motivation in me," says King, adding that Smith would bet him on just about anything, including how low he could get his 40 time at summer football camps. "Other kids are self-motivated. I was just out there having fun. He wanted me to take it somewhat seriously, but have fun at the same time. So I had to take it somewhat like business because I had things on the line. But I was still having a lot of fun doing it."

Smith says his stepson is a kid who likes to prove people wrong, which is why the wagers worked so well. It helped that there were some in the Pittsburgh area who thought King was a soft track star looking to cash in on his speed in a different sport, a tag that still irritates King. In a way, that will to disprove doubters might have played into King's choice of colleges. By the time he finished his junior year of high school, a year in which he rushed for 1,763 yards and scored a whopping 29 touchdowns, King estimates he had about 55 scholarship offers. To say he could have gone anywhere is an understatement. He began collecting letters from coaches in a box that eventually weighed more than 200 pounds. It made sense that he wore jersey number 1 at Gateway.

"He's the single best player I've ever coached," Smith says of his stepson, who backed up his junior year output by rushing for 1,902 yards and 33 scores as a senior, leading Gateway to the Western Pennsylvania District 7 Class 4-A title and earning 2004 Gatorade Pennsylvania Player of the Year accolades. "He has to be one of the best athletes I've ever been around, including my playing days and pro tryouts I've been on. He has speed I've never seen before."

Tom Bradley knew he had a rare talent in his recruiting territory. He'd first met King as an eighth-grader, when Smith had scored sideline passes for the Penn State-Miami game that opened the 2000 season. A year later, King ran a 4.3-second 40-yard dash at Penn State's summer camp, and Bradley had his boss Joe Paterno green light a scholarship offer, the first King received.

Yet despite family ties, this recruitment would be anything but easy. Penn State struggled in 2000 and again 2001, running up consecutive losing seasons for the first time since 1931-32. King was just the fleet-footed playmaking threat the Nittany Lions needed to reenergize their offense—the same fleet-footed playmaking threat who rarely chose old-school, three-yards-and-a-cloud-of-dust Penn State. For a kid like King, Penn State clearly was not the most marketable of destinations in those days.

Bradley was not deterred. He had King in town for the Nebraska game in 2002, a Penn State blowout victory under the Beaver Stadium lights. King could see the impact success had on this school and its fans. Heck, he felt the stadium shake.

As the time came to get serious about picking a school, King was rumored to be leaning heavily toward Florida, a breeding ground for

Playing for JoePa

NFL skill position players. Michigan was tempting, too; King still looked up to guys like Mundy and Breaston, and Wolverines coach Lloyd Carr hoped to use that connection to steal yet another Pennsylvania star for the Maize and Blue.

Tempting as it may have been, Smith never played the Penn State card with his stepson. He didn't have to. Everything King needed to know about life as a Nittany Lion he could gather from what Smith had taught him through the years. Besides, Smith wanted this to be King's decision to select a school "where he felt he was most important," Smith says. "Where he felt comfortable. Where he knew after football, they could help him and do something for him."

That's where Bradley saw his opening. Beginning in December 2003, the Penn State defensive coordinator wrote King one, sometimes two letters every single day. Not form letters, not dictated and typed notes on *Penn State Football Office* stationery, but handwritten notes, the stuff old friends send each other. He wrote about the impact King could have on the Penn State program, how one player of his rare talents could reverse Penn State's slide of losing seasons (four out of five between 2000 and 2004) and return a once-proud program to its rightful place among the nation's elite. But beyond anything he wrote or said, it was what Bradley didn't write or say that sealed the deal.

"I felt real comfortable with Scrap," King says, using Bradley's nickname. "He always kept in touch with me and was an easy person to talk to. When he came on visits to see me, I didn't have to hold anything back or act like he was a recruiter or anything. I knew who he was. He would come in, punch me in the chest, and we'd joke around. Stuff like that."

King had met Paterno, been in awe the first time like everyone else. But JoePa wasn't the lead salesman on this pitch. It wasn't Bradley either, though he delivered the message. It was simply the promise of potential, of what Penn State could be, and who King could be within that restoration project.

"It was a gut feeling, like this is where I should be," says King, sounding eerily similar to Smith explaining his own reasons for choosing Penn State. "When I came up for my [official] visit, everybody was hanging with everybody, and everybody was getting along. It just felt good being here, and I had to run with it."

So on a mid-November day in 2004, King ran with it to the media, telling anyone who'd listen that he was off to turn around the program of his stepfather, the place where Marques Henderson had helped win a national title, the school Harvey Sr. loved so deeply. "To the public eye, they're not very good right now, but they're close to being good," said King that day of a then 3-7 Penn State team. "They're one or two playmakers away. It's like a sleeping giant. Someone has to awaken them, and I hope to be that guy."

Left at the altar that day was Florida (dropped in part because of Ron Zook's firing), Ohio State, and Michigan, the rumored frontrunner till the end.

"When he visited Michigan," Smith said later, "he came home and said he thought something was missing. Then, when he went to Penn State and came home, he said, 'I knew what was missing. It's that family-type atmosphere.'"

※ ※ ※

In 2006, Terry and Alison celebrated the 10-year anniversary of their wedding day, an occasion Smith calls "one of the proudest moments of my life, [Justin] giving his mother away to me as his dad as well as me marrying his mother."

Before King leaves Penn State, he'll celebrate another 10-year anniversary—that of the first time he told his stepfather he was choosing to be a great football player over just a good football player.

Bradley, Paterno, and the rest of Penn State's coaches are now charged with drawing more greatness from that well, but it's Smith who continues to drive his stepson. The two might not be able to trek out to a field for backpedaling drills every day, but they're as tight as they ever were. In 2005, Justin's freshman season, he and his stepdad spoke almost daily, Terry prepping Justin for games and breaking down performances afterwards, while Justin asked questions and sought continual advice.

Playing for JoePa

Going from offense to defense, back to offense, then to a bit of both might have overwhelmed another freshman. But King looks back on Penn State's 11-1 Big Ten championship season as a "big, fun ride." A fast ride no doubt, but one he handled because of the base of football knowledge Smith had poured into him.

"Terry helped me understand football," says King, who doesn't talk much about his birth father, but says that he does talk to him and that his birth father has been to see him play. "Terry helped me understand concepts, and once you get all that stuff done, you can figure things out by yourself. All you have to learn is terminology. Same thing with the offense; same thing with the defense.

"Terry always emphasized trying to be the smartest player you can be. It doesn't matter how much talent you have. If you can't pick up the coverage or you don't know the plays, you can't do anything. And the more you know about your opponent, the more comfortable you are and the slower the game moves."

There's that word again: comfortable. It wasn't a false sense of fitting in that King felt on his high school visits to Penn State and all those dealings with Bradley. It was real. Perhaps it's the egoless locker room in the bowels of Beaver Stadium, where a star like King receives equal treatment as a third-string tight end. That's a Paterno characteristic, the mark of a man who's made his career without names on jerseys.

Perhaps it's that when a coach rides a player at Penn State, the player will always know why he's getting an earful. Penn State's a tight ship, but like any good family, the lines of communication are always open. It's one of the lasting imprints on Smith, and it's worked with youngsters like King the way it's worked for kids in 40-plus years of the Paterno era at Penn State. It's why Smith can safely say, "My whole coaching style is based on my experiences as a player. I want to coach the kids the way I wanted to be coached. If I yell at a kid, I know how I felt being yelled at, so I know I better pick the kid back up and comfort him behind that yelling."

King is one of the more humble college players you'll meet, so you know he isn't trying to tout himself when he says he hasn't been yelled at by Smith on a football field in about five or six years. And it isn't

Terry Smith & Justin King

Justin King.

because he doesn't make mistakes between the hashes. It's because through all their time together, all the workouts and Gateway games and screening sessions in the family living room, King's learned right and wrong, good and great, without Smith needing to show him the difference. It's why Smith can walk Justin through a technique by phone, Justin can implement it on his own, and they can compare notes the next day.

And Smith sees everything. He didn't miss a game in 2005, and he made most of them in '06 as well. That's what family does, regardless of cost or time commitment.

"I think we're completely different," says Smith, who still bribes King with cash, only now he's added a 3.5 GPA as the newest money-making milestone. "He's on the fast track. He's so much better than I was. Even academically he's probably going to be able to graduate in three years. . . . Going into college he said, 'I have a three-year plan that I'm just going to sacrifice my life for school and football, and then after three years, I'm going to reevaluate where I am and make decisions from there.' He's a sharp kid, he's very humble, very quiet. He doesn't even want to talk. But he'll work his butt off."

Somewhere in there you realize why Smith had to be rooting for King to pick Penn State all along, even while he kept his mouth shut. Penn State was the place where Smith could continue to focus on King's football development, because he needn't worry about what kind of person his stepson would be when he left the program. That was Smith's experience in State College. That is King's, too. And King, though young in age, understands that well because it's who he was raised to be.

"Family's very important," Smith says. "Penn State—it's such a close-knit group. They do things the right way. They're not going to compromise their integrity for anything or anyone. It gives you a great foundation for life. This is how the real life's going to be. You need to work to get somewhere, and you have to crawl before you walk. You have to work your way up the ladder and be determined. Sometimes you'll get a setback, but here's how you handle that setback. It prepares you for life."

That way, Justin, with some help from Terry, can prepare himself for greatness.

six

THE SANDUSKYS

THE SANDUSKYS' STORY is a tale of two brothers, a saga of determination. For the Sandusky boys—Edward Joel, or E.J., and Jon—playing at Penn State was a longtime dream. After all, their dad, Jerry, was a two-way player at Penn State from 1963-65, then a longtime defensive coordinator under Joe Paterno. The problem was neither of Jerry's sons was Penn State material. Physically, they didn't belong there.

The Sanduskys' story is similar to their father's story. Like his sons, Jerry, too, was unsure of himself upon arriving on campus in 1963. Far from a prized recruit, Jerry, a receiver and defensive end, was in awe of the sheer size of the average Penn State football player. But also like his sons, he possessed a certain determination to find a way to fit in, even excel.

Each of the Sanduskys, from father to sons, was faced with the same question: Can you handle the challenge of an elite football program? The answer for all of the Sanduskys was an emphatic yes.

Jerry Sandusky was hit in the helmet with the first pass ever thrown to him at Penn State. If he needed a wake-up call to the reality of the challenge that stared him down, then he had received it loud and clear. The '64 team he played on lost four of its first five games.

Playing for JoePa

Yet the team finished strong with big wins over Ohio State and Pitt, which served to brighten Jerry's outlook.

Jerry eventually gained his footing at State, lettering three years for the varsity squad while playing both tight end and defensive end. Once his playing days were over, Jerry became a graduate assistant to Earl Bruce, then took on the job of coaching the offensive tackles before becoming the linebackers coach. He eventually was named Penn State's defensive coordinator and became a major presence on teams that won two national championships in the 1980s and enjoyed continued success upon entering the Big Ten in the 1990s.

By the time E.J. was ready to plunge into Penn State football in the late 1980s, then Jon in the mid-1990s, their father's reputation as a superb coach had long been established. With State churning out players like Greg Buttle, Chuck Zapiec, Ed O'Neil, Kurt Allerman, and Lance Mehl under the tutelage of Sandusky, the school earned the nickname, "Linebacker U." One important graduate of Linebacker U who needed no instruction from Sandusky, however, was Jack Ham.

Jerry is fond of sharing the story of Jack Ham's arrival at Penn State. The coaching staff had watched film on the superb linebacker, which confirmed what they had seen in his first practice session. Everyone was in agreement: Jack Ham was the real deal. And so an urgent call went out to Jerry Sandusky, who was not present at the meeting. When Jerry arrived at Paterno's office, he was ready to talk coaching advice as it pertained to Ham, a future pro football Hall of Famer.

"Joe called my dad into his office," recalls Jon, who has heard this story several times, "[and Joe said] 'All right, Jerry, this is what I want you to do. Leave him alone. Don't change him, you'll mess him up.'"

Jerry Sandusky remembered: "Obviously," Jerry says, "it wasn't hard to coach a future Hall of Famer."

Sandusky spent 35 years as a player, assistant coach, and defensive coordinator at Penn State. He coached in 28 bowl games, appropriately finishing his career with Penn State's 24-0 shutout of Texas A&M in the 1999 Alamo Bowl. On the field, few coaches worked harder. Says son, Jon: "His attention to detail . . . his

The Sanduskys

Jerry Sandusky.

preparation was amazing. I think he felt confident going into every game that they had worked harder than anybody else."

Jerry says his final year at Penn State was an emotional roller coaster. Introduced to the fans at the team's final home game against Michigan along with the graduating seniors, Sandusky hugged everyone in sight. "Hugging them, [it was like] I was hugging every player that I ever coached," he says. "Being able to hug our son, Jon, I was hugging all of our family and our extended family."

Football has been just as eager to embrace the other Sanduskys. Jon and E.J. can't remember a time when football wasn't a part of their lives. "Our vacations were mostly scheduled around my father's speaking engagements, his clinics, the bowl games. And to us, that was just normal," Jon says. "We loved it—loved being part of it, the day to day in the fall."

For a man who breathed football, Jerry did a grand job of not bringing the wins and losses—and the ups and downs associated with each—home to his family. This had a tremendous impact on Jon. He realized his dad had a way of separating his professional life from his family life, and he always looked forward to spending time with his father.

"We didn't fret when he was coming home," Jon says. "He was going to be the same [win or loss]. He didn't make a big deal about football as other guys do. He understood he was working with young kids and they were going to make mistakes; the coaches were going to make mistakes."

Partly through his father's Second Mile program, which encourages at-risk children through nurturing contact from adults, Jon was able to gain a proper perspective on how football fit into his family's life. "I took a step back and said, 'Wow, there's a lot more important things in life—there's a lot more people in need.'"

✳ ✳ ✳

The Sandusky brothers loved growing up in State College around a thriving football program, even if they don't remember certain highlights. For example, there's the time six-month-old E.J. partied at the 1969 Orange Bowl. "Apparently there was a pep rally so loud that the chandeliers were shaking, and I slept through it," E.J. says.

At age six, E.J. became a regular at Penn State football games. Matter of fact, he didn't miss a game from age six through his senior year in college, a stretch of 17 years. "I remember going to games at the old stadium when the south end zone was open, and the track was still around the field, and they had temporary bleachers in the end zone," E.J. recalls. "Like me, [assistant coach Dick Anderson's] and [Paterno's] kids would bounce around on the pole vault pit as a diversion during the game. As kids, we pretty much sat in the end zone. And even when they enclosed the stadium, we all sat in the same section, about 25 rows up."

There was always some kind of activity to keep the coaches' kids busy. "My father would take us into the Penn State locker room on Saturdays and Sundays and we'd play indoor soccer games, or we would go work out," E.J. remembers. "It was basically like having a big playground."

The Sanduskys

The playground was one perk; being allowed to practice with the team was another. E.J.'s conditioning for each upcoming football season at State College Area High School was surely unique, as he ran alongside Penn State football players. That got E.J. thinking. There were some Division II schools interested in him as a player, but the Penn State aura was too strong. He had an interest in coaching as a profession. What better place to observe and learn than at Penn State, watching Joe Paterno, his own father, and the rest of the Penn State football staff? "So that's why I decided to go to Penn State," he says. "I knew I would have to be extremely lucky . . . to have an opportunity to play there."

E.J. joined the Penn State team as a walk-on in the spring of 1988 after a period of so-called "greyshirting," the unofficial term for allowing a player to go to school part-time and extend his eligibility for an extra year. Jerry Sandusky thought it would give his son a better chance of making the team.

E.J.'s first taste of Penn State football was brutal. Following Penn State's 35-10 loss to Clemson in the 1988 Citrus Bowl, Paterno decided to shape up his team. "Joe just absolutely took it out on our team during the winter workouts," Sandusky says. "We got killed." But E.J. survived winter workouts, then spring ball, and redshirted in the fall of '88. "So it was almost like getting two redshirt years," he says. "Basically I was able to hang around enough and worked hard in the weight room."

The longshot was that E.J. went through five grueling spring training camps, one more than most players have to endure. He says that while in throws of those torturous practices, he had his moments of doubt. Luckily, he also knew how to have fun at his father's expense. "I knew my father's defense, so I knew some of their checks when I was playing on the scout team," E.J. recalls. "There were a couple of times, to mess around with the defense, I called one of their check words. My father's screaming at the defense, 'What are you doing? What are you doing?'

"My father never could figure out who was calling the checks. It was me on the offensive line. Finally my father figured it out."

When he did, he told his son in no uncertain terms: "Don't do it again!"

Playing for JoePa

Those long, grueling practices, though, did benefit from some comic relief. The team would practice for nearly three hours, after which helmets and shoulder pads came off before a 20-minute run. Here E.J. had an advantage, since he was 20 to 25 pounds lighter than most of the Penn State linemen, not to mention faster.

"It was the only thing I could excel at," he remembers, "because I was 240 pounds. I think the other offensive linemen got upset with me, because I would beat them in long-distance running."

E.J. was used to running. He had spent many hours running the stadium steps at Beaver Stadium as fast as he could, always in Section "EJ." He always joked, "They named a section of the stadium after me. There's no G, H or I, it goes directly to EJ."

His hard work was starting to get him noticed by coaches. In the meantime, he himself was noticing the way Paterno and his staff worked. "It was just a great experience, being out there watching the coaches do their coaching, how everything was laid out and organized," E.J. says. "I just loved it."

One day a Penn State coach walked over to E.J. and asked, "Hey, can you snap a football?" The thought process was simple: E.J. was never going to be big enough or strong enough to be an offensive guard or tackle. But he could play at center. Sure enough, E.J. was a natural at snapping the ball. Still, things came slowly for him at his newfound position, as he painstakingly worked his way up the depth chart.

"You have to be aggressive but under control. And you have to see things pre-snap and post-snap and make corrections on the fly," E.J. says. "You have to learn proper angles to block a fast guy. You have to know where he's going to be before he gets there, and be able to see all these happenings in an enclosed area very quickly."

That season, the team was in San Diego for the 1989 Holiday Bowl. There, during a snapping drill prior to the game, Sandusky nearly broke quarterback Tom Bill's finger with a snap. Paterno screamed at E.J., "Hey, Sandusky, if his hand is broken, you're going to walk back to State College!" Fortunately for Sandusky, the quarterback's hand wasn't broken.

E.J.'s big break wouldn't come for two more seasons. In 1991, his fourth season with the team, he had finally worked his way up to

The Sanduskys

E.J. Sandusky, No. 77.

second-string center. In the first game of the year against Georgia Tech, he got the call. "I'll never forget, Dick Anderson says, 'Okay, you're in on the next series.' I look around. 'Who's he talking to?'

"That was the first time I had played a meaningful minute. The year before, I had played in mop-up time in a couple of games as the backup center."

In E.J.'s senior year, he earned the job of starting center. His tuition discount didn't cover graduate classes for the following fall, so Jerry Sandusky advised his son to see Paterno about a scholarship for his remaining time at Penn State.

"I think my father knew that I was going to get the scholarship," E.J. says. "I'm sure the coaching staff discussed that, but my father made me go in and ask for it myself."

At that point, E.J. was thinking seriously about becoming a coach himself. After the 1992 season, he moved to North Carolina to become a graduate/assistant coach with the Tar Heels football team. Two years later, E.J. was the offensive line coach for Western Carolina

Playing for JoePa

University, a I-AA school in the Southern Conference. Just eight months later, something happened to him that had never happened to his father: E.J. was fired, along with the other members of the offensive staff. He was out of work, but not for long.

An opportunity opened for an assistant coach at Albright College, and for E.J., it was like coming home. He was back in Pennsylvania, and his wife was closer to her old hometown of Pittsburgh. One year later, the Albright head coach left and E.J. found himself in charge of the football program.

"I didn't expect to get it," he says. "I couldn't believe it—I was 27 [years old] going on 28."

E.J. was the youngest college head football coach in the country.

✳ ✳ ✳

Like E.J., Jon Sandusky recognized the challenge of making the Penn State football team. "My brother had gone through the system and I saw the way he did things," Jon says. "He had to work his tail off, first of all to make the team, and gradually move up to the traveling team."

Jon was not daunted by the task; he walked on and eventually earned a football scholarship in his junior year. "I thought when I went there I was just going to be a scout team guy, which I was fine with," Jon says. "I just wanted to be a part of the big picture, a part of the team atmosphere. But every year, I got a little better, a little stronger, to the point where they could trust me on special teams and a little bit of defense in my senior year."

All the while, he too enjoyed the "huge honor" of playing for Paterno. "Academics was always the first thing he talked about," Jon says of JoePa. "I mean, that says something. You go in there after a tough loss, one of the first things he talked about: 'How many guys missed class?'

"It's unbelievable. At other schools they're ripping you up and down for what you did wrong in the game. It kind of makes you take a step back and think, 'He does have his priorities right.'"

Jon describes a coming of age that he and other players went through at Penn State. "I don't know if changed is the word," he says,

The Sanduskys

Jon Sandusky makes the tackle.

"but players go through some kind of evolution with Joe. He has an amazing way of teaching life to players as they get older. And I would say that 95 percent of the guys go from boys to men by the time they leave there. They understand the little things that he does, and the method behind his madness."

Jon was a student coach at Penn State for the 2000 season while going for his teaching certification. In 2001, he accepted an internship with the Philadelphia Eagles, before gaining his current job as a pro scout for the Eagles.

"It's a fascinating job, you get a new group of players to look at every season," Jon says.

E.J. is now many years removed from his Penn State experience, yet it's no surprise to hear him say that some of the Penn State football philosophy has rubbed off him, and hence on the Albright program.

"I get on my players about how their actions are a reflection of not just themselves, but their teammates, the football program, and the school itself," says E.J. "We do talk a lot about accountability and representation. So those are aspects that we definitely include in our program that you basically get from Joe."

The Albright players could also learn something important about determination from the Sanduskys. "Physically, we probably shouldn't have been out there, but mentally, just the consistency that we brought allowed us to play more than we ever thought we would play," Jon says. "We were both living examples of [Joe Paterno's mantra]: 'Work hard, stay out of trouble, keep your grades up, and stay healthy, and you'll get a shot.'"

seven

THE
JACKSONS

IF KENNY JACKSON CALLED and invited you to dinner, and he showed you around his home before the meal was served, you might see it. You'd have to look closely, because the framed photo isn't very large, and it's now nearly 30 years old. But it's there, on his desk.

It's Kenny, circa 1978, a fleet-footed high school quarterback with boyish looks and seemingly limitless promise. He's standing outside his family's home next to his father, Robert. Then there's his mother, Sarah, who has an arm around 52-year-old Joe Paterno, the Penn State football coach who was pit-stopping in South River, New Jersey, that day en route to his shore house in Avalon, New Jersey.

Tossed into an album or tucked into a shoebox of memories, this image of Paterno with Jackson and his folks might not catch your attention. But here, on display all these years later in Kenny's State College area home, it shouts to you. It begs you to ask. Fortunately, Kenny isn't shy about sharing how he feels when he looks at the picture. Because in one shutter snap, so much of his career, so much of what he's learned in life, so much of what he stands for today was captured on film. In fact Jackson is so sentimental about this memento from his first encounter with Paterno that he's brought it with him on his life's journeys, from his pro football playing days, to nine years as an assistant at Penn State, to his term as receivers coach for the Pittsburgh Steelers from 2001-03.

Playing for JoePa

"Wherever I go, I always have a picture of him," says Jackson, the first Penn State wide receiver ever to earn first-team All-America honors. "I guess guys with the Steelers used to look at me weird. They would have all this stuff up about themselves, and I would have Joe. [Steelers offensive line coach] Russ Grimm used to call me 'Little Joe.' . . . That's what he calls me to this day."

No two relationships with Paterno are alike, and Jackson—both his personal connection to Paterno and that of his family—is no exception. When you take in the photo on his desk, proudly displayed for his wife, daughter, and strangers to see, you figure Kenny must have remained tight with the old football coach all these years. And in a way, he has. In a way, though, he hasn't.

"I love Joe enough to know that I don't need to get in his business," says Jackson, who led Penn State in receiving in both 1980 and '82 and remains third all time in school history with 2,006 career receiving yards. "As long as I live, I can't see him not happy. And I know what makes him happy. Football is important to him with those kids, and he loves coaching."

Jackson's respect, admiration, indeed love for Paterno has deep roots in the State College soil. It's founded in the consistency with which Paterno has run his program and his life. Jackson sensed an honesty and strength of character in the Penn State icon way back in 1978. When every major Division I college coach with a blocking sled and whistle came knocking on his family's front door in South River, Jackson wasn't swayed by promises of glory or prospective NFL riches or an overabundance of school pride. He wanted someone who stressed education and meant it. Someone who wanted him to excel first at life and second at football, the same priority Robert and Sarah had always believed in as they were raising their children.

Joe was that man, and Penn State was his home.

✳ ✳ ✳

South River is a working-class bedroom community 36 miles southwest of New York City. It is, as it was when Kenny Jackson was growing up there, a microcosm of America's melting pot: whites,

The Jacksons

blacks, Poles, Italians, Portuguese, Irish, Germans, Russians, all coexisting in one zip code. Jackson recalls there being two predominantly African-American sections when he was a kid, including the one he grew up in.

Jackson was actually born in Neptune, New Jersey, 30 miles southwest of South River, but moved when he was five years old. His was a conjoined family: Sarah married Robert after the death of her first husband, and together they had four children of their own—Kenny, his twin brother Kevin, older brother Roger, and a younger sister—on top of the five children they'd had from previous marriages. For several years, 11 people lived in one house.

"It was like the Waltons," says Roger, two years older than Kenny. "It didn't even seem crowded. We were all in it together. Me, Kenny, and Kevin slept in the same room along with our older brothers. It was three in one bed, two in the other. One of us would sleep down at the other end of the bed and the other two slept up front."

With nine kids, there was a strict division of chores, the older children assuming the more physical work like caring for the lawn and garden, the younger ones covering smaller tasks like garbage detail. At dinnertime, Sarah usually had to prepare two options for the main course, one for her pickiest eaters (Roger and Kenny), another for everyone else.

Bedrooms and distaste for vegetables aren't all the brothers shared. They were also united in a passion for athletics and the outdoors, both of which they consumed en masse in the streets, fields, parks, and streams within walking distance of their home. There was a park across the street where a basketball game was always on. The brothers used to play tennis with each other there, even though there were often no nets up on the courts. They'd knock the ball back and forth to pass the time. There were swings there, baseball diamonds, even lakes and streams for fishing, which Kenny in particular loved.

Kenny, Kevin, and Roger were creative kids. The boys, closer with one another than they were with their other siblings because of proximity in age, once used the netting from old infant playpens to fashion homemade hockey nets for their games. "You ever see *The Little Rascals*?" asks Roger in his usual fast-talking, jovial manner.

Playing for JoePa

"They had the little gang with Spanky and Alfalfa and all them. That's how we were in the neighborhood. Unlike kids today who'd rather stay in the house and play Nintendo, we had our forts and our meetings and we'd go out in the morning and wouldn't come back 'til the evening. We'd make tents in the woods, play Army. We were close. Everywhere I went, [Kevin and Kenny] were right behind me, following me. It was funny."

With Robert supporting the family by working full-time at French pharmaceutical company Rhone-Poulenc, Sarah had a huge responsibility running the home, thus she encouraged her kids to amuse themselves outdoors. And the more sports her kids played, the better they became. That's when having each other came in handy. Roger may have been bigger than the twins, but it was always a fair fight in one-on-one hoops.

"My twin and I would never fight," Kenny insists, "but Roger and I fought all the time. You'd foul him to death before it was over."

"We could never finish," Roger adds. "We'd play to 11 and it would be 10-9, and we'd never finish the game because we'd wind up fighting. We didn't want either one of us to win."

By the time the Jacksons got to high school, all three were talented athletes with legitimate college aspirations. Kenny was a speed guy. He ran the 100, 200, and 400 meters for South River High's track team, even competed against a star sprinter named Carl Lewis from Willingboro High. (Kenny later declined a track scholarship to the University of Houston, where Lewis went.) He also played basketball and football, the latter being the true glory sport at a school that had a proud gridiron tradition with alums including NFL stars Drew Pearson and Joe Theisman.

When Kenny was a sophomore and Roger a senior, they pooled their talents to help the South River Rams win a state football championship. The calls and letters began soon after. For Roger, much as he enjoyed football, his heart was set on playing basketball in college. Kenny says his older brother also suffered through some undiagnosed back pain that 1977 season, which swayed him to focus more on basketball at the next level. Passion or pain, whatever the reason, Roger opted to decline the smattering of football offers he

80

The Jacksons

received and instead enrolled at New Jersey's Monmouth College in the fall of 1978.

Kenny, meanwhile, had all the options of a prized recruit. Jim Boeheim offered him a scholarship to play hoops at Syracuse. Larry Brown made him the same offer to play for UCLA, while Digger Phelps hosted Jackson for a weekend in South Bend, Indiana, to talk about Notre Dame basketball while dangling the opportunity to play football as well. It was anything but an ordinary recruiting scenario. For one, unlike a lot of 18-year-olds, Jackson had already firmly established the importance of education in his decision-making process. He credits his father's influence for that: Robert grew up in Tuskegee, Alabama, not far from Auburn and Tuskegee universities, where he witnessed successful African-Americans excelling in academic pursuits. He would always stress the importance of school to his kids.

When Fran Ganter and Joe Paterno began recruiting Kenny, their talk about academics struck a chord. Kenny says the Penn State coaches never even saw him play a down of football because of scheduling conflicts. Instead they spent more time mining his persona for character traits. When Paterno finally did see Kenny play a sport, it was during a South River basketball game.

"I was a pretty good student, so it was easier for me than most students; I had more choices," Kenny says of picking a college. "Joe was always into education. Some [coaches] talk about it. With him it really meant something, and you could tell."

Kenny also identified with the realistic approach Penn State took to recruiting. When he visited UCLA and USC, he was put up in the Beverly Hills Hilton. When he came to Penn State, he slept on a cot in host buddy Todd Blackledge's room.

Then there was Roger to consider. After a year spent playing basketball at Monmouth, Roger changed his mind. Today he doesn't use the word mistake, but he says that at some point in 1978, it simply clicked that he never should have abandoned football. The wheels were set in motion. First Roger transferred to Middlesex Junior College, where he continued playing hoops while trolling for football offers. Then, as Kenny was busy leading South River to another state title in 1979, the brothers began talking about possibly playing college football together, tag-teaming there as they had in their prep days.

When Penn State turned up the volume on its interest in the younger Jackson, "Kenny came to me and said, 'Well, what do you want to do?'" Roger says. "I said, 'Hey, if they want me, I'll go up there, give 'em a tryout, let them see me. Because I don't want to go up there figuring they're just going to let me play because you're there. It isn't supposed to work like that.'"

Roger's quick to admit that he capitalized on the attention his brother received to get what he calls "a second chance to play football." But he's also quick to deflect the "package deal" labels that were affixed to him by coaches and media members. As he saw it, he had the talent to play anywhere, and that would bear out once he chose a school.

For his part, Kenny sold his brother's abilities to Penn State and everyone else, hoping someone would see the talent Roger possessed and give him a chance. While he insists he would have picked Penn State anyway, it helped that Paterno and the staff took the time to assess Roger individually, watch old football tape, come to one of Roger's basketball games, and ultimately offer both brothers scholarships at the same time.

"Joe trusted me when I said, 'Look, he isn't just coming to Penn State. He can come there and play. You keep looking at me, but I'm telling you, he can start at Penn State,'" Kenny says. "My brother was influential. He was coveted by a lot of different people at the time, but he trusted Penn State."

The entire Jackson clan trusted Penn State, and it turned out to be the start of a considerably successful relationship.

✳ ✳ ✳

Joe Paterno never made any promises. Not to Kenny, not to Roger, not to Robert or Sarah. He simply let Penn State football speak for itself. That had multiple effects. For one, Kenny, who played right away as a freshman in 1980, saw exactly how much emphasis the coaching staff placed on classes and grades.

The Jacksons

Kenny Jackson.

"Joe didn't use us," he says. "He said, 'Make sure you go to class,' and if you didn't graduate, it bothered him. I couldn't take a BS class. He'd get pissed about it. I wanted to take a horticulture class, because I like flowers and plants. He thought it was BS. He comes from the concrete, the blacktop. He doesn't know."

That same "blacktop rules" approach meant nothing was guaranteed when it came to playing time, which opened the door for Roger to prove he wasn't an add-on, but a special player in his own right. "[Talk of me being a package deal] was no big deal," Roger says. "It meant nothing. It was a joke, because I knew I had the talent."

He proved it by earning a starting cornerback job in 1981—he had to sit out a year before being eligible—and leading the team with five interceptions that season. None was more pivotal than the one he grabbed off Dan Marino against Pitt in the regular-season finale. Penn State trailed 14-0 and Marino was looking for more when Jackson's pick in the end zone saved a Pitt touchdown and halted the Panthers' momentum. The Lions went on to score 48 unanswered points and upset the No. 1-ranked team in the land. The good vibes flowed forth from there into a bowl victory against USC, and, eventually, to a national championship in 1982, Paterno's first at Penn State.

Meanwhile, while the Jackson brothers were making champions of the Nittany Lions just as they had the South River High Rams, they were also making the most of their time together—for better and for worse. Kenny and Roger lived together on campus in 1980 and '81, but unlike their childhood days when they had split a bed and spent every waking hour together, this dorm arrangement wasn't exactly the smoothest of setups. Sure, they still hung out together, partying together off-campus—Roger insists they didn't drink, just danced and laughed—or playing cards down the hall in the room Blackledge, the starting quarterback, shared with running back Curt Warner. But within their own quarters, they were more *Odd Couple* than tight-knit brothers.

"I always wanted everything in its place, and he would come in, mess things up, put things everywhere, wouldn't have his bed made," Roger says. "I said, 'Man, we're in the same room! Why don't you make your bed?' We used to fight about that stuff all the time. Stuff people now would think is stupid, but back then. . . ."

Blackledge and Warner would stoke the battle flames by sneaking into the brothers' room when they were in the bathroom and messing up the joint. Fortunately, Roger was a joker at heart. At one point, to prove his stance on cleanliness, he hung a tablecloth along the ceiling to separate his side of the room from Kenny's.

"We fought every day," Kenny says. "He was a jerk. Still is. I love him, but he was a total jerk. He put up the curtain so he'd have privacy when the girls would come over. You know how it was. You were in college."

The curtain, however, could never keep the brothers apart. They may have verbally jabbed at one another and scrapped during practice, but family's family. Their competitive nature only made them better players. That's why, curtain or no curtain, they spent much of their

The Jacksons

Roger Jackson.

off-seasons those days training together, running cover drills against one another or staying in shape with plenty of pickup basketball back in Central Jersey.

"I never had to go out and find competition," says Kenny, adding that he, Roger, and their father would often sit around the dinner table and talk strategy, fond memories that resurfaced when Kenny later became a coach at Penn State. "Whether it's for clothes, for jobs, or for attention from your parents. [I could compete] every minute."

* * *

It is perhaps no surprise that the Jacksons' post-Penn State careers are as different as blue and white. After Roger's senior season ended with Penn State's Sugar Bowl win against Georgia in January 1983, he was drafted by the Philadelphia Stars of the United States Football League. Rather than stay in State College to finish his coursework and hold out for a shot at the NFL, he left school about 20 credits shy of a degree in restaurant management to play in the upstart league.

He won two USFL titles with the Stars, who featured a host of future NFL players including Kelvin Bryant and Sam Mills. But Roger never made it to the NFL. He took a shot from Mills in practice one day, cracked two bones in his lower back, and never played football again after 1984. When time passed and he didn't return to Penn State to get his degree, Joe Paterno and wife, Sue, the protectors of the program's penchant for scholastic fortitude, began to ride Roger.

"They would call me all the time," says Roger, who, as a way of saying thank you for the second chance at football, took Kenny and his college girlfriend on a 1983 trip to the Bahamas with money he'd earned in the USFL. "'What are you doing? You gotta come up here and finish! You gotta finish' [they would tell me]. I was like, 'I'm gonna do it!' But I never did. I regret that now."

"They were ready to kill him," says Kenny, who played out his final year of eligibility in 1983 and finished his career with 27 school records to his name. Kenny's still fifth in school history with 109 receptions, and his 25 career receiving touchdowns rank second only to Bobby Engram. "They should still kill him to this day, because he never did go back. He had a chance to, but he didn't finish."

While Roger returned to South River to find work, Kenny's career took off. After his second straight All-America season, the summer before which he spent working as an intern at Merrill Lynch in State College, Kenny was selected by the Philadelphia Eagles in the first round (fourth overall) of the 1984 NFL draft. He reeled in 40 passes for 692 yards as a rookie and stuck in the league for eight seasons, seven with Philly and one with the Houston Oilers. As he pondered retirement, he thought about how much he enjoyed helping other players improve. In 1991 he sent a fax to Paterno telling him he thought he could contribute to the program, and beginning in the fall of 1992, he found himself back in Happy Valley as receivers coach for the Nittany Lions. In the ensuing nine years he developed a deeper

The Jacksons

appreciation for Paterno and the Penn State system. It had a lot to do with manners, respect, and, of course, education.

"When you respect education, when you care about it, you keep learning, and it has nothing to do with age," says Kenny, who's now married to a Penn State grad, Ruth Ann, whom he met when he returned to State College in the NFL off-season to complete his degree work. They have a daughter together, Sarah Jane. "As Joe's gotten older, education matters more to him than a football game. He looked at football as education.

"... He doesn't like, 'Yes sir,' 'No sir,'" Kenny continues. "You could argue with him, fight with him, but he's fair. You didn't have to sugarcoat it, but your language was always important. Like you could never say 'pissed.' If I said to him, 'I'm pissed off!' he'd be mad at that."

Jackson also bore witness to Paterno's ultra-competitive side, which sometimes gets lost in the caring, "How's your family?" outer shell. Kenny's favorite tale goes back to the time he and Joe's son, Jay, with whom Kenny remains close, began experimenting with the Atkins diet. When both Jay and Kenny began dropping pounds, Joe had to know what their secret was.

"He got on us, like, 'What are you all doing?'" Kenny says. "We were like, 'What are you talking about? We're just not eating all those carbs.' He was so mad, like we had this conspiracy to be better than him. All we were doing was losing weight."

This particular anecdote gets Jackson laughing about Paterno's lack of tolerance for excuses, exemplified by him screaming "Move it up!" to players who are slow to recover from collisions in practice. Jackson jokes that one day when Paterno passes away, he'll tell all the mourners to "Move it up!"

"Of course, even when he's dead," Kenny says, "we aren't going to believe it. . . . But we'll have a great funeral and just thank God that he's been in our lives."

When that sad day comes, Roger Jackson surely will be there. He may have disagreed with Kenny over the years, and he admits they're not nearly as close now as they were back in the early 1980s. But if he took anything away from his experience with Paterno, it's that you always stick by your family. That was particularly important in 1999 when his father, Robert, was stabbed to death in a robbery attempt. Robert and Sarah had been separated for some time by then, but it obviously rocked the family. The tragic event brought Kenny and Roger closer together again, if only for a brief period of time. It was enough to reaffirm that the brothers would always be there for each other in times of need, even if they now only speak by phone a handful of times per year.

"No matter what happens, stay with your family," says Roger, who's remained in South River since retiring from football and is employed as a crane operator and assistant warehouse manager. He now lives in a different house but on the same block he grew up on. His mother, Sarah, brother, Kevin, and one of his sisters also live on the block. "Being at Penn State, there was so much there you could learn from different people, different ideas people might have. But family's an important thing, and that's what Joe taught us. To this day, he's there if I need him for something. I guarantee he would help me. That's how he is. Even if you weren't a player and he didn't know who you were, he would bend over backwards to help you.

"It's hard to say why anybody would do the things they do, but that's the way he is," continues Roger, who has two daughters and a stepson, Brandon Hodges, a high school wide receiver with skills and a frame that might be confused for a blend of Roger and Kenny back in the day. "His heart was always like that, even when we were up there. He'll get on you, but if he figures there's something he can do to help you, he'll get it done or have one of the other coaches take care of it. Always been that way. And I think to his grave, he'll always be that way."

eight

THE BAHRS

IT ALL STARTED LONG AGO, before Walter Bahr was born. At the beginning of the 20th century in a working-class neighborhood in Philadelphia called Kensington, a building was erected to be used as a boys' club. Through the generations, sons of the neighborhood workers who crafted the building would have an opportunity to socialize and participate in organized sports at the club. And so the Lighthouse Boys Club was born. There, many years after its creation, young Walter Bahr found his way into soccer, beginning a lifelong journey from Philadelphia to the top of the soccer world.

Kensington was dotted with textile mills and blue-collar households, a close-knit neighborhood where sports played a big part in the lives of families. Young Walter played a vast variety of street games that improved his hand-eye coordination and agility. There was "wire ball," a simple game that involved throwing a ball at telephone wires. There was stickball, the street version of baseball. There was "Five Yards," where a football would be kicked back and forth. All these creative street sports helped Walter learn how to handle himself. But none captured his imagination like the organized games played at the Lighthouse Boys Club.

At the club, Walter played baseball, basketball, indoor hockey, and soccer. "The Lighthouse Boys Club had more soccer teams than the rest of the city put together," Walter points out. It was soccer that intrigued him the most. Philadelphia was one of the hotbeds of soccer in the United States during the World War II era, and it was home to many professional teams. Walter was a good enough player that at age 15, he signed with the pro Philadelphia Nationals. Back then, there wasn't much money involved, but Walter was excited because it was a professional league. As a halfback, Walter helped the Nationals win four American Soccer League titles in the early '50s, and was named a member of nearly all of the all-star teams in his era.

In 1947, Bahr made the U.S. National team and remained a key part of the squad until 1958. But it was at age 23, in 1950, that Bahr cemented his name in U.S. soccer folklore. At that time, England was considered king of the world in soccer, and the World Cup was considered a much bigger deal than the Olympics. The Olympics were an amateur competition, while the World Cup featured professionals. The 1950 World Cup was the first big international soccer tournament following the second World War, and the Americans were significant underdogs.

In the first game of the tournament in Brazil, the U.S. national team held its own against mighty England. The teams were locked in a scoreless tie when Bahr's pass was deflected by teammate Joe Gaetjens just beyond the reach of the English goalkeeper to score the first—and only—goal of the game for either team. With that score, the Americans achieved one of the greatest upsets in soccer history.

The game, which has come to be known as "The Miracle on Grass," has since grown in stature, thanks to televised coverage of the World Cup, and has also has inspired a book, *The Game of Their Lives*, and then a movie of the same name. "Each year I do more interviews about the World Cup," Bahr says. "For 25 years, it was a pretty well-kept secret."

Bahr later turned his successful playing career into a long and satisfying career as a coach. "As a player, you think you know everything," Walter says. He learned quickly as a coach that it took more than skills and strategy to be successful in his new profession—it took the ability to handle people. "It takes a while for the chemistry

The Bahrs

Walter Bahr, front.

to show itself," he says, echoing a sentiment that Joe Paterno has expressed over the years.

Bahr coached sports on the high school level for 20 years, with an emphasis toward soccer. He was offered the athletic director's job at Franklin High School in Philadelphia, but turned it down. "It was sort of the kiss of death for any further promotions," Walter says. So he gave up high school coaching and was hired as a part-time soccer coach at Temple University. Then an offer came from Penn State to head up the Nittany Lions' soccer team. The decision should have been an easy one, but it was not. Walter hesitated, as he and his wife did a lot of soul searching. The holdup: If he took the job, it would mean potentially coaching his sons. And Walter was wary of the awkward position that could place him in.

Walter Bahr's three boys—Chris, Matt, and Casey—grew up playing soccer at the Lighthouse, just as their dad had done. The Bahrs were an athletic family to say the least. Chris and Matt would both go on to memorable football careers at Penn State before making their marks as kickers in the NFL for Super Bowl-winning teams. Casey was an Olympic soccer player, and Davies, the boys' sister, earned All-America honors as a gymnast at Penn State. Even Walter's wife, also named Davies, was a champion swimmer.

It was difficult for anyone to question the athletic prowess of such a family. Yet Walter stewed on the Penn State offer, worried about the cries of nepotism that could result from coaching his boys. Chris was already playing the sport at Penn State, and Matt was being recruited by the school. Finally, the Bahrs came to a decision to accept the offer, noting that the benefits outweighed the risks.

From a part-timer, he became a full-time soccer coach at Penn State from 1974 to 1988. During his tenure, the Nittany Lion soccer team advanced to the NCAA tournament 12 times. Walter was inducted into the Soccer Hall of Fame in 1976, and three years later was named Coach of the Year by the National Soccer Coaches Association of America. In 1995, he was elected to the NSCAA Hall of Fame.

Walter enjoyed his time at Penn State, recruiting with contacts he had developed through his many years in soccer. At his time there, he grew to appreciate the tight ship run by Joe Paterno and the sense of achievement JoePa had brought to the university. When he was recruiting for his soccer team, Bahr would often tell parents, "Look, Penn State has a reputation academically, athletically, and my kids went here. If I were doing it over again, I would still send them to Penn State. And I think that's as good a recommendation as I could make."

But just how did his kids end up choosing State, and did they enjoy playing for JoePa as well as their own pa?

✳ ✳ ✳

Heavy-duty telephone wires stretched across the street, creating the perfect "court" for wire ball, one of the three Bahr brothers' favorite outdoor games. As Chris threw the ball high trying to hit the wire, his brothers took off as fast as they could to catch the ball before it hit the ground. If their scramble fell short, then the ball would bounce high off the sidewalk, and Chris would have a "home run."

The Bahrs

The Bahr brothers learned independence from an early age; they entertained themselves and found plenty to do in the neighborhood. They would head to the playgrounds—without adult supervision—and join a pick-up game. This was important to Walter Bahr, who felt his kids had to learn how to handle themselves on their own. "A little skinny kid that gets kicked all over the place, if he wants to play, he has to learn how to handle himself," Walter says. "And you don't learn that with adults around."

The Bahr kids learned to adjust to any type of playing field—level or not. Chris recalls with vivid memory a baseball field with no right field. First base sat snugly against the fence of a private swim club. From first base to second base the fence outlined the infield, and any ball hit into the swim club was an automatic three outs. Plus, the batter had to scale the barbed-wire fence to retrieve the ball. But left field featured no such fence, extending for half a mile. Chris was a left-hand batter who couldn't naturally pull the ball due to the lack of a right field. So he had to learn to hit the ball to left field.

Along with baseball, the Bahr brothers played a wide variety of games on the streets—from handball to two-on-two football—just like their father had done as a child. And like Dad, they were drawn to soccer. On weekends, Walter would drop his sons off at his old haunt, the Lighthouse, to play soccer. "We probably played more soccer than anything because we played it year round," Chris recalls.

So how did Chris and Matt, who favored soccer, become football stars? It happened like this: Chris and a high school buddy were in the park kicking around the soccer ball, having fun. His buddy's father happened to be the high school football coach. When he came by, he was intrigued by the ease with which Chris was kicking the ball. He invited Chris to try out as a kicker for the Neshaminy High School football team. Chris was interested, so he gave it a try and decided to stick with it.

When Chris turned to football, so too did younger brother Matt. The pair would show up for football practice once a week while they continued to play soccer. On Saturdays, Walter coached soccer at the Lighthouse. His sons looked forward to playing soccer for their dad, but Walter refused to coach his sons at the club.

Playing for JoePa

Fast forward a bit, and Chris is searching for a college where he can play both soccer and football. Temple University seemed the best choice, and Chris was ready to enroll. Then came an unexpected development—Chris' dad was hired as a coach at Temple University. Walter was still adamant that fathers shouldn't coach their own sons so Chris decided to look elsewhere. He checked Penn State's schedule, and found very few conflicts between the soccer and football teams. Welcome to Penn State, Chris.

"I used to fly to football games by myself at times, because we played soccer on Friday night, and I'd have to hop on a plane or drive wherever they were playing football [the next day]," recalls Chris.

Chris' soccer background was evident in his football work. He was actually in the middle of a football evolution at the time, as more and more kickers were using the newly innovative soccer-style kick. At Penn State, he was known for his long, accurate field-goal attempts.

"The soccer style was becoming more in vogue," Chris remembers. "I think people realized it was a more accurate method to kick. If you look statistically for kickers prior to soccer style, a guy would lead the league kicking 60 percent of his field goals. And now, [if you only make] 60 percent of your field goals through week three, you're out of work."

Chris was in the spotlight, yet the pressure of thousands of screaming fans never got him flustered. "It's not the pressure of the fans, it's the pressure of the 60 guys sitting on the sidelines, watching," Chris says. "I block everything out and concentrate on making a good swing at the ball."

For the most part, his dual roles on the soccer and football teams went off without a hitch. But there was still some inevitable discord with his football coach. During one soccer game, Chris suffered an injury to his side and was barely able to walk. Penn State was playing Iowa the following day, and Chris flew out to be with the team. When Coach Paterno saw Chris hobbling on the field, he was displeased, to say the least. Chris wasn't able to kick in that game, or for several weeks following. Paterno sidelined Chris as a punishment; even though he may have needed Chris' kicking expertise, rules were rules

The Bahrs

Chris Bahr, No. 99.

and Chris' soccer injury was a detriment to the football team. No one on a Paterno team receives favoritism.

A similar incident occurred when Penn State was playing Air Force. This time it was a game conflict, as the Penn State soccer team was playing West Virginia the same day. Chris felt the football team was strong enough to handle Air Force without him, so he chose to play in the soccer game. "They handled Air Force fine and it turned out we lost to West Virginia anyway," he says. "So I didn't kick (a football) for a few weeks there, either."

When he did play, Chris set football records. He held the Penn State record for field-goal percentage for 50-yarders (six of 15, 40 percent) and field goals attempted in a season (33). His 44-yarder against Louisiana State in the 1974 Orange Bowl helped secure a 16-9 win for the Nittany Lions and their first 12-0 season. Paterno declared his team national champions that season, even though they were ranked no higher than No. 5 in the country in both wire service polls. All his players received a championship ring.

"I don't think people realized how good that team actually was, because we played what was perceived as a softer schedule," Chris says. "We had a lot of talent there. For 20 of those guys to play professional football afterwards, you have to have some talent."

Starting with Heisman Trophy winner John Cappelletti, the Lions were loaded in 1973. Tom Shuman was the quarterback and the defense featured Randy Crowder and Ed O'Neil. "Cappelletti was fun to watch," Chris says. "He seemed to do what he wanted to do. It was a very talented team around him."

In the opening game that season at Stanford, Chris was preparing to kick when he noticed the guy kneeling down to take the snap was none other than Cappelletti. "He actually held for me in the beginning of the year, for the first few games. Then they decided he had more important things to do," Chris says.

At the conclusion of Chris' junior year, he started considering a career in the NFL. "It never even entered my mind that I would do it for a living," Chris says, "I did it because I enjoyed doing it." One year later, Chris would be drafted by the Raiders, who were then in Los Angeles. He played professionally for 14 seasons, most of them with the Raiders, and contributed key field goals as they beat Philadelphia in Super Bowl XV and Washington in Super Bowl XVIII.

In the off-season, Chris didn't want to waste his time, so he enrolled at Chase Law School in northern Kentucky when he was playing for Cincinnati. He graduated from Southwestern Law School in Los Angeles when he was playing for the Raiders. It took him five and a half years from the time he started to earn his law degree. Now a financial advisor, Chris loved State College so much that he chose to come back. He and his family now live in the State College area and get to as many games as they can.

✳ ✳ ✳

Penn State actually wasn't Matt's first choice. Although he was recruited by the Nittany Lions, he initially thought of going to the

The Bahrs

Matt Bahr, No. 10.

Naval Academy. Like brother Casey, who played for the Middies, Matt liked the soccer program there. "I was going there to play soccer and play football too, for (former Penn State assistant coach) George Welsh," he says. "But they were changing the soccer coach and that seemed like too much of a chance to take." So Matt accepted an offer from Penn State, and went to play soccer for his father and football for Paterno.

Matt credits his attitude and preparation for his success at Penn State: "I'd go out there and go through a checklist: feeling the turf around the ball for my footing, getting back in a comfortable position, and telling myself not to freeze in the starting position. I tried to remember: head down, start slow, and accelerate at the target and follow through it."

Just like his brother, Matt used a soccer-style swipe at the ball. He was so successful that he surpassed Chris' kicking records at Penn

Playing for JoePa

State. But Matt wasn't concerned with records. He subscribed to Coach Paterno's philosophy for the team. "Like Joe said, 'The bottom line is to win. Did you help your team, were you part of the effort?' And if so, good things would happen," he says.

In Matt's junior season in 1977, he kicked 14 field goals for the Lions, earning a reputation for last-minute heroics. Against Pitt, he kicked three of four field goals, including a 20-yarder in icy conditions to pull out a 15-13 win for Penn State.

"The game sticks out only because I was successful in what I felt were very unfavorable conditions," Matt says. "The Astroturf field was very icy."

In 1978, Matt kicked a school-record 22 field goals and made every one of his 31 extra-point attempts while gaining All-America honors. The Nittany Lions won their first 11 games that year and were ranked No. 1 in the country before losing to second-ranked Alabama, 14-7, in the Sugar Bowl.

"I had some great teammates and we came up a little short at the end," Matt says. "But that's why they play the game—that's the fun part."

Matt would sustain his game-winning ways in high-pressure situations in the NFL. One of the high points of his pro career, he says, was playing for the New York Giants in the 1991 Super Bowl against the Buffalo Bills. The Giants trailed 12-10 at the half, but went ahead on a touchdown in the third period before losing the lead again in the fourth. It was a spotlight moment for Matt Bahr. With the entire nation watching and the game on the line, Bahr kicked a 21-yard field goal with 7:20 remaining to lead the underdog Giants to a 20-19 advantage. The Giants hung on for victory in Super Bowl XXV when Bills kicker Scott Norwood famously missed what would have been a game-winning field goal as time expired.

"We were severe underdogs against the Bills," Matt recalls. "But that goes back to the Penn State experience, and a game against Alabama. We were underdogs but that didn't mean that we didn't feel we had a good chance of winning."

Matt says there's a different mentality to being a kicker, going into the breach in the last minutes to save your team. "You knew the job was dangerous when you took it. It wasn't like someone said, 'Hey, by the way, you might have to kick at the end of the game.' That was just part of the deal. I don't think anybody ever said, 'Wow, I never expected that,'" he says.

But what he did expect was that Paterno would be watching him. The coach's eyes were everywhere, and that pressure is what Matt says made him a better kicker. "Joe is amazing: He could be 300 yards away on the practice field, you make one mistake and you hear about it. You can hear that voice railing at you from across the way, so you knew his eyes were always on you."

Accuracy was the name of the game for Bahr in the NFL, where he was successful on more than 73 percent of his field goal attempts. Even more remarkable: In 482 career extra-point attempts, Matt missed only 10 of them. He enjoyed a 17-year career in the NFL, winning Super Bowl rings with the Pittsburgh Steelers and the New York Giants.

Like his brother Chris, Matt prepared himself for life after football. During the off-season, he worked during the day and went to school at night, following the advice given to all football players at State. For the majority of professional players, a career is brief at best. That's where Matt feels people get confused.

"The average lifetime in the NFL is 3.2 years," he says. "That means one-third of the league turns over every year, and never plays again. But you can talk 'til you're blue in the face to some kids, it doesn't sink in."

Today, Matt is a design engineer living in Pittsburgh. He also has an Internet-based business making custom uniforms for sports teams, and is involved in a national fitness program called Fit For Life, which focuses on obesity. "We have to find a way to get the kids out of the house away from the media and get them active," says Matt, who never had that problem himself as a child.

For Chris and Matt, the Penn State experience continues to resonate in a positive way in their lives. "The longer you're away, the more you appreciate the program Joe Paterno had and the way he conducted himself," Chris says.

Of course, the boys had another college coach to look up to as well, and he wasn't a shabby role model, either.

nine

THE HARRISES

FRANCO HARRIS HAS ACCUMULATED a lot in his 57 years of life: plenty of good memories, plenty of good friends, plenty of yards, and plenty of touchdowns. In turn, he's received plenty of love from fans who have followed his football career. One thing Franco Harris does not have much of, though, is regret.

Harris was born into a military family of simple means. He turned talent on the football field into four years of free education at Penn State. He turned a co-starring backfield role with the Nittany Lions into an NFL paycheck. He turned a Pro Football Hall of Fame career with the Pittsburgh Steelers into the birth of a business. He turned a passion for the food and service industry into one of America's leading companies in the bakery nutrition category.

Harris has not failed at much, and as such, there is little for him to look back upon and say, "I could have done this better," or, "I could have made more of that opportunity." But early in 2007, speaking from his office at Super Bakery's base in his adopted hometown of Pittsburgh, Harris isn't interested in talking about success. He's talking family. Specifically, he's talking about his younger brother, Piero—Pete to those who knew him best. And as Franco speaks, something in his subdued, gravely voice tells you he's about to admit to something.

Franco Harris has at least one regret. It's Pete, who was only 49 when he died of a heart attack in August 2006. He'd been an executive chef at PGA National Resort and Spa in Palm Beach Gardens, Florida. It was a good job, a great job really, a high-profile post for Franco's kid brother who, like Franco, had majored in food service and housing administration at Penn State. But it was also a demanding job—long hours and work on the weekend. And therein lies Franco's regret.

In recent years, when Franco would get together with his brothers and sisters, he'd always think of Pete. When he'd plan trips with his mom, Gina, he'd ask Pete to come along. But Pete usually had to work. And so Franco wouldn't push him. Next time, he figured. We'll see you next time.

Now Franco's left to cherish those rare times when his kid brother did come along. "We would do a function at the Super Bowl, and he would come," Franco says, "we" being Super Bakery, the now 20-employee company he founded in 1990. "In July [of 2006], I had a party here in Pittsburgh for the [Major League Baseball] All-Star Game, and he came up for that weekend. Then, a couple of years ago he went to Italy with my brother and mother. That was his first time going to Italy. . . ."

Franco's voice trails off, his brain scouring its innermost recesses for other recent memories that include Piero. Instead Franco talks about his own trip to Italy in 2006 with his mother, two of his sisters, and one of his brothers. They made the trip after Pete had passed away.

"We're always doing a lot of family stuff like that," Franco says. "When you do it, you think, 'Wow.' It makes you reflect a lot more on Piero now. Knowing there's so much more that we're doing and so much more that we're enjoying.

"Then again, his schedule,"—Franco stops and laughs, a mix of sarcasm and disappointment that he can't hide—"it wouldn't allow him to do things like that."

✳ ✳ ✳

Time is all you have as a kid. Time and energy. That's what made growing up in the Harris household so much fun. Franco was born in Fort Dix, New Jersey, the Southern Jersey base of the U.S. Army's 9th Infantry Division during and after World War II. He was the third

The Harrises

child born to parents Cad and Gina, who moved the family to nearby Mount Holly in 1954, when Franco was four years old.

In Mount Holly the Harris clan eventually grew to total 11 members. In chronological order, the family's nine children went like this: Daniela, Mario, Franco, Marisa, Alvara, Luana, Piero, Giuseppe, and Michele. Cad worked two jobs to cover the bills, one in a hospital on the base at Fort Dix and, for many years, a night job in a local cafeteria. Gina was home with the children, keeping house—first a two-bedroom place, then a three-bedroom home, a necessary upgrade for the few years that all 11 Harrises were living together under one roof.

"The baby always stayed with my mom and dad, but the rest of us were in bunk beds," Franco says of those years. "There wasn't very much money at all."

Yet the Harris kids didn't want for much. They had each other, and they had a community at their fingertips that was loaded with kids who were always up for some sort of action. Dodgeball, kickball, basketball, baseball, softball, hide and seek. You name it, the Mount Holly kids played it. Franco talks fondly about sprint races they used to run, especially the first time he beat older sister Daniela in a head-to-head heat. "That was a big day," he says, smiling.

Most of the games were unorganized pickup contests, the stuff of vacant lots and slow-moving cross streets, though Franco did join a CYO baseball league when he was eight or nine that served as his first formal sports experience. Giuseppe, 10 years younger than Franco, was also a talented baseball player. In fact, when he reached high school, he traveled to Pittsburgh to meet with the Pirates, a sitdown Franco had arranged through his connections. Giuseppe, though, ultimately decided to play college football instead. Maybe that explains why when he ponders his childhood, some of his fondest memories are of the pickup football games he'd play with older brother Pete, younger brother Michele—his siblings call him Kelly—and neighborhood friends.

"Not just Mount Holly, but we used to go to other towns on the weekends and play streetball," Giuseppe says. "It was never touch. It was streetball, man. Sometimes we played on grass, sometimes we played in the street. And a lot of people ran into signs, because that's the way it was."

Playing for JoePa

Speaking of the way it was, when Franco was growing up, he never wasted time dreaming about some glorious pro football career that awaited him after college. The concept of even going to college, let along earning a scholarship for athletic excellence, was completely foreign to his family.

"Coming from Italy, my mother knew nothing about sports," says Franco, who played his first organized football as a seventh-grader. "And my father, who was from Mississippi, didn't play any sports or anything. I was just lucky the school system in Mount Holly had great sports programs and a great education system. That really made a difference. That and I was naturally athletic, so I was able to pick things up fairly easily."

Franco was a sophomore at Rancocas Valley High School when the light went on. That year older brother Mario, then a senior at Rancocas Valley, was offered a partial scholarship to play football at Glassboro State. It was eye-opening on many levels. Mario had only started to play high school football two seasons earlier as a 10th grader at Rancocas Valley. As the oldest son, Mario was focused on following his father's footsteps by pursuing a career in the military. That's all Mario knew. That's all the Harris family knew. Even after he was formally offered the partial college scholarship, Mario remained determined to join the Marines. Only after a professional convincing job from the Glassboro State coaches did the eldest Harris son decide he'd give college a try.

"I was in shock," Franco says. "Everybody was in shock. Because no one had ever mentioned the word college to us in our whole life. And it was quite strange that you could go to college for free and play football."

Franco himself grew up wanting to be an Army Ranger, but after Mario left for college, Franco began to think differently. He made high school All-American as a junior, and after that 1966 season, the football recruiting letters began to stream in. The interest level grew to a point that Franco knew he could earn more than the partial ride Mario had been offered—he could land a full four-year scholarship. He determined if given that opportunity, he wanted to study hotel and food management, which would enable him to travel and see the world as he would have done in the Army. All of which helped him narrow down his list of suitors to Penn State, Michigan, and Cornell, three schools with excellent hotel and food management majors.

Franco took his time deciding, in part because the wooing process was so foreign to him, especially the perks. He flew out to visit Ohio State in 1967, and that was the first time he'd ever been on an airplane. When other coaches came to Mount Holly to meet with him, Franco would request that they go out to eat rather than have Gina whip up some of her famous spaghetti that Franco had grown up on.

"I liked it when they took me out to dinner," he says. "We never really went to restaurants growing up. I mean *never*. We never went out to eat once. So being recruited, it was like, 'Oh my gosh. People eat rare steak? I've never seen a lobster before.' It was like, 'Wow.'"

It was tough to pass on Cornell, which had sold Franco on hotel and food management as the industry of the future. Penn State had a strong curriculum too, and it had Joe Paterno. Paterno's assistants George Welsh and Bob Phillips were the ones actively pursuing Franco, but when Paterno himself came to the house in Mount Holly, the magic was on.

In hindsight, it comes as little surprise that Paterno hit it off with Franco's mother, Gina, who was born in Italy and had met Cad in Italy at the end of World War II. Says Franco, "There's always that chemistry there when Italians get together."

But it was more than that. "Personally I really liked him," Franco says of Joe. "I thought he was a very sincere person who cared about his athletes. You could feel that the football program was very important to him, the education was very important to him, and you as a person were very important to him."

Franco picked Penn State, and in that instant, a legacy was born.

❋ ❋ ❋

In the life cycle of Penn State football, the Harris family spanned those crucial years when the Nittany Lions rose to national prominence once and for all, then laid the foundation for the school's first undisputed national championship. It started with Franco, who arrived as a freshman in 1968, while Penn State was in the midst of a winning streak that dated back to October 14, 1967, and wouldn't be snapped until September 26, 1970. When he lettered for the first time in 1969, Franco spent the season splitting carries in the backfield with Charlie Pittman—the team's leading rusher in 1967, '68, and '69—and a fellow talented sophomore, Lydell Mitchell.

Pittman was one of several players to leave a lasting impact on Franco in his four years within the Penn State football family. "What happened during the time I was there was just phenomenal," Franco says. "From my freshman year on, it was just great. And I guess they had guys there that started to set the standard, guys like Charlie Pittman. Seeing a talent like that run, it was like, 'Oh my gosh.'"

Franco was no slouch himself. He gained 643 yards in 1969 for the 11-0 Nittany Lions, more impressive when you consider he only took 115 handoffs. That nets to a 5.6 yards-per-carry average that season, best on the team. His 10 touchdowns were second only to Pittman's 11.

Harris never led Penn State in rushing during his three years on the team, but he scored 25 career touchdowns (24 rushing) and topped the 2,000-yard mark for his career, something only 15 other Penn State ball-carriers have done in school history. His three teams (1969, '70, and '71) went a combined 29-4 and won two bowl games, the Orange Bowl after the '69 season and the Cotton Bowl that capped the '71 season, Franco's final college game.

"To go from high school to a program like Penn State, it's night and day as far as the level of play and the expectations of you and demands on you," says Franco, who says he feels fortunate to have blocked for Mitchell in 1971, when Lydell tore off 1,567 rushing yards and 26 rushing touchdowns. "I look at the hitting I did, and just how physical it was, and how demanding Joe was . . . to get things right. When you're going through it you say, 'Man, phew, this is tough.' But it's like anything. When you look back on it, you realize you got through it, and because you got through it, you are a better person and a better athlete."

The Harrises

Franco Harris.

That's the message Franco forwarded to younger brothers Piero and Giuseppe about Penn State when each began receiving football recruiting attention as undergrads at Rancocas Valley High. On the one hand, you could argue that Franco's achievements with the Steelers boosted the amount of exposure his brothers received back home. After all, Franco was the NFL's rookie of the year in 1972, when he caught the famed "Immaculate Reception." And he'd led Pittsburgh to two Super Bowl victories—two of four rings he'd win in his career with the Steelers—before Pete or Giuseppe ever played a down at Penn State. On the flip side, Pete and Giuseppe were talented athletes in their own right, bona fide Division I-A recruits with or without the Harris name. Pete, for example, played football, basketball, and baseball at Rancocas Valley, earning honorable mention all-county honors from the *Burlington County Times* as a quarterback in 1973 and '74.

What's more is that while Franco did talk to his brothers about his experiences, he never used the hard sell, and he never placed calls to Penn State or any other colleges to ask for special consideration for his brothers. In fact, if there's anyone in the family who does deserve credit for pushing Pete and Giuseppe, it's their mother, Gina. "I remember after I got my scholarship," Franco says, "my mom was just ecstatic that I got a full ride. She would tell the three youngest boys, she'd say, 'Go out and kicka tha football, go, go, go. Go out and kicka tha football.' It was funny."

When it actually came time for Pete and, two years later, Giuseppe to select schools, "I told them I really did like the experience [at Penn State]," Franco says, "but in the end, I would always say, 'It's your decision. Just because it worked for me and was great for me, doesn't mean this is where you have to go.' Everybody has to have his own reasons and comfort zone for why he picks a certain place."

Of the two brothers, Giuseppe struggled more with his decision. He'd flown out to visit Arizona State and had fallen in love with the campus—it helped that an East Coast snowstorm left him stranded in Tempe for a few extra days—and the program, run at the time by Frank Kush. Kush, who coached the Sun Devils from 1958-79 and won 176 games in that span, "was really a great man," Giuseppe says. "He treated me very well."

On the day Giuseppe committed to become the third member of his family to play football at Penn State, Kush was in the Harris house, making his final recruiting pitch. Turning down Kush and Arizona State was "the hardest decision of my life," Giuseppe says. But ultimately, he adds, "In the end it all comes down to family. It always comes down to that."

The Harrises

Pete Harris, No. 27.

(Kush, meanwhile, was fired by Arizona State in 1979 in the wake of a lawsuit filed by a former Sun Devils punter who accused Kush and his staff of mental and physical harassment that forced the player to transfer. The harshest allegation in the suit said Kush had punched the player in the mouth after a bad punt in a 1978 game.)

When he arrived in Happy Valley as a freshman, Giuseppe says he felt no pressure to play up to the standard set a decade earlier by Franco or the level at which Pete was playing in 1978. Of course, had he felt any pressure, no one would have blamed him. By 1978 Franco was nearing the end of a stretch of nine consecutive seasons in which he made the Pro Bowl. And as a junior in 1978, Pete had arguably the greatest season a Penn State safety has ever had. He led the nation that year with 10 interceptions, tacking on two fumble recoveries for an 11-1 Penn State team that had gone undefeated in the regular season before falling to Alabama in the Sugar Bowl. Pete's 10 interceptions tied a single-season school record, a mark he shares to this day with Neal Smith, who had played with Franco.

Pete, though, had his share of difficulties, too. After he received first-team All-America accolades for his 1978 efforts, his grades slipped. They plummeted to the point that he nearly flunked out of school. A former teammate of Pete's says Pete went to see Paterno hoping the coach would give him another shot, but instead Pete found out just how committed Paterno was and is to education. The coach refused to bail him out, and instead told him he couldn't play football if his grades weren't up to snuff.

So Pete sat out the 1979 season, toiling away to revive his GPA, which he finally did in time to make it back for his senior year of eligibility at Penn State in 1980, when he picked off three more passes to give him 15 for his career. He's still tied for second in school history in that category.

"I can't speak for him, but I'm sure it was tough for him" to sit out the 1979 season, says Giuseppe, who as a cornerback led Penn State in interceptions during the season Pete was off the team. "I'm sure it's like anybody who's athletically driven. You can't play, but you want to be in there. You're young, you're 20, 21 years old, and you really want to get out there. But he picked it up and came back. That's all that matters.

"He was a great brother, and I'm glad I followed him up there. He was always there when I needed him and vice versa. Like I said, that was the reason I chose Penn State more than anything else. I mean, how many kids can actually say they went to college with their brother and played football with him? I thank Penn State for giving me the chance to play with Pete. And I miss him dearly."

✳ ✳ ✳

In hindsight, the 2006 Orange Bowl seems even more special than it was at the time. Sure, it was Penn State's first appearance in a BCS

Giuseppe Harris, No. 26.

bowl game. It was Paterno versus his friend and colleague Bobby Bowden, the Florida State coach who remains ahead of Paterno for the top spot on the all-time list of Division I-A coaching victories. The game itself was thrilling, a triple-overtime defensive slugfest that saw the Nittany Lions prevail, 26-23. But for Franco and Giuseppe, it's a moment they now cherish dearly, for they will always be able to close their eyes and picture themselves sitting in the stands at that game, talking with Pete, laughing, cheering, reconnecting.

Playing for JoePa

That's a big word for Franco these days. Reconnecting. He admits there have been years in his life when he's fallen out of touch with Penn State more than he would have liked; times when he got bogged down with work like the rest of us. But in recent years he's reached out to the school, bonded with the program that prepared him for life and the college that prepared him for life after football.

"I've reconnected," he says. "That's what I tell people: It's a great institution, a great football family that we have up there, and you have to stay connected."

The Harris family reunion at the Orange Bowl was the fruit of Franco's efforts. These days he's always on Giuseppe to get more involved with Penn State on a number of levels. And he's setting an example as a big brother, not only as a former Nittany Lion football player, but also from an academic and research perspective. His Super Bakery Inc., for which both Giuseppe and Franco's older brother Mario now work, was the first company to be approved by the USDA to sell nutritionally fortified donuts and cinnamon buns to school systems under specific guidelines. When the company began work to design its Super Muffin, Franco decided to partner on the project with the Food Service Research Kitchen in the school of hotel, restaurant, and recreation management within Penn State's College of Health and Human Development. Franco has also made a gift commitment to Penn State of $150,000, half of which benefits the Food Service Research Kitchen, half of which went to start a scholarship fund for minority students in his former major.

Franco now has a plan cooking back home in Pittsburgh. He says he'll be opening a new restaurant there, possibly sometime before the close of 2007. It'll be a small café-type place on the north side of Pittsburgh, not far from where he lived for 20 years of his life and where he still owns a home. His restaurant will serve Mediterranean fare, but the name remains to-be-determined—at least he's not telling anyone at the moment.

It's all positive, all good stuff, until that word pops up again: Regret. See, Pete had once tried opening and operating a restaurant in Pittsburgh. But the business struggled, and Pete eventually walked away from it. This was before he landed the job at PGA National

Resort. Now, years later, Franco says one of the many reasons he wishes his brother was still alive is that Pete would have been Franco's first choice to run the new restaurant.

"You always do that and you always think, 'Why didn't we do more?'" Franco says. "'Why wasn't there enough time?'"

That's a question even Franco Harris can't answer.

ten

THE DUFFYS

ROGER AND PAT DUFFY shared the typical sibling rivalry growing up:

"I'm better than you."

"No you're not. I can run faster."

"Yeah, well I can throw farther."

Each built his case, but in truth they were quite comparable. After all, Roger and Pat are fraternal twins.

"We were always very competitive," says Roger. "Basketball, football, baseball, you name it, we were always out there," fiercely competing against each other.

The brothers would eventually grow into big, powerful linemen for Penn State. Roger later went on to a distinguished 12-year career in the NFL. "I don't know if I would have gotten to the NFL or Division I football without that constant sibling competition with my brother," Roger said upon his installation in 2006 in the Stark County (Ohio) High School Football Hall of Fame.

His father was an important part of that success, too. When the brothers were still in junior high, their father spotted a "For Sale" sign hanging over a stack of 100-pound plates in a sporting goods store. Roger Duffy Sr. asked his sons, "Do you think you could lift those?"

Playing for JoePa

The boys were anxious to try. Roger lifted the plate, struggling with all his strength. "I couldn't lift it and my brother could," Roger recalls. "And that was just fueling the fire between us."

Dad purchased the plates, and the boys began working out every day, lying on the cold cement floor of their basement on their backs, benching the weight. "We finally graduated to a weight bench," Roger remembers.

The brothers lifted routinely, yet Roger still lagged behind his brother, who egged him on. Roger refused to quit, and finally the day came when he could lift the same amount as Pat. With that accomplished, they moved on to Strong Man territory. Their mom's Volkswagen offered up a new challenge.

First Pat would dead lift the end of the old blue car. Then Roger would try, each challenging the other. The feat proved too easy; the boys were soon lifting the back end over and over again, announcing the winner as the one who could complete more reps. It was hardly an activity that would gain approval from a weight coach, but fun nonetheless.

"It was silly stuff," Roger says. "Luckily, we didn't hurt ourselves."

When the Duffy brothers were in grade school, they pleaded with their dad to let them play football, as many of their friends were doing. Roger and Pat were bigger than their friends, and they wanted to play, too. They begged Roger Sr., but the answer was always, "No!" Dad believed his sons were too young to play organized football. "Wait until fifth grade," he told them. Wait they did, until seventh grade.

In high school, the brothers' sibling rivalry morphed into something far more positive and beneficial. "Dad was a big advocate of helping each other out, rather than have the sibling rivalry," Roger says. The boys still pushed each other to the max, whether it was while training, lifting, or playing, but they did so with the thought that it would make both them and their team better. Suddenly, they had a goal more significant than simply outdoing each other. "If there was a day I didn't go out and run or lift, Pat would be doing it," Roger says. "I felt like I'd better get out there and work."

Roger and Pat attended middle school and high school in football-crazed Canton, Ohio. They were featured on a strong line for Canton

The Duffys

Central Catholic, a mid-size parochial school—Roger at guard and center, and Pat at tackle. "Most of the guys played both ways," Roger remembers. "We had 40 guys come out for the team, but only about 15 actually played."

The Duffys were big boys, even at that age: 6-foot-3, 280 pounds. "I think the next biggest guy was 195 soaking wet," Roger says. Even though they were bigger and stronger than the rest of the players on the team, they didn't take their size for granted. They worked as hard as anyone else in the weight room. Their coach, a local legend named Lowell Klinefelter, would have it no other way. Coach Klinefelter, whom Roger says shares a lot in common with Coach Paterno, was a hard-nosed character who gave the boys a dose of tough love, earning their respect and keeping them on track. By their senior year, the twins could each bench press more than 400 pounds—a far cry from days spent on their backs in their basement.

Colleges all around the country were interested in the Duffys, who basically could have written their own ticket to the school of their choice. Ohio State had an obvious edge on the others, what with its long tradition of winning excellence under coach Woody Hayes. But Paterno wasn't simply going to pack his bags with such prized recruits on the line. He sent his first-year defensive backs coach, Ron Blackledge, to Ohio to talk to the twins. Both sides of the Duffy family were from the Pittsburgh area, and they had a history of working in the steel mills. When the elder Roger Duffy received a job promotion and transfer, the boys were very young. Roger, his wife, Margaret, and the boys ended up in Ohio. But their roots and their loyalties were in Pennsylvania. So Paterno knew he had an "in."

The odds were raised for Penn State in 1986 as Ron returned, this time with Joe in tow, to visit the Duffys' home. Always up front and honest, JoePa told it like it was: He was going to be around for the Duffys' college career, they could count on him. But after that? "Mr. and Mrs. Duffy, I plan to coach for five more years," Paterno told them. "After that time my youngest son will graduate from high school, and Sue and I will do some traveling." Fast-forward 20 years, and Paterno still has a couple of years left on his contract. "I always share that story with people," Roger says, "and they get a kick out of that."

Playing for JoePa

The Duffys returned to their roots for a recruiting visit to Happy Valley. The boys hung out with the Penn State players and found them down to earth, but it was the coaching staff that truly impressed them. They quickly fell for the gorgeous campus and were lulled by Penn State's own recent winning tradition. By the visit's end, they had made up their mind: They were going to Penn State.

On campus, the twins caused a bit of confusion. Although not identical, the Duffys looked enough alike that people often mistook one for the other. "We had the glasses and wore our hair the same way," Roger says. "I think I was a half-inch taller, but if we weren't standing next to each other, you couldn't tell."

A case of mistaken identity led to romance on the Penn State campus. Cathy Kamenski, a softball pitcher at Penn State, had classes with Pat Duffy in the first semester. On occasions, they would stop to talk. One day Roger was walking across campus when a lovely young lady that he had never seen before greeted him. After chatting a bit, Roger asked the woman who she was, and after an awkward moment, the mystery was solved.

"She mistakenly thought I was Pat," Roger recalls. "That's how we actually got to meet each other." The intriguing stranger eventually became Mrs. Roger Duffy. "It was kind of funny how that worked out."

At Penn State, the Nittany Lions' strength coach, Chet Furman, would occasionally work out with the twins. Furman soon discovered the sibling rivalry that had long since given the boys an edge. "If Pat went first, I would ask Chet, 'How many reps did Pat do?'" Roger says. "I always wanted to do at least one more."

The 1986 season began without immediate reward for Roger, who had to wait until the eighth game of the season for his first crack at playing time. "I was kind of fortunate, because I got thrown into the West Virginia game," Roger recalls. "The clock was running down, we were up by a big score."

Pat was red-shirted and sat out the '86 season. He wasn't able to travel or play in any of the games, but he did get in some reps on the scout team. For one season he was on the defensive side of the ball and went up against his brother regularly in practice. Of course, they both enjoyed the competition.

Roger Duffy, No. 78.

Meanwhile Roger was learning from the upperclassmen. "I saw how hard those guys worked, how they did the film study, how they handled themselves off the field as well," Roger says. He had several good examples to follow, as the Nittany Lions won the national championship in 1986 with a roster including D.J. Dozier, Shane Conlan, Chris Conlin, and Tim Johnson.

In 1987, Roger was backing up Mike Wolf on the offensive line, when Wolf suffered an injury in the fourth game of the season against Boston College. Roger seized the opportunity and remained a part of State's starting line for the balance of his career. His brother Pat, however, was stuck in a waiting game. It wouldn't be until his senior year, in 1990, that he was finally named a starter on the offensive line for a strong Penn State team that finished with a 9-3 record.

The Lions got off to a rocky start that season, losing to Texas by four points and Southern Cal by five. "We were able to pull it together and win our last nine games," Pat says. The only other blemish on the Penn State season was a seven-point loss to Florida State in the Blockbuster Bowl. The highlight of the season undoubtedly was State's victory over Notre Dame at South Bend. Going into the game, the Fighting Irish were ranked No. 1 in the country, and Penn State was No. 18.

"I remember Coach Paterno was talking to us in the pregame meal," Pat recalls, "and he said, 'You know, we really believe you guys can just go out there and beat this team.' We had a solid game plan, like we did week in and week out. He put a lot of faith in the team there, which paid off in the end. We were able to get that W in South Bend."

With four seconds left, the score was knotted, 21-21. The Nittany Lions lined up for a 34-yard field goal attempt by freshman kicker Craig Fayak. As the seconds ticked down, Fayak booted the ball through the uprights for a 24-21 Penn State victory.

"That was the most memorable game for me," Pat says. "They were in the top spot. We were just able to get in there and grind out a victory." The win bumped the Lions into the Top 10 at the time, a testament to their grueling schedule that year. Along with Notre Dame, Southern Cal, and Texas, the '90 Nittany Lions also faced Boston College, Alabama, West Virginia, Maryland, and Pitt that season—one of the toughest schedules in their history.

Despite their fine record, the players believed they could have done better. "I was a senior," Pat says. "Along with three of the other starters on the offensive line, we never had the opportunity to start. So I guess you could say we didn't have the playing experience. But after the first two games, we started to get more comfortable in game situations, totally different than practice. You get a little experience under your belt, it's different. If we could have had those first two games back, if we played them again we probably would have had a little different outcome."

While Pat was going through his memorable season, Roger was already going through another kind of challenge with the New York Jets in the NFL. He became, in his words, "a jack of all trades." Being used primarily as a center, Roger also played guard, tackle, and even

Pat Duffy.

long snapper on occasion. "They only carried seven linemen active for games, so I had to learn more than one position," Roger says. "I think what helped me stay in the NFL for 12 years was my versatility." Roger played eight years with the Jets and then four with the Pittsburgh Steelers, staying remarkably free of serious injuries in all that time.

The "professionalism" of Joe Paterno's classy program at Penn State was a steadying influence for Roger in his time in the pros. "At Penn State you presented yourself well, as far as knowing your assignments, doing your film study," says Roger, whom Paterno called "the best center I ever coached" in a 1996 interview. "No detail was too small to learn. And the work ethic was important: Practice hard and smart as well."

JoePa saw to that. "You'd think with all that territory [at the practice fields], you'd be safe," says Pat. "But if you messed up on something, you'd sure know it and you'd hear it from wherever [Joe] was standing. You'd hear him yelling and giving you some words of encouragement."

If Paterno wasn't present, then he was there in spirit along with his hard and fast rules, which have stuck with Roger to this day. "Something I'll always remember is the rule about wearing hats in a building," Roger says. "You'd walk through the hallway with your baseball cap on and he'd say, 'Hats off in the house.' We're in a huge training complex, locker rooms, weight rooms, and you treat the training facility like your home."

That kind of discipline carried over to every aspect of the college life—and beyond. "If you're going to work hard in the classroom, you're going to work hard in your job. You're going to work hard being a dad to your family. It becomes a part of who you are, what you're made of. You handle yourself in a professional manner, both on and off the field," says Roger.

That's precisely what he did in the pros over the next 12 years. "With the Jets, we didn't do much winning," Roger recalls. "I had four head coaches in eight years, and obviously you're not going to win too much when you're turning over coaching staffs and offensive schemes. But it was a good organization. They took care of the players and the wives and the families."

He felt particularly at home with the Steelers after he was traded to Pittsburgh following the '97 season. Like the Jets, the Steelers usually treated their players like family under the Rooney regime. Roger also found an old friend in Furman, who had been the weight coach at Penn State but now was working for Pittsburgh.

In 2001, Roger's last season in Pittsburgh, the Steelers lost to the New England Patriots in the division championship game, leaving Roger just short of a Super Bowl appearance. "Even though I wasn't a starter then, just being part of that was exciting," he says. "A town like Pittsburgh loves their team."

After football, Roger wound up as a financial planner, while Pat now works in the industrial supply field after a brief fling at pro ball with the Miami Dolphins. Both reside in Ohio.

Like many other former Penn State football players, both brothers carried lessons from the Penn State experience into the everyday working world. "I'm very proud to be part of the Penn State tradition," Pat Duffy says.

For the Duffy twins, that goes twice.

eleven

THE GUMANS

ANDREW GUMAN LOOKS BACK at his boyhood and can't believe how quickly things flew by. Seems just yesterday Guman was a California kid with a Penn State winter coat and a mouth full of confidence, ready to tell anyone he met that his beloved Nittany Lions would win on Saturday. When he looked up he was a freshman playing football at Penn State, the school where his father's photo still appeared in posters that listed the program's greatest running backs.

The way he tells it, it's like a dream in fast-forward. . .

First Andrew grew, matured, and contributed on defense as a Nittany Lion, earning playing time as a freshman and sophomore before starting some games as a junior. He made some big plays on the field and some headlines off it on the way to becoming a team leader. Eventually, people quit confusing him with his dad, Mike, one of 34 running backs in Penn State history with more than 1,000 career rushing yards.

More time zipped by. Then, in his senior year, he took a shot in a game against Ohio State and wound up with a collapsed lung that nearly cost him the balance of his senior season. Just before the last grain of eligibility slipped through the hourglass of his career, his body rallied and pronounced Andrew healthy for his last game as a Nittany Lion.

Playing for JoePa

Whoosh. It all just went so darn fast. In a blink Andrew had gone from freshman to senior. In another blink, his college football career was over. His NFL dream too raced by, flickering and fading like a reflective highway sign splashed by the headlights of a passing car.

Of course, life went on. Andrew found work and moved away from his family in Allentown, Pennsylvania, away from the state he'd called home for a decade and a half. Sure, he thought about reversing field, trying to get back to that place where NFL scouts still lingered, where he might still have a chance to extend his football life. But he'd already made up his mind once.

No more football. No regrets.

Then one day it happened, as it does for so many Nittany Lions who are now ex-Nittany Lions. Andrew found himself in Beaver Stadium, that glorious sprawl of blue and white that shakes and waves and bounces to the beat of Penn State football. It was September 2006, nearly two years since his last game as an undergrad. He was sitting in the stands next to his girlfriend when the stadium jumbotron blared to life, releasing its standard pregame video highlights package of great moments and revered players in Nittany Lion lore.

It all rushed back to him. The locker room. The uniform. The tunnel. Cleats on concrete—click, clack, click, clack. Blue Band. Butterflies. Green grass. Fight songs. Boyhood adrenaline. The unmistakable roar of 110,000 loyalists.

Andrew opened his eyes . . . and closed them again.

"It was hard," he says. "I didn't want to watch."

The game started. He knew these guys who were playing for Penn State; they were his friends, guys he'd lifted with, guys he'd hung with in their apartments. He settled into his seat and began to cheer with the same passion he'd cheered for Ki-Jana Carter and Bobby Engram in 1994, or Curtis Enis and Aaron Harris in 1996. When it was over, he realized he had found peace with his renewed status as a fan of his favorite team.

"The thing that hurts—not hurts—the thing that I miss the most is Penn State," says Andrew, now 24. "The atmosphere. The Penn State program. Just being a Penn State football player. Not the NFL. Not even playing the sport. Just being part of it."

The Gumans

✳ ✳ ✳

Mike Guman didn't have to force his only son to become a football fan. It just happened, beginning with Los Angeles Rams games. After four years in Penn State's backfield, Mike was selected by the Rams in the sixth round of the 1980 NFL Draft. He played for L.A. for nine seasons, a 6-foot-2, 216-pound H-back who could do a little of everything, from power running in the trenches to catching passes in the flat. He credits that versatility for extending his NFL career.

In 1982 Mike's wife, Karen, a Penn Stater herself, gave birth to their first child, a boy. Andrew doesn't retain a lot of memories from those early years in California, but he distinctly remembers going to watch his father play and being scared to walk down to the sideline. His dad would beckon him to leave the stands and come to the field, and Andrew's heart would race. One game Andrew was so frightened, he froze in his seat instead of going to meet Magic Johnson, the Lakers star who was watching from the Rams sideline that day. Mike snagged Andrew an autograph anyway.

When Mike's NFL career ended, he and Karen decided to return to the area where he had been a three-sport star in football, basketball, and baseball at Bethlehem Catholic High School. They settled in Allentown, Pennsylvania, and focused on raising their children: Andrew, who was five and heading into first grade at the time of the move, and his four younger sisters, Emily, Joanie, Rebecca, and Abigail. Mike had earned his license in the securities business while he was still playing football, taking advantage of a Merrill Lynch-run program facilitated by the NFL Players' Union. Settled in Pennsylvania, he broke in on the retail side of the business, and today is vice president of sales in Pennsylvania for Oppenheimer Funds.

When Andrew started grade school, his interest in football blossomed. Once, for a school project, he was asked to decorate a bear that illustrated what he wanted to be when he grew up. Andrew put the bear in a football uniform. Mike fueled his son's enthusiasm by taking Andrew and his sisters to games at Beaver Stadium in the mid-1990s. They'd drive out for a game or two a year. In time Andrew could recite all the best players' names. There were also occasions when Mike and Karen made the drive to State College on non-football weekends, like when Mike would participate in a charity event for Second Mile, the foundation started by former Penn State defensive coordinator Jerry Sandusky.

"We'd go up, make a weekend of it, go to the pool, stay in the Nittany Lion Inn," Andrew says. "It was the greatest thing in the world."

While Mike opened Andrew's eyes to Penn State football, the elder Guman took a decidedly hands-off approach when it came to discussing his own accomplishments as a Nittany Lion. But not everything could not be concealed. When Andrew would go into the Penn State locker room with his dad on those trips, he'd see photos of Mike with teammates like Matt Millen, Bruce Clark, and Chuck Fusina. Those guys were legends, and there was Dad standing among them. Andrew later got his hands on highlights of the 1979 Sugar Bowl, and there was Mike again, carrying the ball, lugging the Lions oh so close to what would have been coach Joe Paterno's first national championship.

For Andrew's 14th birthday, Mike rented a limousine to take the family two hours east to Giants Stadium for the 1996 Kickoff Classic, Penn State versus USC. After Curtis Enis ripped off 241 yards to lead Penn State to a 24-7 thrashing of the Trojans, Mike took Andrew into the victorious locker room. The Gumans met Enis and fullback Aaron Harris. Outside the locker room Mike caught up with then USC coach John Robinson, who had coached him with the Rams.

On their way out to the waiting limo, the Gumans passed the Penn State team buses, where Mike also saw Paterno and paused to say hello. It was Andrew's first time meeting the Penn State coach.

"I remember him saying, 'Oh, you're a Guman? When you get older, we'd love to have another Guman here,'" Andrew recalls. "That always stuck in my mind."

Mike laughed it off. It isn't that he discouraged Andrew from playing football in the yard, or living and dying for Penn State football every fall Saturday. It's that he left the options in Andrew's hands. "If he didn't want to play football," Mike says, "I didn't care. It was his choice to do what he wanted to do."

The Gumans

What Andrew wanted to do was play football. So much so that if Mike was too busy to toss the pigskin around, he'd grab one of his sisters and take her to the yard to catch his spirals. Same thing with tossing a baseball, which is what Andrew was doing one day with younger sister Rebecca when the ball missed her glove and clocked her right in the face—days before her first Holy Communion. "I gave her a black eye, a bad black eye," Andrew says. "It's pretty bad in the pictures. She looks pretty in her Communion dress, but both eyes are swollen, black and blue and puffy. My mom was pretty upset."

The incident didn't slow Andrew's athletic pursuits. He played soccer, basketball, and baseball as a grade schooler, adding organized football to the list in seventh grade when he joined a CYO team in Allentown. Coincidentally, CYO football is how Mike got his start in the game, playing as a fifth-grader against eighth-graders to whom he typically gave up 100 pounds. Andrew, meanwhile, played two years of CYO ball. In that time, Mike didn't coach his son and rarely demonstrated a technique for him in the backyard. He did, however, attend the occasional practice and would offer advice to the coaches. His presence was enough to let Andrew know whether what he was doing was right or wrong.

By ninth grade at Allentown Central Catholic, Andrew was dressing for varsity games and starting as a quarterback for the jayvee squad. Yet unlike a lot of football prospects who receive recruiting nibbles early in their high school careers, Andrew was not yet fully committed to the sport. In fact, he didn't play football at all as a sophomore, electing to focus on basketball and baseball. He played again as a junior, but broke his hand in the fourth game and missed the rest of the season.

It was then, after his junior year, that Andrew realized the weight his dad's name still carried. He began receiving recruiting letters despite having played very little football at Allentown Central. The correspondence arrived from Penn State, Pitt, West Virginia, and others, "and I knew I had the genes going for me," Andrew says. Mike remained impartial on his oldest child's plans: "I felt pretty awkward, to be honest with you," he says. "I didn't want to put any undo pressure or influence on him, making him think, 'Oh, you have to do this because of me.' I didn't want that by any stretch of the imagination."

What Mike could not control was undo pressure that fans, media members, and coaches put on his son to be the same caliber athlete Mike had been. It was only natural. Mike and Andrew are 26 years apart. Mike had been one of the Lehigh Valley's greatest sports products. Many residents who had seen the elder Guman play were still around when Andrew was establishing himself as an athlete. Some of the comparisons that surfaced were positive. There were similarities, some recruiters said, in how father and son looked and ran on a basketball court or football field. But when word got out during Andrew's senior year that Penn State had come calling with a scholarship offer, negative comparisons gained momentum.

"'Does he deserve it? Is it because of his dad? Is it politics?'" Andrew says, repeating questions he heard or read at the time. "I was naïve to a bunch of that. Some of it hit me like, 'Why, what did I do? Why do these people have to say that stuff? I'm just trying to do my best.'

"I guess I just took it in stride, tried to deal with it myself. I didn't bring it up to my parents. I didn't want to make it a conflict between my dad and I or our family."

Internally, however, it was another story. Andrew had a college decision to make, and if he elected to take Paterno up on his long-ago offer—"We'd love to have another Guman here"—it would mean flying right into the storm of a father-son comparison.

✳ ✳ ✳

To fully understand how Andrew arrived at Penn State, you have to understand how Mike wound up there as a freshman in 1976. Despite growing up a three-hour drive east of Beaver Stadium, Mike knew very little about the Nittany Lions as a kid. Ask him the players he recalls watching on TV and he'll throw out names like Johnny Rodgers, the 1972 Heisman trophy winner from Nebraska, or Joe Washington, Oklahoma's All-America running back of the mid-1970s. His favorite team? Notre Dame, the team his family pulled for, the team you would have pulled for too if you had received 12 years of Catholic grade school education.

Like Andrew, Mike participated in multiple sports: He stuck with football, basketball, and baseball for all four years of high school. Playing alongside his friend John Spagnola (who would also go on to an NFL career) in 1974, Mike's Bethlehem Catholic team went 11-0 and finished with a No. 4 state ranking.

But baseball, not football, was his true love. A left-handed pitcher, Guman was drafted by the Texas Rangers and strongly considered playing minor-league ball after high school. Had the dollars been there, he likely would have hung up his football cleats for good. But Guman says the value of the baseball contract wasn't worth passing up a free college education and the shot at playing Division I football.

Once set on football, Mike took recruiting trips to Penn State, Michigan, North Carolina State, Pitt, Maryland, and Notre Dame, going everywhere but Michigan with his parents, Don and Betty. "Mom and dad were great," Mike says. "They didn't put any pressure on me." It helped that Don, once a three-sport athlete himself, knew a thing or two about impartiality in college football. When he retired from officiating in 1994, Don had spent 37 years as a head linesman in everything from midget ball to major college bowl games, his final game being the 1994 Orange Bowl, when Florida State beat Nebraska for the national championship. (He never refereed a Penn State game while Mike was in school, but he worked two games in the 1980s in which controversial calls went Penn State's way, causing at least one opposing coach to question that impartiality.)

Looking back on his recruiting trips, Mike didn't come away with positive feelings from his weekends at Notre Dame or Pitt, two of the more serious contenders for his services. At Michigan, a trip he made with fellow recruit Matt Millen from nearby Whitehall High School, the guys stayed in a classy hotel off campus. "We were ordering shrimp 'til the cows came home," Mike says, laughing at the memory.

Penn State, on the other hand, added no sugar to the mix. Mike spent his PSU visit sleeping on a cot in Keith Dorney's room. (Dorney, by the way, hails from Emmaus, Pennsylvania, a 15-minute drive from Mike's hometown of Bethlehem.) There was no room service-delivered shrimp cocktail, either; meals were consumed in the dining hall with the rest of the student body. Mike appreciated the genuine college experience. He also liked the ability to potentially play football close to home, which would allow Don and Betty to get to every home game, just as they'd done throughout his high school career.

If the deal needed sealing, there was Joe Paterno. As the story goes, on one of Joe's trips to Lehigh Valley in 1975, he stayed in a Holiday Inn at which Mike's sister, Connie, worked. During his stay, Paterno spoke at a testimonial banquet, and in his speech he raved about the hotel's dining area bun service. Coincidentally, Connie was the waitress at that Holiday Inn whose job it was to hand out bread to guests. She loved the compliment. So too did her family.

"I think one of his greatest strengths is his ability to recruit," says Mike, who received a 1975 in-home visit from Paterno and John Chuckran, Penn State's Lehigh Valley recruiting coordinator at the time. "He'd come into your house—and you can ask former Penn State players this—and in your home, he didn't care about you. He went to your parents. He recruited your mom more than anything. Your mom and your family. He's a very smart man."

Mike's only stipulation was that he be allowed to play baseball in college. Paterno said okay, so long as Mike played spring football as a freshman. That flexibility was enough to convince Mike to join one of the more star-studded recruiting classes in Nittany Lions history. His pal Millen, who initially verballed to Colorado, signed with Penn State, making a reality something he and Mike had talked about doing during their recruiting travels together. Paterno's haul also included Matt Suhey, Bruce Clark, Pete Harris (Franco's kid brother), Lance Mehl, Irv Pankey, and others.

Mike says he knew there was a lot of talent coming to Happy Valley in 1976, "but we were 18 years old, and you're cocky, you think you have everything," he says. "You find out you have to have a lot of chemistry, too, to be good, and there's a lot of competition. I mean, college football is hard. You come in there and you're all-everything in your area and so is everybody else. Everybody wants to play, but only 11 guys get on the field at one time."

The Gumans

Mike Guman, No. 24.

In 1976, Guman got on the field early and had an immediate impact. After Penn State struggled in a win against Stanford and lost three straight to Ohio State, Iowa, and Kentucky, Paterno made changes. Sophomore Chuck Fusina went in at quarterback; freshmen Millen and Clark became starting linebackers; and Guman, who had been a reserve defensive back, was switched to offense.

In his first game as a Penn State running back—October 9, 1976, against Army at rain-soaked Beaver Stadium—Guman carried the ball 25 times for 107 yards and four touchdowns. Penn State won the game 38-16 and ripped off five more consecutive victories before losing to No. 1 Pitt in the season finale and Notre Dame in that year's Gator Bowl.

Playing for JoePa

Guman's teams never looked back from that stumble at the start of '76. Penn State lost just once in 1977, finishing 11-1. At one point during the 1977-78 seasons, the Nittany Lions won 19 straight games heading into the 1979 Sugar Bowl, a 14-7 Penn State loss to Alabama in which Guman was famously stonewalled at the goal line on a fourth-and-goal run that would have tied the game.

Despite that missed shot at a national title, despite an 8-4 senior season that failed to meet expectations, despite practices so frequent and demanding that Mike once told his parents, "Get me out of here!" Mike walked away with a positive experience. "I remember a lot of things, and all are good," he says. "You don't remember the bad times. You just remember the fun stuff, the good stuff, the memories, the guys you played with, some of the antics in the locker room. Big victories, good wins, bowl games we played in. . . . [Paterno] is a tough guy to play for. He's demanding and he runs a tough program. It's hard. It's physical. But I was out there with my buddies playing for a purpose, and there was nothing better than that. That's what I miss about football."

Mike also left Penn State recognizing that there was something special about the way Paterno operated a football program. "Don't get me wrong," he says. "They're there to win. That is the priority. That makes everything work. But it's not at any cost. I think that's what makes them a little bit different.

"[Paterno] has a formula that he thinks is appropriate for college sports, and he doesn't deviate from that. His kids get through school, they learn a lot in the program, they turn out to be great citizens and contributors to the communities they're living in. Whether they register the amount of wins other people want, he doesn't change the way things are done. I admire him for that. In a world when the temptation is to win at any and all costs, he tries to do it the way he believes is the right way to do it."

✳ ✳ ✳

By the time Andrew was heading into his senior year of high school, he'd had about enough of the negative comparisons between his athletic skills and those his father once had. It bothered him to the point that he decided he wasn't going to do what his father had done. He did not want to play for Joe Paterno at Penn State. That would only intensify comparisons between father and son.

In the summer of 2000, Andrew and his folks took unofficial visits to Maryland, Duke, and Virginia. He had interest in Pitt, West Virginia, and Northwestern, too. Fran Ganter, then Penn State's offensive coordinator, offered Andrew a scholarship, but entering the fall, "I was thinking, 'Why not go do my own thing and go to my own school, create my own identity,'" Andrew says.

Later that fall Andrew received a call from Ganter, asking if he had made up his mind yet about college. Andrew told him he was still considering other schools, to which Ganter replied, "You know, Andrew, this scholarship could go to someone else." And there it was, reality shaking Andrew through the phone line. Another recruit might have blown off Ganter's reminder as coachspeak. Another recruit might have reacted negatively to that perceived ultimatum. But this was a kid who'd dreamed of playing football for Penn State. He didn't need Joe Paterno at his dinner table to convince him where his loyalties resided.

Ganter's words sent Andrew's mind racing. Could he really pass up Penn State? Would he jog in place while another recruit stole his dream to become a Nittany Lion? Andrew was sitting on a plane with his father, en route to see a Pitt-West Virginia game, when he got his answer—the plane never took off. They sat on the runway for two hours. As father and son left the plane to return to the terminal, Andrew turned to Mike and said, "Dad, I'm going to Penn State."

"In my head I was like, 'Let's just let all that other stuff go about following in footsteps and shadows,'" says Andrew, whose first act after making his decision was to buy a Penn State hat from a store at the airport. "'Let's do what I really want to do and just go to Penn State.'"

As it turned out, Andrew's Penn State experience the next four years could not have been more different from Mike's term there in the '70s. Andrew's teams went a combined 17-26 from 2001-04, including 3-9 in 2003—the worst record of any Joe Paterno-coached team—and 4-7 in 2004. Andrew, who sprained an ankle early in 2001 but still played enough in reserve duty and on special teams to burn his freshman eligibility, took the lean years particularly hard.

Playing for JoePa

Understandably so. This wasn't the Penn State story he'd fallen in love with as a kid watching games next to his dad on the couch. These weren't the Nittany Lions who'd routed Oregon in the 1995 Rose Bowl or smacked around USC at the Meadowlands on his 14th birthday trip. All he'd ever associated Penn State with was success. Never failure, never defeat. Three total Big Ten wins in his junior and senior years combined? An ugly 6-4 Homecoming loss to Iowa his senior year? One bowl game in four seasons? Unprecedented.

"We were trying so hard," he says, "putting in all this effort, and we just couldn't get anything to work. It's not like it was one game or one series or one play. It was two years! And it was the same cast of characters over that time span.

"It wore on us. It wore on Joe Paterno. You saw this great man, this great coach who has been so successful his entire life come to a point where he had no answers. He took the brunt of it, despite the legend he is. And you felt for him. This guy's not losing the games. It's these 100 players in the room who are not performing."

Football's a team sport, we all know that. But for all his teams' woes those years, Andrew carved out for himself a productive college career. He started four games at safety as a junior and finished with 47 tackles. He developed into a team leader as a senior, finishing third on the team with 67 stops (43 solo), despite missing two and a half games with a lung condition called pneumothorax, the result of the collapsed lung he sustained in a loss at Ohio State.

Off the field, he was the model Penn State product, earning a 4.0 GPA in the fall semester of his junior year and garnering first-team Academic All-America honors as a senior. At the time he was just the 21st different Nittany Lion in school history to reach such elite academic status.

Andrew also grew as a person in his four years at Penn State. Some of it was navigating those tough times on the field without his teammates pointing fingers in the locker room, something he's adamant did not go on. Instead there was much unity, as Andrew came to appreciate the brotherhood of the program and the enjoyable aspects of the Penn State team concept—perhaps even more so as the losses mounted.

The Gumans

Mike and Andrew Guman.

Then there was Andrew's relationship with his father, who, true to the way he'd raised Andrew in the sport, was hands off about Andrew's growth at Penn State. "He allowed me to experience things for myself, rather than him trying to live it through me again," Andrew says. "Looking back, I really appreciate the way he handled it."

The reward for Mike was that by not forcing anything, it became more natural for Andrew to come to Mike when he did have questions or issues to discuss. "Sometimes with your kids," Mike says, "it's hard to tell them things. They don't listen. But the older Andrew got, as maturity set in, he would call and we'd have great conversations on the phone. He would confide in me and ask my opinion on certain things. And I'll treasure that. That meant an awful lot to me."

Adds Andrew: "College football at Penn State sort of rectified the whole negative connotation I had of being associated with my dad. Playing at Penn State and having some success allowed me to create my own identity. It allowed me to be who I was as a football player and it allowed my dad to be the person he was."

✳ ✳ ✳

The last two years have been conflicting for Andrew. He played his final game in a Penn State uniform on Senior Day 2004, a rout of Michigan State for which he wasn't sure he'd be cleared to play until the week of the game. It was an emotional day: hearing his name called in the pregame ceremony for seniors; holding back tears as he emerged from the tunnel at the south end of Beaver Stadium; playing like he was on fire, jumping around after every play, a frenzy of regretless energy.

In the ensuing spring he went undrafted, signing as a free agent with the Detroit Lions. He stayed in Detroit all summer and played in every preseason game that August, acquitting himself well enough to think he'd stick with the practice squad if he didn't make the team.

He didn't make the team. Nor did he make the practice squad. Instead Andrew returned to Allentown, to the house he'd grown up in, to await a call from the pros that didn't come. He spent the bulk of his free time helping to coach his former high school team, souring on the NFL business by the day.

Meanwhile, back in State College, Penn State jumped out to a 6-0 start, led by Michael Robinson at quarterback and a nasty defense with Andrew's pal Paul Posluszny at the helm. After a heartbreaking mid-October loss at Michigan, the team ran the table to finish 11-1. It was cathartic success for the Penn State program and its followers. However, the emotions were mixed for Guman, who, stuck in a career holding pattern, had nothing to distract him from his thoughts.

"Each game I was so excited to watch them," he says, "and then it was like, 'Oh man, they're good now. They're winning.' I was happy for them, but I'm not out there. It was tough. It was really tough. . . . It was difficult to grasp what was different [in 2005] that led to them having success versus the previous two years when we didn't. I was trying to figure out some type of logical reason to make it easier to understand."

Andrew eventually grew tired of waiting for the phone to ring, and he rifled through his Penn State connections to land an interview with Long Island-based Honeywell. It yielded an offer to become a financial analyst in the company's finance undergraduate rotational program. He took the job and started around Thanksgiving, moving into an apartment on Long Island.

About one month into the job, Mike called Andrew. Andrew's agent, Brett Senior, had called Mike to say the Detroit Lions wanted

The Gumans

Andrew to come back and try out for a special teams slot that had opened. This was Andrew's shot. He tossed around the possibilities: If he performed well, he could be playing in an NFL game in a week or two. He might get sent to Europe in the off-season, maybe come back and make the team the next year. He could also fly to Detroit, impress no one, and wind up back at Honeywell—if they'd take him. When he was hired, he'd answered "yes" to the question of, "Are you finished with football?"

Andrew talked to his dad about it. Mike wanted Andrew to be sure he was weighing both options carefully. Andrew said mentally he'd moved on, that there were too many what-ifs to derail the career momentum he was gaining at Honeywell.

"I said, 'That's fine,'" Mike recalls. ". . . If it's out of your system, then great. I just don't want you to second-guess yourself a couple years down the road.'"

Andrew assured him he knew what he was doing and asked his father to trust him. "I didn't really have that passion that I felt I needed to be successful," Andrew says. "I could have gone out there and gone through the motions, but I didn't have the passion behind it, so what good was it in my head? I said, 'It's not worth doing.'"

"Great," Mike told his son. "I'm behind you 100 percent."

Andrew won't lie. There are still times when he wakes up on a fall Saturday and the butterflies return. He says he still fights himself sometimes. A lot of what he misses, though, lives on in Happy Valley. A lot lives on in him. He left the Penn State experience with a set of ethics and standards superior to most former college football players. Mental toughness, discipline, teamwork, it all traces back to Joe Paterno's system. Shaving every day, no earrings, hats off in buildings. Same deal.

"Being a Penn State football player separates you," Andrew says. "You do things a little more strictly, with a little more discipline, even if it's a little more difficult. And that inspires pride. Family members pass that down onto cousins, nephews, grandsons. It's what those younger kids look up to.

"It's what I saw in my dad, how proud he was to be part of Penn State. If he hadn't felt that way, we wouldn't have gone back to games.

Playing for JoePa

I wouldn't have known what Penn State was all about. I wouldn't have compared everything to Penn State when I made a college decision. Dad never would have taken the time if he didn't have a love for Penn State inside him that reflected upon his family."

Especially upon his only son.

twelve

THE
NORWOODS

JORDAN NORWOOD WAS HIDING. Not even his father could find the Penn State receiver. Minutes earlier, Penn State had completed its extraordinary comeback season with a triple-overtime 26-23 victory over Florida State in the 2006 Orange Bowl.

On a stage set up on the field, the Penn State players were high-fiving and hugging. A crowd was swarming the area. Jordan's father, Penn State safeties coach Brian Norwood, was in the press box. He had watched his son make a team-high six catches for 110 yards in the major New Year's Eve bowl game—an amazing performance by the freshman receiver in a tight game.

At the final gun, Jordan's father came dashing down from the press box to the stage where all the players were celebrating, looking for his son. No luck. Then he finally spotted him, standing alone on the fringe of the celebration, without his jersey or shoulder pads on. Father approached son, congratulating him on a good game.

"Don't you want to put your shirt on?" Brian asked Jordan.

"No," his son replied. "I take it off, and nobody knows who I am."

Brian understood his son completely. He knew he was not someone who enjoyed the hugs and the pats on the back, or being in the spotlight. "Jordan loves feeling good about how he's contributed, but he's not one to look for publicity," says Brian. "He's always been quiet and reserved. He's very confident, but he has no need to be built up."

It was a special moment for both of them. The two men stood there, talking to each other and appreciating the moment—both glad to be sharing in it together. "It's something I appreciate and am truly thankful for," Jordan says of having his dad on the Penn State staff. For the Nittany Lions, there's nothing odd about such an arrangement, though; the program seems to have made a habit of it. Joe and Jay Paterno. Jerry Sandusky and sons. Fran Ganter and sons. Larry Johnson and sons. And now the Norwoods, too.

*** *** ***

Brian Norwood's father was raised on a tobacco farm in North Carolina, part of a sharecropping family. Brian's father, Nathaniel, wanted to play sports, but the baseball season conflicted with the farming season, and he couldn't budge his family's commitment to farming. So he did the next best thing: "There was a baseball team that represented North Carolina," Brian says. "He was a ball boy for the team."

Nathaniel eventually found his way to the Air Force, which led his family from the fields of North Carolina to Hawaii, where Brian spent his teenage years. "The people there embraced my family and we embraced the culture," says Brian, who enjoyed Hawaii enough to stay there for college at the University of Hawaii, and later to marry and start a family.

In college, Brian was a cornerback for most of his college career. He was a good enough player to get a serious look from the Calgary Stampeders of the Canadian Football League. "It was just for a very short period," he says of his time with the team. "I made it through the beginning part of camp. I was one of the last cut, and I was going to be on the taxi squad or the team. But I got sick. I was diagnosed with juvenile diabetes."

As far as Brian was concerned, the illness turned out to be a blessing. While working for United Airlines, Norwood felt the familiar tug of football, and decided to attempt to find a coaching

The Norwoods

position. He landed one as a graduate assistant at Arizona in 1990. From there he coached at Richmond from 1992-94 and at the U.S. Naval Academy from 1995-99. At Navy, Norwood helped to turn out some fine defensive backs, including second-team All-America Sean Andrews, who tied for most interceptions in the country in 1995 with eight.

Navy led to a coaching gig at Texas Tech for two seasons, then Penn State came calling. Norwood and Penn State coach Larry Johnson were old friends, and he used that connection to explore the opening at State College. "It just so happened when Larry called, Coach Paterno was on a trip to Hawaii," Brian recalls. "He and my head coach in college had become good friends, so everything just sort of fell into place."

At Penn State, Norwood quickly made a name for himself as a developer of superb safeties, such as Shawn Mayer and Yaacov Yisrael. "Penn State is probably the institution that is most similar to the Naval Academy," Brian says. "We have the same values at Penn State. [They recruit a] similar type of young man. . . . There are things that you expect a young kid to do. It goes along with being a Penn State football player: discipline, loyalty, and hard work.

"It's not an easy place for the young players. Coach Paterno really stresses the academics and doing things right, and in turn the players have a great opportunity and have great success on the football field."

※ ※ ※

Sports have always played an important role in the Norwood family. Brian and his wife, Tiffiney, have five children: Gabriel, Jordan, Levi, Brianna, and Zaccariah. Each child is involved in sports, at Jordan's urging. It's a trait he picked up from his father, who felt it was important to be involved in physical activity.

"I think I started playing football when I was in first grade," Jordan says. "Flag football. I've played ever since then, only missing my sophomore year in high school when I moved up here."

Before settling in the State College area, Jordan had lived in Hawaii, Arizona, Virginia, Maryland, and Texas as he followed his

Playing for JoePa

father's career moves around the country along with the rest of the family. The one constant in a life on the move was sports. When he was a student at State College Area High School, Jordan played both basketball and football, and he had no problem balancing the two sports. He made his mark as a star point guard, leading the Little Lions to the 2003 Class 4-A state title, and twice was selected defensive player of the year in the Mountain Athletic Conference. Due to a broken thumb, he saw limited football action as a senior. Yet even so, he was surprisingly productive: 21 catches for 273 yards as the Little Lions swept to the state semifinals.

As it has been for other Penn State athletes, playing at State College Area High School was excellent preparation for big-time college football. "Things are kind of run the way Penn State does," Jordan says. "That goes along with how we ran a football practice in high school and just the demeanor we took into games, things that were reflective of Penn State football."

Although he grew up with a strong football background, Jordan was divided for the longest time on his choice of sport for college. In football, Jordan was hardly a "name" recruit. But some coaches, including Paterno, were still interested. It helped that he peaked at the end of his senior season. His personal best came in a three-touchdown game against Erie Cathedral Prep. "That was just a game that stuck out for me," he says. "It was maybe my second game back from a thumb injury. . . . I had three touchdowns and maybe 130 yards receiving."

What drew Paterno's interest was actually Jordan's play on the basketball court. The coach was impressed with the kid's athleticism and encouraged him to come to Penn State. Football aside, Jordan was happy to stay home, close to his family. Of course, having his father on staff was an added bonus. "He told me he was there if I needed anything," Jordan says, "and I have been taking advantage of that."

Brian was fully confident that his son would succeed in football at Penn State. So was Jordan, who exudes a quiet confidence. But during Jordan's first practice at State, he presented his father with a small problem. "The first practice we had, we were doing one-on-ones, and for the first five or six snaps that he was up, I wasn't watching my guy,

The Norwoods

Jordan Norwood, No. 24.

I was watching *him*," Brian says of his son. "I never thought about that factor. So I'm in practice. I'm saying, 'C'mon, Jordan, c'mon.' It took me one practice for me to get out of that mind-set."

After initially "greyshirting," Jordan made a quick splash in his first season with the team, playing a featured role in Paterno's "Kiddie Corps" of receivers in 2005 that helped turn the Nittany Lions around. From 3-8 the year before, Penn State finished No. 3 in the country with an 11-1 record and that pulsating Orange Bowl triumph.

"It was a pretty exciting year, with some of his catches," Brian says of his son. "The whole family was excited. It was fun to watch."

It seemed that whenever a big play was needed, Paterno's freshman receivers were up to the challenge. Jordan did his part with a number of clutch plays against stiff competition in Michigan and Ohio State. Although he wasn't a starter and missed two games during the season, the game-breaking receiver still managed to corral 32 catches for 422 yards—an impressive average of 13.2 yards a catch.

"He's a little bit like Bobby Engram," quarterbacks coach Jay Paterno says, comparing Norwood to one of Penn State's greatest wide receivers. "He doesn't have the great size (5-foot-10, 160 pounds), probably isn't a 4.4 guy, but he really can get open."

Jordan is thrilled by the comparisons to Engram. "Those are great, big shoes to attempt to fill," Jordan says. "All that means is that I have to keep working hard and be able to contribute to the team as much as possible." He continued to do just that with six catches for 154 yards in the Blue-White game in the spring of 2006. During the 2006 season, Norwood had 45 receptions for 472 yards, second-best among Penn State receivers.

✳ ✳ ✳

Jordan isn't the only sibling in the family to make sports headlines in the past year. His brother, Gabe, played a key role for the George Mason basketball team in a surprising run to the 2006 Final Four. The two brothers have enjoyed rooting for each other—Gabe in the stands at the '06 Orange Bowl, Jordan in the stands for George Mason's historic upset of Connecticut in the '06 NCAA tournament.

Paterno excused both Jordan and Brian so they could cheer for Gabe in person. Paterno found himself in a rooting mood, too. In a Sunday practice during the Connecticut-George Mason tilt, Paterno was told that Gabe's team was on the verge of knocking off the Huskies. JoePa cut practice short so the Penn State players could rush to the locker room and watch the end of the game. They cheered as the Patriots pulled off the upset of the tourney.

Not too shabby a year for the Norwoods—just don't expect Jordan to make too big a deal of it.

thirteen

THE CONLINS

KEITH CONLIN NEVER GETS TIRED of telling stories. He's collected and refined a lot of good ones over the years, from anecdotes that'll make your sides split with laughter, to tales tinged with more somber backdrops. When it comes to stories about Joe Paterno, Conlin probably could fill a book. And if he ever did decide to put fingers to keyboard, he'd start at the end, since therein lies the message that ties it all together.

It goes a little something like this: Conlin, a mountain of a man who had started at tackle for Penn State's undefeated 1994 team, was out of football by '99. He'd graduated from Penn State in 1996, a year after the Nittany Lions took care of Oregon in the Rose Bowl to seal a 12-0 season. He'd been drafted in the sixth round by the Indianapolis Colts, but after injuring himself in camp, the Colts cut him that August. Conlin, one of eight brothers and sisters, then returned to coach at his alma mater, LaSalle High School in Wyndmoor, Pennsylvania.

That next winter—on February 2, 1999—Keith's mother, Mary, passed away from cancer at 62 years young. Anyone who knows anything about college football will tell you that February is the holy season in recruiting. It's when programs ebb and flow, collecting fresh high school seniors like shells washed upon a beach, battling their

145

rivals for those gems still undecided on their school of choice. In 1999, national letter of intent day—the day when kids make their college commitments official—fell on Wednesday, February 3. Three days later, the Conlin clan gathered in a funeral home near Philadelphia. As the crowd assembled in late morning, in walked Joe Paterno, along with many of his longtime assistants and some of their wives. Some former Penn State players were there, too.

"Everybody who coached me and my brothers," says Keith, the second of three Conlin brothers to play Penn State football, "they all got on a plane, flew down there, went to the funeral, and then flew back to Penn State to be with the recruits. There were people there who were in shock that [Paterno] was there and that he would do something like that. A class move by a class guy."

Keith will never forget it. In fact, in the months and years that followed, as he went from assistant coaching gigs at The Catholic University of America to Hampden-Sydney (Va.) College, Conlin preserved the gesture by retelling the circumstances to friends and strangers alike.

"Hey, what's Paterno like?" they'd ask.

"He was at my mother's funeral on one of the biggest recruiting weekends of the year," Conlin would tell them. "If that doesn't give you an indication of what's important to him, I don't know what the hell does."

✳ ✳ ✳

Paterno entered the Conlins' lives in 1982, when Penn State was pursuing Chris Conlin, a stud offensive line prospect at Bishop McDevitt High in Wyncote, Pennsylvania. Penn State assistant Dick Anderson was the point man courting Chris, but as tradition demanded, when it came time to confirm the high school senior's commitment, Paterno made dinner plans himself at the family's home.

The Conlins lived in Glenside, Pennsylvania, an 8,000-resident northern suburb of Philadelphia. Joe and Mary had moved from nearby Oreland several years earlier and bought a house with enough space to accommodate a 10-person family: five boys (Ken, Chris,

The Conlins

Craig, Keith, and Kevin) and three girls (Carin, Kim, and Courtney). The two oldest, Kenny and Karen, had their own rooms in the home. Kim and Courtney shared another room. The four youngest boys bunked in the attic, a renovated space the family lovingly nicknamed "the dormitory."

"It was just one big room, kind of like a loft," youngest brother Kevin says. "That was an eye-opening experience in my life, coming home and having your older brothers beat you up, make you tougher."

The house had seen many memorable meals before Paterno arrived to lock up Chris. Nothing was better at the Conlins' than Sunday dinners, because Sunday was the one day each week when Joe would not go to work at his tire shop in Oreland. Instead, Sunday was family day. Joe, Mary, and the kids would rise early, dress in their Sunday best, head to mass, then stop for breakfast on the way back. They often spent the rest of the afternoon entertaining family and friends, which meant lots of adults in the house and even more kids running around outside.

The yard was a kid's paradise. There was a hoop set up for basketball, "21" being the frequent game of choice. A Wiffle ball game was always afoot. They even had an in-ground pool. "My parents invested a lot of money in the backyard," Kevin says, "figuring with the whole family there, we wouldn't need to go places."

Joe and Mary invested in their own future, too. They started Moon's Tire Service in 1964—Moon is Joe's nickname—initially working out of their home in Oreland before buying a shop in Oreland in 1967. Joe did the grunt work while Mary handled the bookkeeping. The business thrived during the next two decades, with as many as 12 employees working there at any given time. Of course, having five sons at home ensured that Joe never had to look far for an extra shop boy.

Kenny, Chris, Craig, Keith, and Kevin spent hours of their boyhood summers toiling in the tire shop. They did what any other employee would do: changed tires, drove the truck, swept the shop. It was hard work and broiling hot days spent wearing full-length outfits and work boots. "We'd basically work for pennies," says Chris, who as a newborn baby earned the nickname Buck or Bucky (short for

Buckwheat) for his dark-skinned, bushy-haired likeness to *The Little Rascals* character. "From 7 or 7:30 (a.m.) to 5 (p.m.) every day, and then Saturday from 8 to 12. In the summertime, it was brutal."

Brutal indeed. Yet years after departing Penn State, the boys say the hours they spent slogging 600-pound tires in sweltering heat made them appreciate the opportunity to play college football and pursue an education. Buck tells the story of arriving at Penn State before fall semester in 1983, his freshman year. He was 18 and lonely. He'd never been so far from home for so long, and the wide abyss of college intimidated him. We've all been there.

Joe Conlin saw it differently. When Buck called Mom and Dad to say he wanted to come home, Joe didn't try to reason with him. Instead he quickly shot back, "I'll be up there in three hours. You can go to work with me tomorrow morning." Buck paused, thinking back to those long, hot days. "Ahhhh, that's okay," he told his dad, choosing to suck it up instead.

That poignant anecdote, a classic in the Conlin memoirs, repeated itself again with each son. "The shop kept us out of trouble in the summertime," Keith says, "but it's also the reason we all went to college. You're sitting there getting beat up and you say to yourself, 'Hell, I can't wait to go to college. I don't want to do this the rest of my life.'"

Especially since the boys didn't exactly rake in a fat salary at Moon's. "You'd ask where your paycheck was at the end of the week," Keith says, "and Dad would say, 'You just ate it last night.'"

Right. Almost forgot those family dinners. If Sunday was like a fine-dining, sit-down experience—"Shirts and ties," quips Joe—the rest of the week was like the buffet line at a bustling East Halls cafeteria. Only there was no soda at the Conlins' home. It was milk, orange juice, or water—your pick. Even after Abbott's Dairies stopped delivering milk to the greater Philadelphia area, it made an exception for the Conlins, who used to burn through 25 gallons of milk a week. That's more than three gallons per day, so much of the white stuff that the family devoted an entire refrigerator, one of three in the house, solely to milk. (There was a meat man, too. He'd make weekly Wednesday night stops in Glenside to restock the Conlins' meat

The Conlins

Chris "Buck" Conlin.

freezer and save Mary from having to lug home steaks and chops for her large family.)

"Everybody had to be there for dinner on Sunday night, which was awesome," says Buck, who now lives near Ft. Lauderdale in Cooper City, Florida, with his wife and daughter. "During the week it was kind of difficult because we were all playing sports. Sometimes you had a game or something so you couldn't make dinner. But the best time was being together at dinner, and if we were all together, it was a great memory. Unfortunately, if you didn't eat fast enough, you didn't get to eat a lot."

Buck's nod to the extent of the family's athletic involvement is no exaggeration. Perhaps it was the natural intra-familial jockeying amid chores and games that bred such competitive children. All eight kids played sports at some point. Karen, Kim, and Courtney, each of whom attended Gwynedd-Mercy Academy High School, gravitated to softball and basketball. Oldest sons Kenny and Buck attended Bishop McDevitt, Ken excelling in baseball (he later played in the Baltimore Orioles farm system) and Buck developing into a Division I-A football prospect.

Craig's strength was basketball; in his 20s he played professionally for several seasons in Europe. It was during Craig's high school years, though, that Joe and Mary decided to make a change. Unhappy with the academic-athletic balance at McDevitt, they enrolled Craig at nearby LaSalle High, one of the top prep schools in the Philadelphia region, known specifically for its blend of academic and athletic excellence. The Conlins fell in love with LaSalle and later decided to send their youngest two sons to the all-male school.

It was at LaSalle where Keith first drew recruiters' attention, much the way Buck had a decade earlier. And though Keith visited a handful of other schools and professed serious interest in Florida State, deep down, it made sense that he'd pick Penn State. After all, Dad did look Keith in the eye and tell him, "Go where you want, but keep in mind, your mom and I will get to your games once or twice a year at Florida State. We'll make them all at Penn State." It wasn't guilt; just truth.

Or maybe Keith's reasoning was grounded in memories of family tailgates outside Beaver Stadium in the mid-1980s, sharing meals and hanging out with Buck's friends on the team. Buck used to sneak him into the locker room and shove free Nittany Lions swag into his hands.

Or it could have been the glow of a program so committed to its values, the same values that reminded him so much of home in Glenside.

Or, it could have been because of Mom.

* * *

Paterno and his assistants would have chartered a plane to attend Mary Conlin's funeral, if nothing else because three of her sons had helped the Penn State program succeed for many years (Chris from 1983 to '86, Keith from '92 to '95, and Kevin from '93 to '97). But in this case, it was more personal than that. This was no courtesy call.

The Conlins

This wasn't something a head coach did because he's a head coach and the mother of some former player passed away and it was right and decent and par for the course. Rather, in the 18 years since Paterno first picked up a fork and knife at the Conlins' dinner table, Mary, Joe, and their family had become like family to Paterno, his wife Sue, and many of the Penn State assistants.

Mary made chicken cutlets for dinner that night in 1982. Paterno remarked how they were the best he'd ever had. But Mary, perhaps unlike the hundreds of recruits' mothers to set a plate before Paterno in the last half-century, never met a compliment she took quietly. Thus, when Paterno genuinely praised her chicken, Mary instead smelled a recruiting pitch, and snapped back, "Get the hell out of here."

That was Mary Conlin. In 1991, in the seconds after Paterno offered Keith a scholarship, did Mary jump for joy? Did she hug her son or shake Paterno's hand and thank him? Nope, she saw a chance to tease the old coach. "I gotta know, Joe," she said. "You gave my boy a scholarship. That's great. But are you dying your hair?"

"I'm like, 'Oh my God,'" recalls Keith of those uncomfortable moments. "My dad's jaw hits the floor. But [Paterno] gave it right back. He's like, 'Are you dying yours, Mary?'

"My mom would give it to Joe all the time," Keith continues, "ask why his hair is so black and he's 70 years old, stuff like that. My dad and I would just cringe. But [Paterno] loved it. Everybody kissed his ass all the time, and she just kept it real."

No piece of Conlin-Paterno history encapsulates that sentiment quite like this one from Penn State's 1993-94 Citrus Bowl trip. That season, 9-2 Penn State flew to Orlando to take on Tennessee on New Year's Day 1994. The night before the game, New Year's Eve, Penn State's players gathered for a team snack. Curfew beckoned, and the coaching staff insisted on a quick and quiet bite before sending their kids off to bed.

Mary and Joe were in town for the game, and that evening they partied at a nearby New Year's Eve bash. Mary rarely drank alcohol, but on that night she indulged with a few glasses of champagne. That's when she decided to say a quick good night and good luck to her sons. (Keith was a second-year tackle that season while Kevin was there during his redshirt year.) She found them sharing a snack with a roomful of teammates.

Keith remembers it like this: "So my mother's in there giving her two sons hugs and kisses. 'Happy New Year,' 'I love you,' this and that. And Paterno's standing there and says, 'Mary Conlin, get the hell out of here!' She looked at him in front of 125 players and said, 'Shut the hell up you old fart!' He got sooooo red. And I'm sitting there like, 'I'm gonna die. He's gonna kill me. I'm done.' I looked at my mom. I thought, 'Who's gonna hurt me worse? Joe or Mom?' It's like, if I tell Mom to get out of here, she's gonna kill me. But if I go and piss Joe off, I'm really dead. So I went with my mom."

Good choice. After all, Mary was the rock of the family. She always told it like it was, refusing to take any garbage from anyone. "Whenever there was a problem," says Kevin, "it was never my dad raising his voice. It was always her. It was never, 'Wait till Dad gets home.' You got your whupping right there."

In many ways, Mary ran the Conlin family akin to how Paterno ran his Penn State family. Perhaps that's why the two so respectfully butted heads and traded barbs all those years. They were so similar.

* * *

"Buckwheat" Conlin need not think hard to conjure some of his favorite images of Penn State. For all the wondrous success on the field, the All-America season he had in 1986, the national title he helped the Lions capture, his favorite times were those postgame tailgates with his extended Penn State family.

It was always the same group: the Conlins—Mary, Joe, and several of their kids; the Knizners—Buck's teammate, Matt, and his parents; and the Kuzys—Buck's teammate, Rich, and his folks. Those three families would set up camp together at every home game, run up flags or banners, light the grill, toss on some burgers and dogs, prepare the porkroll sandwiches, pop open a few beers, and get to talking. Others often joined the mix. Mitch Frerotte was Buck's roommate for four years, and he and his family often joined Camp Conlin in the victorious postgame shadows of Beaver Stadium. Mike Russo and

The Conlins

Keith Conlin, No. 53.

Mike Wolf later became "room dogs" with Conlin and Frerotte, and thus the tailgate turnout grew.

In the early years, the Conlins would leave Glenside at 4 or 5 a.m. for a day of football and fun, packing into the conversion van Joe had bought just after Buck signed in 1983. Later they began shoving off on Friday afternoons, determined to maximize their tailgating experience. Those were impressionable trips for Keith and Kevin, kicking it with Buck's buddies like Tim Manoa and D.J. Dozier, laughing with the Knizners and Frerottes. They would tour the locker room, say hi to equipment managers Tim Shope and Brad "Spider" Caldwell, and walk out loaded down with free T-shirts, gloves, and sweatpants.

"Even though all those guys—my brother, Mike Wolf, Mitch Frerotte, Tim Manoa—were from different areas, no matter what, when my family showed up, everybody was family," Kevin says. "It left a mark in my mind that it was always going to be like that."

Playing for JoePa

That family environment remained intact when Kevin arrived at Penn State. But unlike Buck and Keith, Kevin, who played guard and center for Paterno, was not a highly sought after prospect in high school. His recruiting experience was much more strenuous and unsure.

For Buck, a guard/tackle at Penn State, saying yes to Coach Paterno made sense, even though he had a handful of big-time suitors. He had always loved the tradition and plain uniforms of schools like Penn State and Alabama. And between Dick Anderson's avid pursuit of him as a prep player at Bishop McDevitt and Paterno's promise to Joe Conlin that he'd make his second-oldest son into a man, Penn State emerged as Buck's pick.

Keith, like Buck, was a jumbo-sized prospect in high school who also played guard and tackle for the Lions. He was talented, a physical force on the defensive line who had schools all along the East Coast sending him mail. He was cocky too, at least in high school. Keith tells the story of going one on one with Buck one summer in the family backyard in Glenside. Buck wanted to get in some reps in assorted pass sets to stay sharp for the upcoming NFL season. Keith wanted to show he could hack it against his big brother. Both threw on some pads and took to the yard. "I came out of my stance the first time and Buck hit me, picked me up, and tossed me like a little girl," Keith says, becoming more animated. "I swear I'd never been treated like that in my life. My little brother Kevin had the look of fear in his face. Buck's like, 'Who's next?' Kevin's like, 'What the heck! I don't want to go!'"

Of Keith, Kevin says, "Growing up he was a lot bigger than I was. I was the short, fat kid and he was the tall, skinny kid. I guess I was always trying to compete with Keith, cause he was always the biggest kid there."

Keith, however, was never too big on himself to forget Kevin. Like a good older brother, he encouraged his kid bro to challenge himself. When it came time for Kevin to choose a college, Keith urged him not to settle for a Division I-AA suitor, but to accept an invitation from Paterno to walk on at Penn State.

"I knew I always wanted to go there," Kevin says. "I was lucky enough to have an avenue with my two brothers that gave me an

Kevin Conlin.

opportunity to walk on. It was kind of ingrained in me as a child that I was willing to do whatever it took to play at a place like that. I would push myself. I knew I would have to wait a long time, a lot longer than everybody else, but I knew I would always push forward. It was just second nature, being in my family, that I would work as hard as I possibly could."

Kevin, like Buck years before him, also had second thoughts about staying in Happy Valley once he'd already joined the program. "That's when having a brother like Keith there was so beneficial, because I could go talk to him and tell him how I was feeling," says Kevin. "He was like, 'Look, everybody goes through that same time, everybody wants to come home.'" Keith even told his brother the story of Buck's bout of homesickness, and how the offer to come work at Moon's Tire Shop quickly changed his mind.

"Keith was great," Kevin says. "Our bond became strong at that point—because he was there. A lot of people make decisions to leave schools like that before talking to somebody who's been through it. I was lucky to have someone like Keith there to help me out."

* * *

A decade's passed since a Conlin suited up for a Penn State team. (Keith, however, returned to the program in 2005 as an assistant to strength and conditioning coach John Thomas.) Hard to believe how time flies. On November 22, 1997, the day Kevin played his last game in Beaver Stadium, his entire family gathered in University Park to witness a bittersweet Nittany Lions victory. On the field, Kevin was focused on making Senior Day a winning day, and he most recalls beating Wisconsin 35-10 with help from a Hail Mary touchdown pass caught by wide receiver Joe Jurevicius on the last play of the first half. It was a play Paterno had forced the Lions to practice week in and week out, a play run so frequently, it never failed to produce groans from the depths of the practice field. This time, in Kevin's final home game, it paid off.

"For five years we worked on it and worked on it," says Kevin, who now has two kids, is a high school teacher, and coaches high school football not far from where he grew up. "Just shows you how you have to prepare. Might not be this game or next game or even this season, but you gotta prepare for every single situation."

That chilly November night, as the endless darkness of Happy Valley enveloped Beaver Stadium, the five Conlin brothers huddled together on the turf. As postgame shadows bent and flickered around them, the men shuffled into a semicircle and faced the camera. Craig on the far left, then Keith, then Kevin in the middle still in his home blue uniform, then Buck to his left in a black leather jacket, then Kenny wearing a white road version of Kevin's No. 59 jersey. Snap.

The Conlins

The moment meant so much to so many Conlins. Buck can look at his copy of the photo and picture his playing days, how as a freshman in 1983 he was treated like family by upperclassmen Ron Heller and Dick Maginnis, and how three years later he would do the same for freshmen on the 1986 national title squad. His lone regret is having used his eligibility in 1983, which prevented him from a redshirt season and a fifth year of classes. He left Penn State in 1987 for the NFL, and five seasons in that league plus 14 years of Arena football (three as a player, 11 as a coach) later, he still has no Penn State degree. "[Paterno] was very upset, and I think he probably still is upset about the handful of guys from that '86 team who never graduated," says Buck, who is now a construction superintendent living in Miami, Florida. "He used to say, [doing his best high-pitched Paterno impersonation] 'I'm gonna tell your parents!' But I understood what he was saying. I wish I would have graduated."

Keith can look at the same photo and smell the glory of the 1994 season, that magical offense that worked so hard and so well together. "We were all blue-collar kids," Keith says of fellow offensive linemen like Marco Rivera and Jeff Hartings. "Marco's father was a butcher. Jeff's father was a chicken farmer. My dad was a tire man. We knew what the hell hard work was."

Keith, whose first memory of Paterno is lifting $5 off him for an ad in his grade school yearbook when the coach came to Glenside to recruit Buck, still teases Paterno that he's never won any national or conference title without a Conlin. (Of course, on top of 1986 and 1994 plus the 2005 Big Ten title for which he was an assistant, he counts unrelated Shane Conlan, a redshirt in 1982, as a brother.) And the coach will jab back, much the way he and Mary Conlin used to go at it.

Kevin, he sees the same photo as inspiration, for it was during his time as an undergrad that he began studying the Penn State system to assist him in his current job at Abington High School. "I always knew I wanted to coach," he says, "and I think high school is the ultimate level, because you not only get to coach kids, but you can really mold them into becoming men. That's the best experience in coaching: not winning games, but seeing kids come back as adults and men."

Playing for JoePa

Joe "Moon" Conlin, the family patriarch, when he looks at the same picture, he can see instantly that Paterno delivered on his promise for his sons. He made Conlin men of Conlin boys, and in the process, he made Joe and Mary forever part of the Penn State family.

"Buck and Dad," says Keith, thinking back to the last time his dad and Paterno saw each other, "they came to practice one day before the Orange Bowl [days before Christmas 2005]. When he saw my dad, Joe ran over. I could see him getting choked up. He just has that much respect for my mom and dad."

He has that much love for one of Penn State's favorite families.

fourteen

THE SUHEYS

WALKING INTO BEAVER STADIUM as a high school recruit, Kevin Suhey stood in awe as he came face to face with his past. Staring him down were photographs of his grandfather and great-grandfather, hanging among pictures of Penn State's lineage of All-Americans. Bob Higgins, Kevin's great grandfather, was a receiver at Penn State from 1914-17 and in 1919; he later served as head coach from 1930-48, including the Lions' historic, undefeated season in 1947. Steve Suhey, Kevin's grandfather, played guard for the Lions in the 1940s.

That's remarkable in and of itself, that two generations of Suheys preceded Kevin at Penn State. Except that's not the whole story. Kevin isn't a third-generation Penn Stater, he's a *fourth*. His father, Paul Suhey, was a linebacker for State from 1975-78; and Paul's brothers, Matt and Larry, also suited up for the Lions as running backs in the mid-to-late-'70s. So really, that makes Kevin the sixth member of the Suhey clan to play at State, which he sums up in one word—"amazing."

"Fourth generation," says Paul. "I don't think that's going on anywhere else in the country."

The "whole story" begins with Steve Suhey, an All-America lineman on that storied '47 squad who married Higgins' daughter, Ginger. They had seven children, including Paul, Matt, and Larry,

159

who all played football at Penn State. Then came Kevin, a quarterback. And the family tree isn't done branching out yet: Joe Suhey, Matt's son, made a verbal commitment to the Nittany Lions in December 2006. So not only are the Suheys continuing to add new generations to their Penn State heritage, they're doing so with multiple players in each of the last two generations.

Paul says that Kevin had an opportunity to play college football for other programs, but Penn State was the place for him. "We weren't going to argue with him," says Paul. "We thought that was a pretty good decision, too."

The roots of this tree are entrenched in Penn State soil. Higgins was the stuff legends are made of, the subject of countless stories for both his contributions as a player and coach. And to think, Higgins—a native of Corning, New York—actually had to convince his skeptical parents that football could make for a good career. Once on the field, the hard-nosed hit man became an All-America end noted for his fierce play. Teammates remembered Higgins, also a fine kicker, for his ability to catch opposing ball carriers from behind, often tracking them halfway down the field. But it was his game-breaking offensive abilities that catapulted him to legend status. Case in point: A Higgins 85-yard touchdown catch against Pitt was immortalized in Knute Rockne's *Great Football Plays*. Perhaps even more remarkable was the time Higgins duplicated a touchdown catch against Lehigh in 1915. The teams were deadlocked in a scoreless tie when Higgins caught a pass from Stan Ewing and ran 15 yards for a touchdown. But the play was called back, as the Lions had 12 men on the field. With extra yardage tacked on for the penalty and time running out, head coach Dick Harlow called the exact same play, and Higgins scored yet again to hand Penn State a 7-0 victory.

Upon graduation in 1920, Higgins started his coaching career at West Virginia Wesleyan, then moved on to Washington University in St. Louis. He later returned to Penn State as an assistant under Hugo Bezdek in 1928. Two years later, Higgins was named head coach.

The Suheys

Bob Higgins.

There were times Higgins probably wished he hadn't taken the job. Talent was scarce because of a "purity" campaign at Penn State that didn't allow for athletic scholarships, yet alone meal tickets. Higgins' early years at Penn State were difficult. He didn't post a winning season for seven years, fielding teams that one of his assistants, Joe Bedenk, once said "couldn't beat a good high school team." But his reputation as a player and popularity as a coach helped him survive those losing campaigns. It wasn't until the 1937 season that a Higgins-coached Penn State team had a winning year, and not until 1947 that the Nittany Lions went to a bowl game.

"Hig," as he was known, was criticized for his "unimaginative" single-wing formations and preference for old-fashioned power football. He answered his critics with this retort: "A good coach can do as much with the Single Wing as he can with the T-Formation." Ultimately, Higgins proved his point. Relying on power football and a stellar defense, the Lions began their ascent with a winning season in

Playing for JoePa

1939 that included a 10-0 victory at Pitt, one of Penn State's toughest opponents in those days. That victory against the Panthers marked the first time the Lions had defeated their in-state rivals since Higgins himself was a player in 1919.

The '39 season marked the beginning of a streak of 49 straight non-losing seasons at Penn State, a stretch that lasted until 1988. Things really began to turn around for Higgins in the 1942 season when the Lions finished the year ranked 19th in the nation. He didn't have to look very far for talent in the '40s, as he mined the coal mines of western Pennsylvania for quality players. He was a determined recruiter, as noted in the story of Negley Norton. A coveted player, Norton had agreed to attend Pitt and was already settling into the players' dorm when Higgins came knocking on his family's front door.

"One night," Norton recalls, "Bob Higgins showed up. My dad had graduated from Penn State. And Bob Higgins said, 'Earl Norton, are you going to let your son go to Pittsburgh?'"

"Guess where I went?"

In the end, Norton was glad he chose Penn State over Pitt. He wound up playing tackle on some strong Nittany Lion teams, including the '47 squad that set still-standing NCAA records for fewest yards allowed in a game (minus-47 against Syracuse), fewest average rushing yards over a season (17.0 yards per game), and lowest average per rush (0.64 yards per attempt). That season the 9-0 Lions finished the year ranked fourth in the country and earned a trip to the Cotton Bowl to face third-ranked Southern Methodist. The game, which ended in a 13-13 tie, was the school's first bowl appearance since the 1922 season.

Maybe the '47 Lions, featuring several World War II vets, were so tough that year because Higgins was so tough on them. "When we would practice or scrimmage and a guy would miss a block or a tackle, he'd tell the guy, 'We broke your plate tonight,'" recalls John "Shag" Wolosky. "That meant you didn't come to eat at the training table. And some of the guys didn't have any place else to eat, and no money to buy food, either. There were guys who didn't eat their evening meal."

The Suheys

Steve Suhey.

Higgins, like Coach Paterno, would not tolerate disrespect among the players. Swearing was not allowed in practice; anything that would earn one of his players an ejection during a game would also earn one of his players a trip to the showers in practice. Then there was the dress code: Higgins' players had to wear coats and ties to class. And curfew was midnight, sharp.

Higgins only coached for one more year following the '47 season. There was a power struggle between Joe Bedenk and Earl Bruce, two of the assistant coaches, for the top spot following the '48 season. Bruce was supported by the coaches, but Bedenk was favored by the university establishment. The students wanted neither, according to Charles "Jiggs" Beatty, a Penn State player at the time. "We wanted a big-time coach for a big-time college," he says. Bedenk eventually won the job, but only for the '49 season. He was replaced in 1950 by Rip Engle, who had turned out successful teams at Brown. Engle brought along with him a little-known assistant by the name of Joe Paterno.

Playing for JoePa

Before Higgins' tenure at Penn State was up he began the Suhey tradition at Penn State by recruiting a young man from Jamestown, New York, by the name of Steve Suhey. When Suhey arrived at Penn State he was a poor kid in need of a helping hand. Coach Higgins lent him that support, inviting the young lineman to live with his family. Higgins had no idea at the time that he would soon be gaining a son-in-law as well as a boarder.

Wartime halted Steve's college career, just as it did for many a player in the 1940s. Suhey joined the fight in the Pacific with the Army Air Corps after the 1942 season. He was gone for three long years, but during that time, he couldn't shake thoughts of Ginger Higgins from his mind. Ginger was the middle of Bob Higgins' three daughters, whom Suhey had met while living at the Higgins' home. Steve and Ginger exchanged letters, anxiously awaiting the day they would be reunited. That day came with Steve's return to State College following the war, and the couple soon married.

With a new wife, Steve resumed his studies and play for the Nittany Lions in 1946. His unyielding style of play and toughness was the epitome of the '47 squad, and Steve was rewarded that season with an All-America selection. Noted for his superior strength and large hands, Steve was also quicker than some of the backs who benefited from his superb blocks.

He was a telling sign of what was to come many years later in the form of three young boys from State College Area High School.

✳ ✳ ✳

Paul Suhey remembers Grandfather Higgins. "We were around him enough as kids," Paul says, "but we didn't quite understand him as a football coach, or an ex-football coach, at that time."

Paul and his brothers simply knew "Hig" as a grandfather who loved to play checkers with them. After leaving football, Higgins remained out of the limelight, never bothering to second-guess the coaching staff that followed him. Health failed Higgins, who suffered from a stroke and was paralyzed on one side of his body. But Paul says his grandfather was still plenty of fun. Not to mention, understanding.

The Suheys

Left to right: Larry Suhey, Paul Suhey, and Matt Suhey.

"We were always rolling around in the grass and playing with a football," recalls Paul. "My grandfather had an autographed football painted with the score [from a big game in his coaching career]. . . . We took it out and played with it. To us, it just looked like a plain, old football. We didn't really pay any attention to all the stuff on it, and we had a catch with it. . . . We actually scuffed it up pretty good.

"My grandfather didn't care. He thought it was funny. . . . We always laughed about that."

Playing sports was a natural way of life for the seven Suhey children—four brothers and three sisters—while growing up in State College in the 1960s. On Saturdays, the children would mimic the action on the field while listening to the radio play-by-play announcer describe the action as the Nittany Lions battled in Beaver Stadium. When the game was over, the kids reverted to whatever sport was in demand that day. With seven kids, Paul recalls having plenty of sports equipment around the house. And fortunately for the Suhey children, the family lived right behind the high school. Their back yard opened up to the soccer team's practice field, which turned into an extension of their own yard.

Steve Suhey was more of the strong, silent type. He didn't often speak to his children about his football career at Penn State, or his

Playing for JoePa

friendship with Joe Paterno when the young coach was living in his home shortly after following Coach Engle to State College. Nor did he say much about his NFL experiences with the Pittsburgh Steelers. He just encouraged his children to enjoy playing sports. He didn't need to force his boys to take a liking to football; living in football-rich State College did that job for him. "We understood our dad played [at Penn State]," Paul says, "but he didn't really brag about it. He just basically allowed us to enjoy Penn State football at the time."

Larry, the oldest, was the first of his brothers to attend Penn State, followed by Paul, who was three years younger than Larry. "I'm thinking, 'Why should I go eight hours away when I can get the same thing two miles away, in my own backyard?'" says Paul. "And I think Larry made me realize that."

When it came time the following year for Matt to make his decision, the standout fullback gave consideration to Ohio State and went on a recruiting trip to Arizona. Then his brothers stepped in, leaning on him in a brotherly way to try to keep him home in State College. "Down deep," Paul says, "I think it probably made my parents happy that we all decided to come here, but they didn't pressure us."

The trio of brothers was able to suit up together in 1976, with Larry at fullback, Matt at tailback, and Paul at linebacker. Unfortunately, the fun lasted but one year. Larry injured his knee and only played for two years at Penn State. Paul went on to play a full four seasons, as did Matt, who eventually enjoyed a fine professional career with the Chicago Bears.

Paul, now an orthopedic surgeon, remembers 1976 as a special time for the three of them. "It was comfortable," he says. "I could help Matt and Larry could help me, and we weren't so much in awe."

In a way, you could say that for the Suhey brothers, their backyard just expanded a bit further come college, from the soccer field at State College High to the environs of Beaver Stadium. The trio set a good example for the next generation of Suheys to follow.

The Suheys

✳ ✳ ✳

Kevin Suhey was a relatively late bloomer in football. That's the way his dad, Paul, preferred it. Kevin could toss the pigskin around the backyard or out in the street with his friends, but he wouldn't get his first taste of organized football for some time. "I don't know if it was as much that he didn't want me to get hurt," Kevin says of his father, "as he wanted me to experience other sports, too."

At the time, the family lived in Jacksonville, Florida, where soccer was a popular sport that was played year-round. Kevin took advantage, but also made time for baseball in the spring. When the family moved back to Pennsylvania, Kevin was in the sixth grade and itching to play football. The Sunshine State had multiple winter sports to choose from, but the lone outdoor sport in Pennsylvania come cold weather season was football. And the team to root for was the Nittany Lions.

"Right about the time I moved back, Larry Johnson was a junior or senior at State College High School," Kevin recalls. "He was the big deal. And then he committed to Penn State and I started to try to follow him there. I started to go to all the games."

That only served to scratch the itch. Finally, Paul granted Kevin permission to try organized football in eighth grade. Kevin was a quick learner, soaking up all the advice he could get from his dad. That landed him the starting quarterback job at State College Area High School, where Kevin eventually racked up some impressive stats. As a senior, he led State College to the state semifinals after winning the District 6 title. He was an accurate passer, completing 64 percent of his attempts for 12 touchdowns and 1,660 yards.

Kevin's first season at Penn State was quite different from that of his teammates. He chose to greyshirt, not starting school until the spring semester. With that downtime on his son's hands, Paul decided to give Kevin a taste of life in the NFL. Paul contacted an old friend from his Penn State days, Matt Millen, who is now general manager and CEO of the Detroit Lions. Millen offered Kevin an internship in the front office—with a twist. When he wasn't busy helping out management, Kevin was spending his time throwing passes to pro

Kevin Suhey, middle.

receivers. Due to NCAA rules, Kevin could not participate in practices, so he got his tosses in before practice. Coach Paterno wanted to make certain that Kevin was receiving an education off the field as well, so in addition to his internship, Kevin enrolled in fall classes at the University of Michigan. When the experience wrapped up in January 2005, Kevin could boast of a unique entry on both his business and quarterback résumé.

Kevin spent the 2006 season at Penn State trying to find his niche with the team. In the meantime, he's been soaking up the same environment that benefited the previous generation of Suheys at Penn State. Under the watchful eye of Paterno, Kevin has learned what it means to work hard and focus on the details. From one generation to the next, that philosophy hasn't changed at Penn State.

When he considers his decision to attend Penn State, Kevin says it was an easy one to make. He knew ever since he was a little kid that he wanted to be a Nittany Lion. "Penn State was kind of in my blood," he says.

It's hard to argue with that.

fifteen

THE GANTERS

IT'S A TIMELESS SCENE: A young boy and his father sitting together at home, following the broadcast of a football game featuring their favorite team. It happens everywhere across America during the fall season. For Fran Ganter, the setting was his parents' home in Bethel Park, Pennsylvania, in the late 1950s. And the rooting interest was Penn State, even though Bethel Park is just a 30-minute drive from the University of Pittsburgh campus.

"When I was little, I remember sitting in the den on a Saturday afternoon," Ganter recalls. "My dad would have one of those TV trays in front of his chair, and he had another TV chair beside his chair with a radio on it, and he would make these big sandwiches, like only a true Pittsburgher can."

Fran's father, Fran Sr., would inundate his son with as much football as possible: The Penn State game would be on the radio, because it was not televised, and the Notre Dame game would be on the television. "We would sit there and he would have the sound turned down on the TV game, watch it, and listen to the Penn State game. For as long as I can remember we were Penn State fans. I can remember when Dick Anderson and Galen Hall, Roger Kochman, Richie Lucas, all those guys played."

If he had a crystal ball, young Fran would have been thrilled to see his future as a Penn State football player and then a longtime coach

169

with the Nittany Lions. For 38 years, Fran was an indispensable assistant to a coaching legend. Two of Fran's four sons, Chris and Jason, would play for that coach, Joe Paterno. And former Penn State and NFL wide receiver Jimmy Cefalo is the boys' uncle.

"I always wanted to be a football coach," says Fran, now the associate athletic director for football at Penn State. "My high school coach, Dan Galbraith, was my idol. I thought he had the greatest job, and I wanted to be just like him."

His greatest hero, though, was his father. A man with a tremendous work ethic, Fran Sr. ran two businesses in Bethel Park—a gas station and a restaurant—to provide for his son and three daughters. "We hardly ever saw him," Fran Jr. recalls. "He worked really, really hard."

Ganter was in Paterno's second recruiting class, a running back with high ambitions. "I came as a tailback and grew into a fullback," he says. But with running backs like Charlie Pittman, Lydell Mitchell, and Franco Harris around, he wasn't playing as much as he wanted. "I always thought the coaches were nuts, because I wasn't playing more," says Ganter, who played from 1968-70 on some of Paterno's early powerhouses. "But as I look back on it as a coach, I was competing with guys who were better than me. Some great, great players were there."

While many of Fran's teammates were heading to the NFL following the 1970 season to continue their football careers, Ganter was headed for the sidelines—as a coach. He majored in health/physical education strictly so he could qualify to work at a high school and coach football. To fulfill that dream, he continued his education to earn a Masters in physical education while doubling as a graduate assistant to George Welsh on the Penn State football staff.

Then fate changed Fran's life. As Ganter was wrapping up his Master's degree, Welsh left to become head coach at Navy. "That left an opening, and Coach Paterno hired me in [Welsh's] place." For Ganter, it was a case of being in the right place at the right time. "Had Coach Welsh not left," he says, "I could be coaching at Bethel Park right now."

Ganter began as an assistant running backs coach, then moved to head coach of the freshman team. There, he learned to relate to

The Ganters

Fran Ganter.

individual players and adjust his coaching style. As a former player, Ganter was understanding of the players' problems and made sure he was available to listen as he moved up the ladder: head jayvee coach, recruiting coordinator, then offensive coordinator in 1984, and, finally, assistant head coach in 2000. As the offensive coordinator, Ganter turned out some of Penn State's best football talents, a list that includes Curt Warner, D.J. Dozier, and Blair Thomas, three of the top running backs in Penn State history.

While fulfilling his self-appointed destiny as a coach, Ganter had the support of his home team. He needed every bit of it. "My family understood the amount of time that a college football coach has to put in, and the amount of time that a coach would stay away from his family, away from Little League games, away from high school games, not being able to see practices, that kind of thing," Fran says.

So Ganter's sisters pitched in, helping Fran's wife, Karen, coordinate the sports activities of the Ganters' four boys. That was no easy task, given the boys' sporting interests. So when Karen couldn't make it to one son's game, a relative was always there to help.

Fran and his wife did receive a weekly reprieve, a chance to catch their breath. Every Thursday evening during the season, coaches and their wives would meet at one of their homes. After relaxing and unwinding from the stressful week, the large group would head downtown to The Tavern and enjoy sandwiches compliments of Paterno. "And that went on for 10, 15 years," Fran says. "It was so much fun."

At least Thursday nights were fun. On Sunday mornings, the mood might change during the coaches' meeting, especially if Paterno needed to let off a little—or a lot—of steam. "He'd get on you on Sunday morning . . . second-guess you, which is his job," Ganter says. "But never would he do that in public."

As for the kids, Ganter says, Paterno would let them have it, which is part of what made Paterno such a great leader on the sidelines. "He just commands a certain respect," he says, "and you can see it in the way the officials handle him."

Fran is also impressed by Paterno's remarkable memory. "When you bring up a game," Fran says, "he'll bring up the down, the distance, the official's name who made the call in 1987. He knows who scored what touchdown to beat us, he knows who was out of position, who dropped the interception, etcetera."

Ganter also credits Paterno with making the correct call when the university decided to join the Big Ten in 1993. At the time, Ganter wasn't in favor of the decision; the Nittany Lions had been independent for their entire history, during which time they had built up a number of memorable rivalries among the Eastern schools. Joining the Big Ten would sacrifice many of those rivalries, particularly Pitt.

"I really was against it," Ganter says. "Now as I look back, Joe was smart enough [to know] what it would do from a prestige and

The Ganters

academic standpoint. The Big Ten is awesome. It really is fun to be in a conference. Now we're playing for a league championship every year. We know these guys, because we've played against them for years."

In 1994, the Lions' second year in the Big Ten, they went undefeated and gained a berth in the Rose Bowl. Kerry Collins quarterbacked a record-breaking Penn State offensive machine that whipped 12 opponents under the guidance of Ganter. The Lions capped their perfect season with a 38-20 Rose Bowl win over Oregon. It was Penn State's first Rose Bowl visit since 1923.

Following the '94 season, Ganter was offered the head coaching job at Michigan State, but he turned it down. The decision wasn't surprising, considering for many years Ganter was generally regarded as the heir apparent to Paterno's job. His roots ran deep in State College, where he was tied to a family of coaches who had shared life's triumphs and tragedies.

He needed the support of that family in 2002. That summer, Fran's wife, Karen, died suddenly at the age of 53. The Ganters were devastated, and yet more bad news was on the way. Fran's mother-in-law, Liz Bruno, was preparing to make the trip to State College to comfort the family when she suddenly passed away of a heart attack. The sudden losses dealt the Ganters a knee-wobbling blow, but thankfully the Penn State family was there for support.

Typically, Paterno was one of the first to be there for Fran and his family. But then, just a little over two weeks after Karen's death, Paterno was dealt his own loss when his brother, George, suffered a heart attack and died. George had played in the same backfield with Joe at Brown and had been a radio color man for Penn State football.

On the field, Penn State was struggling, too, having just gone through two losing seasons. "It's been a long year," Joe Paterno said in 2002. "I worried about Frannie. I worried about the players. I worried about me. We got through it, though."

Following losing seasons in 2000 and 2001, Penn State rebounded with a 9-4 record in 2002 and a bowl appearance. In 2003, one year after Karen's passing, Fran Ganter left the sidelines to work in the university's athletic office. Paterno knew he would miss his trusted assistant. "It's amazing how many times things will pop up and I am always thinking, 'What would [Fran] have done there?'" Paterno said.

Ganter left a career of highlights as offensive coordinator, including two that stand out in his memories: Penn State's first national championship and Penn State's first Rose Bowl in the Paterno Era. Two of Fran's biggest fans got to see plenty of that highlight reel firsthand.

※ ※ ※

Fran Ganter's sons—Jonathan, Chris, Jason, and Ben—revered Paterno and the Penn State program while growing up. Yet while each boy played Division I football, only Chris and Jason ended up on the Penn State roster.

Ben, the youngest, decided on Cornell so he could have a better chance to play football. Jonathan, the oldest, was actually dissuaded by his parents from attending State. The Ganters felt he shouldn't pass up the opportunity to go to Princeton, especially since he wanted to be a lawyer. "We almost had to make him go away," Fran says. "That was really one instance where we really felt Princeton was a better place for him for a variety of reasons. He agrees with us now, but he didn't at the time.

"What's interesting, and I'm bragging, he ended up working in the White House for two years, and then he worked for Attorney General Alberto R. Gonzales for one year in the Justice Department."

At State College Area High School, Chris and Jason made a unique connection on the football field when Jason caught a pass from his older brother Chris during his sophomore season. Jason would reconnect with Chris by following him to Penn State a couple of years later.

Chris' high school career was one for the record books. He passed for 3,700 yards and 33 touchdowns during high school, and as a senior was named first-team All-State by the Associated Press. He was noted as being a tough customer, which Chris calls "a function of growing up with three brothers. We beat the crap out of each other.

The Ganters

was a lot of fighting. But it made us better in all kinds of ways. I wouldn't have given it up for anything."

There were lessons to be learned at home as well from his father. "As far as teaching football, there were no Xs and Os, really," Chris recalls. "He never got specific with the game of football. He just helped us understand the big picture of everything, just related it to life. Those were the lessons that he taught us from his experiences in football."

Despite spending plenty of time around the Penn State program, Chris had his doubts about attending college in Happy Valley. Once he became a sought-after recruit, Chris thought it might be a better idea to go somewhere other than Penn State. He wanted to get away from all the added pressures that would come with playing for the hometown team with his father as the offensive coach. "If I was a linebacker, it would have been completely different. But I was a quarterback and my dad was the offensive coordinator," he says.

Chris visited about 10 schools, but nothing stacked up to Penn State. So he rolled with Plan A and chose the Nittany Lions, thus inviting plenty of criticism from doubters who thought he was only there because his father was a coach and he was a hometown kid. "That was just something I knew going in I was going to hear," Chris says.

The competition at quarterback was stiff at that time. It was the era of Zach Mills and Mike Robinson, and Chris didn't get much playing time. Yet he kept things in perspective: "If you want to go to a school like Penn State, you'd better expect that. I knew I'd have a chance to compete, and that's all I could ask for."

Chris spent his first year on the bench as a redshirt. In 2002, he stepped into the role of third-string quarterback and holder on the kicking team. Still, Chris was a long way from achieving one of his dreams—throwing a touchdown pass in a college game. Running for one, however, was within reach. Against Virginia, in the 10th game of the 2002 season, Penn State had everything well under control. The Nittany Lions' drive had stalled inside the Cavaliers' 30-yard line, which brought out the kicking team. Chris took the field to hold for the kicker, and the team lined up for the kick. But Paterno had something else in mind. Wanting to put the game out of reach, he instead called for a fake field goal.

Chris took the snap from center, pulled up, tucked the ball under his arm, and raced 30 yards to the end zone. Touchdown! Chris pointed skyward, a motion to the heavens. His mom would have loved this moment. Fran Ganter was all smiles as the Penn State players swarmed around Chris. They were a family. They had all shared in Chris' pain after his mother's passing, and now they reveled in his joy.

Paterno was happy, too. He quickly moved down the sidelines to shake hands with both Fran and Chris. The final: 35-14, Penn State.

✳ ✳ ✳

When Karen Ganter passed away, Jason was still in high school. Fran took on the job of getting his sons, Jason and Ben, to school in the morning. It was a difficult time for the family, as the boys missed their mom.

After the loss of their mother, Jonathan Ganter graduated from Princeton and planned to come home to look after his younger brothers. To do so meant rejecting an offer for a Washington, D.C. internship, however, and Fran, Jason, and Ben each asked Jonathan to reconsider. Fran couldn't bear to see his son alter his dreams, so Jonathan went to Washington.

Meanwhile, Jason was a top student at State College Area High School who also excelled on the football field as a wide receiver and defensive back. The three-year starter culminated his career with an impressive senior season that included 54 tackles and five interceptions. He also caught 12 passes for 110 yards and was selected first-team All-Allegheny Conference.

When colleges came calling, Jason decided he would remain close to home, opting to walk-on in 2003 at Penn State. "I've gone to all the games since I was little," said Jason, a safety for the Lions after choosing Penn State. "Playing for Penn State has always been a dream of mine."

And with good reason, as Jason had received a first-person glimpse of Paterno's family-first philosophy well before he joined the Nittany

The Ganters

Chris Ganter eludes a defender.

Lions. Jason remembers with some warmth how Paterno invited the younger Ganter boys to the football team's training table after Karen's passing, so that they could have dinner with their father.

Like his brother, Jason was red-shirted his freshman year. In 2004, his sophomore year, Jason earned playing time on defense and special teams in every Penn State game. In 2005, he won the job as the holder on field goals and extra points, and was on the field in the closing minutes of Penn State's 2006 Orange Bowl game against Florida State. With the teams battling in the third overtime, the Lions lined up for what was supposed to be a fake field goal attempt from the Florida State 12-yard line. But as Ganter waited to take the snap, he sized up the Florida State defensive alignment and didn't like what he saw. He called off the fake, took the snap, put the ball down for freshman kicker Kevin Kelly, and then watched as the ball sailed through the uprights for a 26-23 victory.

Playing for JoePa

* * *

Fran Ganter is no longer on the sidelines, but still very much in the game at State College. As associate athletic director, he is still working with Paterno, only off the field. Just about anything football-related passes through Ganter's office. "There are maybe five or six main areas, from strength and conditioning to medical, to the academic, the budget. I try to keep the little things out of Joe's hair," he says. That also includes making up football schedules and running five football camps in the summer.

Ganter's form of lion-hearted loyalty to the Penn State program is not unusual in the Paterno Era. "The unique thing about Penn State," Ganter says, "you could be 58 years old and decide to come up to see your old school after you've played football here. You'll walk into this office and you'll remember four or five of the coaches that are still here. There are not many places like that.

"You could walk in and feel like you're part of the family. That's another situation that really keeps it all going, and we're lucky that Joe's been here so long."

The same can be said of Fran Ganter, too.

THE
JOHNSONS

LARRY JOHNSON JR. was going to play football at North Carolina, no doubt about it. His father, Larry Sr., knew it. He could see that twinkle in his son's eye, hear an inflection in his voice when Larry talked about the Tar Heels.

It all made perfect sense.

Larry Sr. was born and raised a two-hour car ride down Route 64 from Chapel Hill, home of the University of North Carolina. The Johnson family roots still clung firmly to Carolina soil. Larry Jr. had been smitten with the blue and white—Tar Heel baby blue and white, that is—for as long as he could remember. So when Larry Jr. took his official visit to UNC in 1998, it only confirmed what his father had suspected for years: Carolina was the one.

"We get down there, and he's falling in love with the place," says Larry Sr., who also brought his wife, Christine, younger son, Tony, and daughter, Theresa (Tony's fraternal twin), on the recruiting trip. "He had a great time. The next day I looked at my wife and said, 'You know what? He's going to Carolina. Get yourself ready. Get your tears ready.'"

The tears were not tears of joy. See, the Johnsons reside in State College, where Larry Sr. has been coaching the Penn State defensive line since 1996. Junior was considering attending a school that was almost 500 miles away—that was the source of the tears. But the decision was not yet final. The eldest of the three Johnson children had 10 college football offers, and Larry Sr. suggested they at least take recruiting trips to some of those schools. One of those places was Penn State.

Larry Jr. agreed. Why not take a look? There was no pressure, since his heart was already packed for Chapel Hill.

So Larry did his due diligence, took some additional school visits, including the one to Penn State. He had a great time that weekend, met some cool guys on the team, saw the inside of one of the more storied programs in college football. He met the assistants. He talked to Joe Paterno. Beaver Stadium was palatial.

But it was just a visit. Carolina was still the one.

Or was it?

✳ ✳ ✳

The Johnsons are a tight clan. They don't make rash decisions, and they don't make solo decisions—at least when it comes to life-altering crossroads. This was no different. Larry had a choice before him, and as is often the case when one of the Johnsons has a decision to make, the entire family gathered for a roundtable discussion. It's a simple premise. Everyone gets a turn to speak his or her mind; in this case, all Larry had to do was listen. After that his parents, brother and sister would support whatever decision he made, because it would then be considered an informed decision.

Theresa went first. "Larry, I've been to every one of your games," she started. "Now you know, if you go away, Mom and I will be there, but it won't be the same if we miss it. We won't get there sometimes. But we'll be there and we'll support whatever you're going to do."

When she paused, Larry's kid sister had tears running down her cheeks.

Tony was next. "I basically told him, 'I would like for you to stay in town so I can see you play.'" Tony says today. "I told him I would want to wear his jersey when he became the star running back at Penn State. Then I busted out in tears too."

The Johnsons

Larry's mother, Chris, went next, and the tears returned. Finally, red eyes around, Larry Sr. cleared his throat. He began by ticking off advantages and disadvantages of leaving home to play football at North Carolina versus staying local at Penn State. He told his son, "Don't go away from home to say, 'I'm getting away from home.' Because if you say that, then we've done something wrong as a family."

After the roundtable concluded for the evening, Larry pulled his father aside to talk one on one. That's when Larry Sr. explained one final element of the decision-making process—a final thought to consider. He told his son the reality that awaited him at Penn State if he elected to become a Nittany Lion.

"I shared with him that he'd be in a glass bubble," Larry Sr. says. "I told him, 'Everything you do will be magnified. Everything you say will be blown up. Because you're not only a player, you're a coach's son. So you'd have to be even better. You'd have to be a great student and do everything right. That's tough, Larry.'"

That's tough, Larry. Glass bubble, Larry. Have to be even better, Larry.

Larry Sr. had done it: He'd said it all without actually saying it. He knew his oldest son's makeup. This was a kid who struggled to make friends on his youth football teams growing up because he perceived a separation from his teammates that actually never existed. He felt alone. He felt they were jealous of him, maybe because he was a coach's son. He felt exiled. And as a grade-schooler, he'd sometimes cry about the situation, a situation that was more an invention of his own mind than anything.

Larry Jr. was also a kid who loved to battle. Stubborn maybe, but he was a warrior, and his father knew it. He wouldn't turn and run from a situation just because it might be difficult to endure. He'd welcome the challenge instead.

The day after the Johnsons held their family discussion, Larry stood before a throng of friends, family, and faculty at State College Area High School. With eyes and camera lenses trained on him, he stepped forward. Larry Sr. says until their son opened his mouth, he and Chris had no idea what he was going to say.

Playing for JoePa

"I've made my decision," Larry started, his heart thumping away somewhere deep within his pressed suit. "I'm going to. . ."—he paused, the room clinging impatiently to his voice, ever so eager for an answer—"Penn State."

An instant lightning bolt of cheers and screams filled the room. There was a collective exhale, too. The local star was staying home.

Chris broke into tears. "We knew then," Larry Sr. says, "that the rest was going to be easy, because he made a great decision."

✳ ✳ ✳

Becoming a successful football player is anything but easy. Larry Sr. knows that first-hand. His father, Herman Johnson, was a proponent of stern parenting. He was Larry's role model, but he was also a throwback. Herman, a former boxer in the Army who carved out a life for himself and his family despite having only earned a seventh-grade education, didn't know the meaning of the word easy. Or mercy.

"If you messed up, you paid for it," Larry Sr. says. "He'd grab a board, anything he could get his hands on. It was old-school discipline."

And it worked. When Herman told Larry or his other kids not to cross the street, no one crossed the street. No one crossed Dad.

The Johnsons of Williamston, North Carolina, weren't a wealthy bunch, but they had something much more valuable than stocks or bonds. Larry Sr. learned of it long ago from his father. It's a story he's told his own kids many times through the years, and it goes something like this:

Herman's talking to Larry one day when he says, "Larry, there are two things that I'd like for you to have, and one I can't give you."

"What's that, Dad?" Larry asks in return.

"I can't make you a millionaire," Herman says, letting the words settle in. "But I can give you my last name. I can give you Johnson. And that should mean something to you."

Larry Sr. is still struck by the weight of that anecdote. For in it lies so much about who he and his siblings are as people, and so much about the sort of people he's raised Larry Jr., Tony, and Theresa to be. For Larry Sr., his name was and is a badge of dignity, respect, and discipline. Growing up, being a Johnson and understanding his family legacy helped him gravitate toward some special people who shared many of Herman's qualities and philosophies on life.

In Larry Sr.'s teen years it was Herman Boone, who coached at Williamston's E.J. Hayes High School in the 1960s—he went 99-8 in nine years there—and later became head coach of just-integrated T.C. Williams High School in Alexandria, Virginia. (Boone's time at T.C. Williams, controversial because he received the job over a legendary local white coach, is documented in the inspirational Disney movie *Remember the Titans*.)

Boone, Larry Sr. says, was all about precision, execution, discipline, and tradition. His players wore coats and ties on game days. "Being an E.J. Hayes Tiger meant something," he says. "You looked that way. You carried yourself different. We were clean-cut kids and 'Yes, sir' and 'No, sir' guys."

When he reached college, Larry Sr. faced his first test of that "Yes, sir" system. Larry had his mind set on accepting a full scholarship to play football at East Carolina University. He would have become the second African-American ever to play at ECU. It was a terrific opportunity. But before he could accept, his father stepped in. Herman told Larry he could forget about ECU. He was going to attend Elizabeth City State, no questions asked. That's where Larry's brother, Alekan, was. That's where his sister, Nelly, was. That's where Larry was going.

And a funny thing happened. Larry, a staunch believer in discipline and respect, rebelled. "It was a tough transition," he says, "because I didn't want to be there. Every day for the first two months, I'd walk on the field and I'd try to start a fight and try to get kicked off the team so I could transfer or something. Finally I realized, you know, I could have a chance to play as a freshman if I really work at this thing. It was a defining moment."

After college, three years of which he spent living with Alekan, Larry signed as a free agent with the Washington Redskins. He was the last linebacker cut in camp, and rather than pursue his career on the field with an alternative offshoot like the World Football League, Larry decided to get a job. He'd never coached before, but he wanted to try that direction. He says he always had a passion for kids and for giving back. He just needed a chance.

Enter Herman Boone once more. Larry's high school coach called a buddy in Charles County, Maryland, who agreed to hire Larry as a high school assistant. Poof! Larry had his first real job. He was young, passionate, fiery, and in love with his work. He was doing something for others, which was important to him, and it drove him. He enjoyed it so much he stuck with it even as he was starting his own family.

That's how Larry Jr. and Tony first tasted football—as fans of their father's teams. They would ride the team bus on Fridays and Saturdays to attend games with Larry Sr., running up into the stands, catching candy hurled skyward by cheerleaders after the home team scored a touchdown. "They were around it so much," Larry Sr. says, "it was easy for them to walk right through the door."

When Larry Jr. was eight and Tony six, they began playing their first organized football in a 75-pound league. Their coach? Dad. Larry Sr. felt strongly that his boys' first experiences on a gridiron be positive ones, so he'd run high school practice, then keep his entire staff around afterwards for practice with the little kids.

Larry Sr. calls those times "the best fun of my life," even the day he first explained to his sons that being a coach's son meant acting the part of a coach's son. "They were on the sideline playing with the water buckets, picking daisies, not paying attention," Larry Sr. says. "So I get home and I give them this big speech: 'Okay, look here guys. You gotta understand this. When you're on the field, you gotta do this, do this, do this. You can't be playing around. And if you don't want to play football, just say so.'"

Tony remembers Larry Sr. beginning his speech while the three of them were still in the car on the ride home from practice. "We got screamed at," Tony says, "and we were crying when we walked into the house. Our mother asked us what was wrong and we told her Dad was being too tough on us."

When Larry Sr. asked if his sons wanted to quit football, he didn't suspect they'd take him up on the offer. But that's what happened.

The Johnsons

Larry Johnson Sr.

Larry and Tony wanted out. Chris walked away laughing while her husband thought about what to do next. He paused, then turned to them and said, "Well, you're going to play anyway." That line still gets a laugh out of Larry Sr. today. "That was the only moment I had to try to keep them in football," he says. "Ever since then it was really easy."

There's that word again: easy. But strangely, as the Johnsons' story continues, it seems somehow accurate. Once Larry Jr. and Tony decided for themselves to stick with the game, Larry Sr. didn't have to become one of those face-to-the-pavement sports dads who force feeds football to his kids. It came naturally. The boys took to the sport more as they grew, Larry Jr. as a running back, Tony as a quarterback and wide receiver. They rooted for each other, Theresa too. All three Johnson children loved watching one another thrive in their respective sports pursuits. (Theresa played softball at Penn State.)

Of the two boys, Tony was more easygoing. He preferred basketball to football; in fact, he says one of the reasons he stuck with football so long is that it afforded him the chance to play with his older brother, whom he calls one of his role models. Larry was the serious one, the focused one. As a baby, he used to sleep with the Nerf football Larry Sr. would drop into his crib at night. Larry was the one who'd spend hours on the couch with Dad watching NFL Films footage of Gale Sayers and Marion Motley, studying their moves for his own arsenal. "He was an old-school guy in a young body," Larry Sr. says.

Larry's dream wasn't just to make the NFL. He wanted to be the next Jim Brown, the next Walter Payton. And even as a midget-leaguer, his only request was to "just run the ball." He once took a sweep 80 yards for a touchdown, the final 40 yards of which he ran alongside mom Chris, who sprinted in unison with him down the sideline.

As he watched his kids develop, Larry Sr. told himself that when they reached high school, if he couldn't coach them, he'd be there to watch them play. So in 1995, when Larry Jr. was about to enter ninth grade, his father made a decision. Larry Sr. had been working at T.C. Williams High in Alexandria, the former employer of his friend and mentor, Herman Boone. Larry was commuting at the time from the family home in Maryland, putting in a lot of hours to revive a once-proud program that had fallen on hard times. But in '95, after two years at T.C. Williams, Larry Sr. decided to return to Charles County to become an assistant high school principal. He quit coaching, telling himself that was the sacrifice he had to make to be there for his sons. He became a deacon at his local church, settling into the life he wanted—the life of just being a dad.

It didn't last. A year after leaving T.C. Williams, Larry Sr. received a call from Jerry Sandusky, then the defensive coordinator at Penn State. Sandusky had met Johnson during summer football camps and recruiting trips—three kids Johnson once coached in high school had gone on to sign with Penn State—and they had maintained a close relationship. Sandusky was recommending Larry Sr. for an opening at Penn State to coach special teams and defensive linemen. It was a tremendous opportunity, and it was being dropped right in his lap, through no exploration of his own. Easy, right?

Johnson decided to interview for the post with Penn State head coach Joe Paterno. Larry Sr. had met Paterno briefly a few times before, but nothing like this. This was big. A week went by, and the day of the interview arrived. Larry Sr. decided to take Larry Jr. with him on the trip, and the two drove north from Maryland for the interview.

The Johnsons

"I'm wracking my brains, getting ready for this big meeting with Coach Paterno, the coach of the century," Larry Sr. says. "I was organized. Had my books, my notes, everything. We had breakfast with Jerry Sandusky and Coach Paterno. So we're talking and Coach Paterno looks at me and says, 'Larry, I've heard a lot of great things about you. And here's what we want to do.' He says, 'I'm not here to interview you. I'm here to offer you the job. Go look at the campus and we'll talk later on.'

"When we sat and talked later that day, he didn't ask one question about football—not one," says Larry Sr., still sounding surprised at the course of events. "We talked about family, life, my goals, my inspirations, what I wanted to do, and what he wanted. And the rest is history."

Soon after, Larry Sr. packed up his family and moved to State College. If you're surprised that he would abandon the life of "just being a dad" so quickly, don't be. Something Paterno told him shortly after his arrival confirmed that this position would offer the best of both worlds—career and family. And that was too tempting to pass up.

"[Paterno] said, 'You'll get a chance to spend time with your family,'" Larry Sr. recalls. "'I promise you that because that's important to me.' And I'll tell you, he has not backed away from that. Anything to do with kids, family, games, I've been there. He's allowed me to be a father to my kids. And for that, I really, really admire the guy."

❋ ❋ ❋

That's how it really happened. The ha-ha version, the one Paterno used to drop in press conferences from time to time, was that he hired Larry Sr. to have the inside track on recruiting his kids. But the real laugher is that when Larry Jr. accompanied his father to the "interview" with Paterno and Sandusky, he was nowhere to be found on Penn State's radar of future recruiting classes. Larry Sr. says he recalls telling Paterno and Sandusky that his son played football and ran track, "but they didn't know how good an athlete he was at the time," Johnson says.

They sure found out. Playing alongside his brother, Larry Jr. broke out his senior year at State College Area High. He rushed for 2,159 yards and 29 touchdowns that season. You don't miss a star like that in your backyard. Yet Penn State almost lost him anyway.

Larry Jr. credits Paterno and former Penn State offensive coordinator Fran Ganter with pursuing him aggressively as he neared the end of his high school career, but ultimately "it took more than them to get me to commit to PSU," he says. "It was my family that really helped me decide. And family comes first."

Now, in the rising years of an All-Pro NFL career, Larry Jr. says he has no regrets about having chosen Penn State over North Carolina. Part of that is the afterglow that still resonates from his senior season in 2002, a virtual fall-long Johnson family lovefest in Happy Valley. (That year Larry gained 2,087 yards and became the first 2,000-yard rusher in NCAA history to average more than 7.5 yards per carry.) Part of it is seeing in hindsight the struggles that North Carolina had in the years Larry would have been there. And part of it is plain old maturity.

Larry has no interest in revisiting the trying memories, but there were times when he chafed under what he perceived to be an old-school approach to offense at Penn State. There were times he called out that lack of creativity, times he wondered if he'd ever become the featured tailback in Joe Paterno's system. At some point, it would have been understandable had he questioned his decision to come to Penn State, much the way Larry Sr. wondered why he was stuck at Elizabeth City when he could have been writing his own script at East Carolina. But by now, the good moments have washed away any flare-ups.

"It was the greatest time in my life to have my boys in front of me," says Larry Sr., who also used the pull of family to nudge Tony and later Theresa into picking Penn State, too. "To get a chance to see them play college football is something most fathers don't get a chance to do, and I got to do it from the sideline, which was really special. It was truly a blessing for me."

"We had more pressure on ourselves because we were a coach's kids, and time after time we had to go out there and prove ourselves," adds Tony, who as a wide receiver had perhaps his finest season in 2002 (34 receptions for 549 yards), the same year Larry stole headlines on his march to 2,000 yards. "But my brother and I had been living with that most of our lives, so we got used to it very quickly."

The Johnsons

Larry Johnson Jr.

✳ ✳ ✳

It's been more than three years now since Tony played his last game as a Nittany Lion, closing the Johnsons' chapter on Penn State football. Theresa has since graduated too, and Larry Sr. has eclipsed his first full decade on Joe Paterno's staff. Tony's now living in Kansas City with Larry, running marketing and PR efforts for his big brother and his big brother's numerous charitable efforts. Larry, meanwhile, has been running roughshod over AFC defenses with the Kansas City Chiefs.

As his family spreads his name out into the real world beyond the protective bubble of State College, Larry Sr. has begun growing nostalgic for those 75-pound league games when his kids were in front of him. He misses the days when he could sell Penn State football to mothers and fathers of recruits, then come home and live the actual experience. Despite the distance, he remains very close with his kids. He talks to all three of them by phone several times a week, counseling them on life, on the good and the bad. Like the time Larry wasn't playing much in his first two years with the Chiefs. He was repeating an old routine, withdrawing from the other players, looking to give the team an excuse to trade him. "You just can't do that," Larry Sr. told his son, the advice of someone who had been in that same tough spot once before. "You're doing it the wrong way."

Sometimes, though, phone calls and five or six weekend trips a fall aren't enough. "The toughest thing for me to do is leave the stands now," says Larry Sr., who can only get to Chiefs games when there isn't a conflicting Penn State game the same weekend. "It's tough to get on a plane, fly back to Penn State, and go to work again, because I want to be like every father. I look in the stands, see all these fathers, and I want to be that guy, you know?

"I'm at the point in my career that it's starting to bother me more now than it had before because I miss that. . . . There's going to be a tough decision down the road for me. I know that. I know I'm going to have to deal with that pretty soon."

What makes his struggle more difficult is that the aspects of Penn State that he sells as a recruiter—in February 2006, Johnson was named Recruiter of the Year by Rivals.com—are the same aspects that pull him back. They are the same reasons he wanted his sons to play football and mature into men within the Penn State program. They are the core pillars of Penn State football; they are the core pillars of who Joe Paterno is as a person.

That's why when you ask Larry Sr. about the influence Paterno has had on him personally and professionally, he takes his time answering. He eventually decides to retell the story of his favorite Paterno speech, delivered in a team meeting after a road loss to Ohio State several years ago.

"It was the great Joe Paterno motivational speech I'd been waiting for," Larry Sr. begins. "He talked about tradition, pride, what does Penn State mean, why do we wear no names on our jerseys, why do we wear the black shoes. At that moment I said to myself, 'I want to be like him. That's what I want to stand for. That's the kind of program I want to create.'

The Johnsons

Tony Johnson, No. 11.

"There wasn't a dry eye in the place that day, including yours truly. And I'll tell you . . . he knew what he was saying. He wasn't just saying it. I mean, he was living it. You felt it. You felt it coming from every word he said because you knew that's a part of him. Darn, man, it was just awesome. And that's what I took away from it—a guy who's committed to a lot of things. He believes in family, he believes that education takes you somewhere, no matter what color you are, black, white, green, or purple."

Larry could go on, but he's made his point.

"Every year he has 105 guys on the team," he says, "and they're all his sons. He may not know all of them by name, but he knows all of them by heart, and he knows what he's going to get for them."

Paterno got it for Tony and Larry. Now Larry Sr. must decide how much longer he wants to help sell the Paterno family before he leaves to reunite the Johnson family. And that, clearly, is anything but an easy decision.

seventeen

THE JOYNERS

IT STARTS WITH RESPECT. You see a piece of trash on the ground, pick it up. Don't take shortcuts by walking on the grass. Never wear a hat inside a building.

What does any of this have to do with football? If you're Joe Paterno—everything.

At first you have no idea what Paterno is talking about, Matt Joyner says. "Then, in your junior year, the light starts to go on," he says. "Okay, I'm not learning about football, I'm learning about life. That's what Joe is teaching me. He's not only teaching me about sports, he's teaching me about how you deal with your family, how you interact with people from a professional standpoint, and how you deal with adversity within your life."

Welcome to the Joe Paterno Finishing School of Football. Of course, for the Joyner boys, Matt and younger brother Andy, JoePa's teachings weren't entirely foreign. In fact, they were more of a continuation from the head start they'd received from their father. Dave Joyner, the boys' father, played for Paterno from 1969-71 and enjoyed an impressive athletic career as an All-America in both football and wrestling. He also soaked up the sayings and lessons that Paterno preached. Thus, before Matt and Andy were even dreaming of playing college ball at Penn State, they were absorbing from their father what it would take to play there someday. We're talking about the Paterno Platitudes:

- Respect your peers and your elders.

- Keep plugging away and something good will happen.

- Don't cut corners.

- Take care of the little things and the big things will take care of themselves.

"There are these little snippets that you get from Joe," Dave says, "and those are the kind of things I talked to my kids about a lot, probably ad nauseum. It probably drove them insane, but I think it's absolutely true.

"There were a number of times when there were big things going on in my life, both positive and negative. I was usually able to relate those things to situations on the field, and I was guided through by those appropriate platitudes [preached by Joe]."

Dave says many other players from his era felt the same way, though in some cases, it took them a little more time to recognize the value in the education they'd received from Paterno. "A lot of guys really became converts after they got out," Dave says. "You know, that stuff he was telling us about life really is true. I mean, I don't remember anyone who ever talks about the program in a negative way, and that's pretty unique."

Paterno coupled his commandments by stressing hard work and dedication to achieving team goals. That too stuck with the elder Joyner, who made sure Matt and Andy knew what it was like to sweat and toil in order to accomplish something in life.

"[Dad] would lay out training programs for me," Andy says. "He would go to the track with me, teach me how to block. I never saw anyone work as hard as him. That's how he trained nonstop for wrestling and football."

"My family is one of great determination," adds Dave, speaking of the Joyner lineage and his immediate family in the same breath.

The Joyners

The Joyners were tobacco farmers in North Carolina. Dave's grandmother had an eighth-grade education and raised three kids by doing laundry and running a boarding house. She passed away recently, one month shy of 102 years. She was still living in her own house.

Dave credits his parents for much of what he learned as a kid, and in turn, much of what he's taught his own children. He describes his parents, mom Charlotte and dad Bobby, as both having a "quiet determination"—their actions often spoke louder than their words. Dave's father had been a gifted athlete in his own youth. He played college-level golf at North Carolina State in the days when Arnold Palmer was playing at rival Wake Forest. He also played high school football. Bobby Joyner's athletic career was curtailed by World War II, in which he fought with the 503rd Airborne division, the first Airborne unit out of Fort Bragg, North Carolina.

"He jumped in Burma and New Guinea and the Philippines and was all through the jungles," Dave says. "You know, they didn't call them Special Ops back then, but they kind of did a lot of the same things that our Special Ops people do now."

The 503rd was instrumental in one of America's most significant victories in the South Pacific during World War II, the Battle of Corregidor. A small, rock-strewn island in the northern Philippines located at the mouth of Manila Bay, Corregidor was a strategic point for both the Japanese and American forces. Not long after the Japanese attacked Pearl Harbor on December 7, 1941, they attacked Corregidor, wiping out resistance from American and Filipino forces. The Japanese forced their prisoners to make the infamous Bataan Death March to notorious Camp O'Donnell, during which many American lives were lost.

It wasn't until March 1945 that the 503rd Airborne division helped retake the island for the United States in one of the fiercest battles leading to the end of the war. The Americans attacked by air and sea, and Bobby Joyner was a part of the amphibian forces that landed on Corregidor. As he would later tell his son, many of the American paratroopers ended up falling in the ocean because the island was so small, and the chutes were hard to control. In addition, the planes could only make one low pass over the island because of small arms fire.

Sniper fire poured down on the Americans for the better part of a week. Because they had tied themselves to trees, the Japanese were hard to spot. When the American soldiers did see them, they didn't know whether they were dead or alive. The jungle had a strange, otherworldly look to it in many ways. "Most of the tops of the trees were gone, my dad said to me, because of all the bombing," Dave recalls. "You had all this jungle, but no tree tops."

The Japanese were entrenched in caves and tunnels, and a place called "Monkey Point" mountain, where they had all their munitions buried. "When they knew they were losing the island, they barricaded themselves in Monkey Point. They committed suicide. They blew up the entire mountain.

"My dad said he saw it happen. He was a mile away. He ran and hid behind the biggest boulder he could find, but he couldn't get his legs under it. There were pieces of boulders the size of cars coming down, and his two legs below the knee were sticking out. His legs were crushed."

Bobby Joyner ended up in a hospital in Manila for nine months. He had seven operations, then transferred to a Veterans Administration hospital in North Carolina. He spent nearly a year and a half there recuperating. Doctors saved Bobby's legs, but 45 years later, he had the left leg amputated due to a chronic infection.

That didn't affect Bobby Joyner's mobility, however, or his zest for life. "He used to run 10K races on his prosthesis," Dave says. "You couldn't tell watching him walk that he had a prosthesis."

Dave Joyner says in many ways, his character was shaped by his father's involvement in the war, and his stoic nature. Bobby Joyner had no time to feel sorry for himself and expected the same from others, including his son. Surviving a war made him stronger, as it did other fighting men. Dave passed some of that resiliency from the "Greatest Generation" on to his own children.

"Corregidor, and the history of that, is something that my family holds very dear, just to know what he went through," Dave says of his dad. "I view it as a very significant piece of my upbringing."

The Joyners

✳ ✳ ✳

Make no bones about it. Dave Joyner was very hands-on with his sons' athletic careers. But in a positive way. When it came to football, he didn't allow Matt or Andy to join organized games until they reached junior high.

"He's not a big believer in Midget or Peewee football," Matt says. "Number one, from a health standpoint, your neck's not fully developed yet. And a lot of times, it creates a lot of bad habits that have to be untaught when you get into middle school or high school anyway."

Once the boys were given the green light, Dave watched closely. He helped them during the summer months with conditioning and training to prepare for the upcoming season. But his guidance was needed in other areas, too. "I drove them crazy," he says. "They'd do something like ride their bicycle off the roof of a barn. *That ain't gonna work.* They were crazy enough that they broke enough bones just paying attention and doing the right things. . . . They were busy, active kids."

The same description fits Dave when he was a kid. He recalls being "enthralled by football," and particularly enthralled by Penn State football. He was 12 when he started going to Nittany Lions home games at Beaver Stadium, not long after the stadium was moved across campus to its current location off Park Avenue. But Dave didn't show up with tickets. He'd climb the fence and sneak into the game, being sure to run from any cops who spotted him. At that time there were no bleachers behind the end zones, leaving an open grassy area off each end zone. Dave would watch a little of the game, then join one of the pickup football games going on at one of those plots at either end of the stadium.

Only a few years later Dave found himself as an unproven offensive lineman with those same Nittany Lions. Only there was no hopping fences this time. With Paterno watching closely, Joyner struggled in his first spring practice. There's a saying in Penn State circles that if JoePa stops yelling at you, he doesn't love you anymore. "I really felt loved that spring," Joyner says with a chuckle. "I was never lacking in effort, but things weren't quite falling together. I was missing blocks, my timing was off. And maybe part of it was that Joe was riding me so hard."

His struggles only intensified when the linemen got to the seven-man sled. "I had trouble hitting the sled right," Dave says. "It was such a subtle concept. Joe wanted you to hit through the man, not *to* the man. That was the old principle. Evidently I was hitting to the man on the sled. Joe had this great joy riding that sled, blowing his whistle and screaming at the linemen. And every time I'd go, he'd just scream at me because I never got it right. But at the end of spring, I did all right. I got better."

He improved so much that after losing some practice time to a bout with mononucleosis, he became an anchor on the line for the 1969, '70, and '71 squads, paving running lanes for the likes of Charlie Pittman, Lydell Mitchell, and Franco Harris. Joyner's teams went a combined 29-4. He was part of the undefeated 1969 team, and after Penn State had its 31-game unbeaten streak snapped in 1970, his Lions won 15 straight from 1970-71, a run that ended at Tennessee in the last game of the regular season.

"That was a big downer for me," Dave says of the 31-11 defeat at the hands of the Volunteers. "I left from there to go to the Kodak All-American festivities. So I was bound to a real happy event, but I was not feeling that way."

Penn State dropped from No. 5 to No. 10 in the polls following the loss, and its stock slumped even further in the estimation of East Coast football critics. The Nittany Lions needed a good showing four weeks later against Texas in the Cotton Bowl if they were to win back any respect. Trailing 6-3 at halftime on New Year's Day 1972, Joyner, playing his final collegiate game, recalls jogging off the field next to Paterno.

"We're going in and Joe runs up to me at the sidelines," Joyner says. "He and I are kind of like the last ones off the field. We're running into the locker room and he says, 'How's it going out there? What should I do? What should I say at halftime?' And I said, 'Joe, don't say anything. We're just fine.' It was like a heavyweight fight. We're pounding them, and I could tell they're ready to break. So he came in and just said, 'Keep plugging.' He didn't try to do anything. And sure enough, you know what happened in the second half."

Dave Joyner.

The Nittany Lions outscored the Longhorns 27-0 after intermission. Final score: Penn State 30, Texas 6.

✳ ✳ ✳

Matt can relate to his father's success in big games, having played in the game that gave Paterno his 300th career victory, a 48-3 victory over Bowling Green in 1998. Matt, who played safety and on special teams for Penn State, also has some favorite Paterno stories of his own. "We were playing Rutgers at the Meadowlands, and it was my first year traveling," Matt says of his freshman year in 1995. "I knew you had to be five minutes early to team meetings at home. Nobody told me it was 15 minutes when you were on the road. So I was up in my parents' [hotel] room hanging out, and I looked at my watch: 'Okay, seven minutes to go. I better get in the elevator and go down.'"

When Joyner got downstairs, the rest of the team was already seated in a conference room, munching on a snack. "As I started to walk into the area, [defensive lineman] Terry Killens is sitting there and he's waving his arms at me. It looked like he was waving me to get out. I realized I didn't have my tie on. You had to wear a coat and tie. Joe is very strict about that.

"So I start to turn around and walk toward the elevator. Sure enough, from behind, I hear these footsteps and Joe is screaming at me. 'Joyner, what are you doing? Get over here!' He left a squad meeting to chase me."

So Matt did what any resourceful Joyner would do with JoePa on your heels. He ducked out of the way and tried to hide. "He came around the corner and started shaking me," Matt says. "Down in the lobby, the whole bar was completely silent. And he was yelling at me, 'I'll never take you on another road trip! Get your butt in here! You're a freshman and you're holding up the whole meeting!' I was so embarrassed."

Joyner sat down next to linebacker Jim Nelson at the first table he could find. "Whenever I got yelled at, I always had a little smile on my face," Matt continues. "I've been that way since I was little. That's how I deal with it, I guess. But Joe saw that and said, 'Wipe that smile off your puss.' I was a freshman. I didn't know that a puss meant a face. I thought it meant something bad. I'm like, 'What did he just say?' I had no idea what he was talking about. I tried to cover up my mouth to keep from laughing more."

That's when Nelson leaned over to Joyner. "Dude," Nelson said, "next time you get into trouble, don't sit next to me."

Needless to say, Matt was never late for another one of Paterno's meetings. He also learned the hard way about Joe's feelings on cutting corners: "It was preseason," Matt says, "and I was walking to grab lunch between practices. And I figured, what the heck, I'll just cut across the grass at the commons there. And sure enough, Joe happened to be pulling into the parking lot." Paterno rolled down the window of his car and screamed at Matt to get off the grass. In no uncertain terms, Joe equated the move to taking shortcuts in life.

Then there is Paterno's rule on wearing hats indoors. "You can't wear a hat in a building, that's just the way it is," Dave says. "That's part of the old common courtesy. It was late in Matt's career, game

The Joyners

Matt Joyner.

night, and Matt comes out of our room at the Nittany Lion Inn after visiting and he puts his baseball cap on. I said, 'Matt, what are you doing? You've got a hat on!'"

Matt refused to remove the cap. "We take the elevator down," Dave says. "We're in the rotunda there. Matt's got his hat on, and the door opens and there's [defensive coordinator] Jerry Sandusky standing there. You wouldn't believe how fast this big-talking football player's hat came off when he saw Jerry standing there. His hat came off so fast and went under his arm that it was just incredible."

Andy actually was the first of the Joyner brothers to play for the Nittany Lions, going to Penn State as a walk-on in the spring of 1992. His career was cut short by a variety of physical problems, including a serious knee injury. "I blew my knee out cutting on the turf in my junior year," he says. "Needless to say there were a lot of expletives coming out of my mouth. As I lay on the ground, the first person I saw when I opened my eyes was Joe, standing above me and asking me if I was all right. I just hoped he didn't hear the expletives. He never would swear. It was kind of his mantra."

Playing for JoePa

The injury prevented the brothers from playing together at Penn State, something they'd missed out on in high school, too, since they attended different schools. Still, his brother's presence in the program at PSU is what drove Matt to pick the Nittany Lions. He'd hoped to have a shot at playing against Andy, a wide receiver, in practice in the one year that their careers would have overlapped.

"He was on offense and I knew I was going to play defense," Matt says. "I thought, 'Here's my chance to hit him.' We've been competitive all our lives, and that's why I was as good as I was. Andy set the bar high for me. And I always wanted to hit my brother on the field. That was my dream."

Even though that matchup never materialized, playing football at Penn State was still the realization of a longtime dream for both brothers. They grew up going to games with their parents, at least when they could fit them in amid their busy athletic schedules. Both boys played several sports; Matt says he played as many as six organized sports at a time growing up. Still, Matt and Andy say they felt no pressure to match Dave's accomplishments in football, wrestling, or anything else.

"My dad never made us feel that way," Matt says. "He always encouraged us. We could play whatever sport we wanted, we just had to do something every season. He didn't care what it was, even if it was playing in the band. So in that respect, I didn't feel any pressure from my parents at all, ever. I never really felt like I had to live up to anything.

And, Matt says, his father was never critical: "Every game my dad said, 'You played a great game.' He was always positive. And we were never allowed to quit. My dad's big thing was, if you start something, you finish it. Even if it was right at the beginning and you hated it, my dad didn't care. He said, 'You committed to something, you have to honor that commitment. And you have to be loyal to that team.' That comes from Joe, too. Joe's big thing is loyalty."

At Penn State, the loyalty factor works both ways. That was one of the main reasons Dave wanted his sons to go there. "Andy was hurt a lot—seven operations—and he wasn't able to contribute as much as he wanted to," Dave says. "Yet [the Penn State coaches] were paying as

The Joyners

Andy Joyner.

much attention to him as they had to the John Cappellettis and Ki-Jana Carters of the world. And they weren't paying attention to him because he was my son. They were paying attention to him in spite of him being my son. He got yelled at if his grades were not right. . . . I wonder in a lesser program if anybody would have paid attention to Andy Joyner."

Even though Andy's knee injury kept him from playing football after his junior year, Paterno took him to the Rose Bowl game at the end of the 1994 season. A classy gesture for sure, and it didn't end there. As Andy pursued his academic and then professional career, Paterno wrote him several letters of recommendation, including one that Andy credits with getting him into Dickinson Law School. "It was such an honor that he would do that, because I'm not a star," says Andy, who is now working in investor relations for an oil and gas company.

That support is another reason Matt, now a national sales manager for a firearms manufacturer, wound up completing the family legacy at State. "If Matt goes to another school and is a star," Dave says, "I'm sure they're going to pay attention to him. But what if Matt's a nobody on the field, which can always happen. Are they really going to pay attention to him? I was never as comfortable that was going to happen anywhere else but Penn State."

Dave also felt comfortable that in choosing Penn State, both his sons would witness a consistent philosophy delivered through Paterno's strong leadership. "I was here for my tenure, and for my sons', and I watched how the program worked," says Dave, a longtime surgeon, orthopedic physician, and chairman of the Health and Safety Committee for USA Football. He's also done some work with Team USA Olympians. "The very core issues of the program didn't change at all. I'm not saying Joe and the coaches and the kids didn't change and adapt to a new world. They did, and that's appropriate. But the very core never changed, and to me, that was very reassuring."

Same goes for Paterno's incredible memory, a major link that ties together his teams and players from years gone by. "I remember when I was in high school," Matt says, "right before my senior year, and we were at the MS dinner in Hershey. It's a big thing. A lot of the players and coaches come down, and my dad's on the board. We were talking to Joe and Joe leans over to me and goes, 'So, did your dad teach you how to hold like him yet?'"

Paterno was referring to a costly holding call against Dave in an Orange Bowl game three decades earlier. And as sharp as the coach's memory is of players and moments, so too do his players vividly remember Joe and the things he drilled into them over the years. Dave speaks fondly of the advice Joe always gave about taking pride in what you do, even when it comes to the little things.

"That's one of the major ones," Dave says. "You know, discipline is self-motivating. When you walk around and you see a piece of trash on the ground, pick it up. You're not just helping to clean up, you're helping your internal self-discipline. It makes you stronger. And to this day, I can't walk by a piece of paper and not pick it up."

Paterno's "tuck" rule also remains strong in Dave's memory: At football practice, shirttails have to be tucked in. "You get yelled at if it's not. You ask yourself, 'Why in the world is that important?' Does

The Joyners

that have anything to do with your playing? On the surface, no, it doesn't. But it begins to make sense to you that if you care enough about that small rule, then you become self-disciplined. It's just a place where a line is drawn, and you need to pay attention to those small details to make yourself what you need to be."

Paterno and his rock-solid philosophies haven't changed much over the years, Dave points out. "He's basically the same, and that's good," Dave says, "because that means that love him, hate him, agree with him, don't agree with him, you pretty much know what you get. Whether he's right or wrong, he does what he thinks he should do. Not all of us agree with him sometimes. But with Joe, you know where you stand."

And the reason for Paterno's success? Joyner might come closer than anyone in explaining it. "His magic is that he has this ability to make you rely on yourself internally," Dave says. "His real talent is internal development of those intrinsic things that day in and day out make us different. I think they recruit people that are somewhat like-minded, whether the kids realize it or not. And then Joe and his staff are able to enhance that already internal quality somebody saw somewhere."

With Paterno, it always comes back to basics, Joyner says: Respect everything, don't take shortcuts, take care of the little things. Seems Paterno's finishing school is still in session long after class is over.

eighteen

THE KULKAS

WAS JOHN KULKA THE ANSWER to a coach's prayers? It was the start of the 1966 football season at Penn State and head coach Joe Paterno was worried. He had just taken over for Rip Engle as head coach, and Penn State faced one of its toughest schedules in school history. The problem: The Penn State squad was depleted. Nearly every position on the offensive line had to be filled.

"We're going to have to play so many inexperienced people against tough opponents, I don't see how we can be really outstanding offensively—at least early in the season," Paterno said at the time.

Enter John Kulka. He filled one of the offensive tackle positions and became a leader. His brother, George, joined the Lions one year later on the defensive side. With a strong offensive line, the Nittany Lions turned things around quickly in the late 1960s. The Kulka brothers played on Paterno's first bowl team, in 1967, and then Joe's first unbeaten team in 1968. George would later play on another unbeaten, untied team in 1969.

Some 25 years later, a third Kulka, Todd, would add a new chapter to the Kulka football family when his 1994 Penn State team notched its own undefeated season.

Not a bad legacy for one family.

Playing for JoePa

It all started with the Kane connection. Kane High School, located in northwestern Pennsylvania between State College and Erie, was a small school but had produced some major football talent. As John Kulka recalls, there wasn't a whole lot for a kid to do in Kane, Pennsylvania, but there were plenty of sports to choose from. The Kulkas' focus was football, and the two brothers trained together, each pushing the other. John played on the offensive line for the football team, while George played both tight end and defensive end, due to limited numbers.

John Kulka visited Penn State when he was in State College for a high school track meet. He walked around the campus and when he saw the facilities that the athletes were offered, it was love at first sight for the Kane discus thrower. He was already a Penn State fan anyway. Every year, the booster club in Kane had arranged for a trip to the Penn State-Pitt game. It was a special trip and the high school team always looked forward to it.

"At that time, it was always played at Pitt," remembers John. "It was a big, old concrete stadium and the bus trip down was always fun."

John hadn't started playing football until junior high school, but he learned the sport quickly, and by his senior year he was good enough on the gridiron to attract the attention of Penn State recruiter J.T. White. John followed the lead of another Kane player, Tim Montgomery, and decided to attend Penn State, in part because the school's civil engineering program—John's interest—was one of the best in the nation.

Like his older brother, George had the same interest in civil engineering. The comparisons between the brothers don't end there. George also threw the discus on the high school track team and excelled on the football field. He had other scholarship offers to consider, but when White came calling the following year, George chose Penn State.

Along with a good engineering program and a good football program, Penn State had something else George liked—his older brother. "It was nice to have a brother there, because he was already established," George says.

The Kulkas

John Kulka.

By 1966, Engle had turned over the head-coaching duties to Paterno. The rookie head coach had enough confidence in John to give the sophomore the nod at starting center. It was a learning experience for the young man. In the first quarter of the season opener against Maryland, Penn State quarterback Jack White completed a 21-yard pass to Jack Curry, only to have it called back because Kulka was too far downfield and ruled to be an illegal receiver. Kulka didn't make too many mistakes after that, however, and Paterno was victorious in his opening game as head coach, 15-7.

Though the Lions won that game, they were in for a rough season. By the time Penn State was to play Pitt in the '66 season finale, the Lions had a losing record of 4-5. Support was dwindling for Paterno.

Playing for JoePa

The Lions needed to beat archrival Pitt to preserve Penn State's string of nonlosing seasons that stood at 27. The week before the Pitt game, Penn State had been shellacked by Georgia Tech, 21-0. The Nittany Lions' offensive line needed to improve its play against Pitt, and it did. Bob Campbell dashed through gaping holes created by Kulka and the offensive line, leading Penn State to a 27-0 lead by halftime.

The Lions led 41-12 early in the fourth quarter when Paterno did something totally out of character: He ordered a trick play to make sure of the win—a fourth-down pass from punt formation. This got the Lions a first down and led to their seventh touchdown of the afternoon in a 48-24 rout. Kulka keyed the offensive line, leading to three touchdown runs by Campbell.

The Lions showed marked improvement in 1967, the year that defensive end George Kulka joined the team. After losing two of their first three games by a total of three points, the Lions won seven straight. Their 8-2 record put them in the Gator Bowl against a high-scoring Florida State team. The game ended in a 17-17 tie but was deemed an important measuring stick for Penn State football. The '67 season was a turning point in the Lions' storied history, and things would only get better as State posted an 11-0 record in both '68 and '69.

With those two impressive teams as the centerpiece, the Lions put together a 31-game unbeaten streak spanning four seasons. Paterno, a relative unknown beforehand, was now a national figure with professional job offers who had verbally jousted with President Nixon over the national rankings. The Lions did everything in that period but win a national championship, which Nixon personally and controversially handed to Texas.

Penn State was solid on defense and offense during that time. John Kulka, tri-captain for the '68 team, was on a strong offensive line that paved the way for Charlie Pittman, Penn State's first All-America running back, who credited Kulka and Dave Bradley for his success. In praising Penn State's offensive line, position coach Joe McMullen also singled out Kulka and Bradley. "You only notice those tackles when they miss a block," McMullen said. "When (quarterback Chuck) Burkhart gets up from underneath a pile of the wrong-colored

The Kulkas

George Kulka.

jerseys, or Campbell or Pittman get smeared for a loss, then people take notice. But when they do their job, nobody notices and they don't get many thanks."

The Nittany Lions capped their 11-0 1968 season with a thrilling 15-14 victory over Kansas in the Orange Bowl to earn the No. 2 ranking in the polls. The Lions needed a two-point conversion at the end to win the game, and they were lucky to get two chances to complete it. After their first two-point conversion failed, they were given a second chance when the Jayhawks were penalized for having too many men on the field.

John was in the middle of it all. "That penalty call was relatively quick, and we were able to get another play in before we had time to think about it," he says.

Kulka credits Paterno with never folding under the pressure of that '66 season, then leading Penn State to greatness in the ensuing seasons. Kulka says that following the rules of Paterno's "Grand Experiment" gave him and his teammates some much-needed focus. "Everybody knew what was expected," says John. "That was part of the philosophy that he instilled."

George agrees, noting that Paterno's emphasis on success in the classroom kept his mind occupied off the field. "I didn't do as much socializing because I was studying when I was away from the football program," he says. "It was difficult." That difficulty extended to the playing field as well, where George Kulka wasn't sure where he would fit into the Penn State scheme. "I tried a few positions, but I ended up being a defensive end," he says.

On a pretty good team, no less. The '69 team ran the table, including a 10-3 Orange Bowl victory over Missouri. Not a bad way to wrap up a college career for the Kulka brothers.

✳ ✳ ✳

Todd Kulka, John's son, recalls Saturdays spent in the lettermen's lot outside Beaver Stadium, tailgating with his family and their friends. For John, those afternoons brought back many memories as he socialized with former teammates. The talk was always football, while the adults sat back with drinks in their hands and the kids stuffed their mouths with hamburgers and hot dogs. It was family time for Paterno's extended football family.

Taking part in those tailgates as a teenager, Todd dreamed of one day joining in the party—after he had earned his own letter at Penn State. At State College Area High School, Todd was a three-sport letterman in basketball, football, and baseball, but his focus was on the latter two sports. He played linebacker and receiver on the football team, and was a centerfielder on the baseball team.

At first, Todd was intrigued by the path of his older brother, Tim, who had played baseball for the University of Maine. Todd accepted a baseball scholarship from Mary Washington College, a small school in Fredericksburg, Virginia. But he missed Penn State too much. Not long after enrolling at Mary Washington, Todd began to yearn for all the trappings of a big-time football school that he had grown up adoring. After one semester of college, Todd became disenchanted

The Kulkas

Todd Kulka.

with Mary Washington. He gave up his baseball scholarship and headed back to State College to attempt to walk on to the Lions football team.

"It's the long way around and you don't get all the perks of being a scholarship guy," says Todd, talking about being a walk-on.

That was 1992. Mary Washington baseball coach Tom Sheridan thought Todd's chances of making the Nittany Lions football team as a walk-on "was about one in a million." But Todd was willing to take that chance. He put in the necessary work and then some. After a blur of never-ending days, he made the team as a linebacker to start the '94 season.

Penn State was emerging as a Big Ten powerhouse in its new conference. In beating Illinois that season, the Lions wiped out a 21-0 deficit for the biggest comeback in Paterno's coaching career. The Lions finished the year 12-0 with a 38-20 victory over Oregon in the Rose Bowl. With Kerry Collins quarterbacking, the Nittany Lions set NCAA records for scoring with 47.8 points a game and for total offense with an average of 520.2 yards a game.

"I think everybody on all parts of the team contributed and got people ready to play, and everybody executed," Kulka recalls. "There weren't a lot of shenanigans.

"Being part of that group, that camaraderie, all the things that go along with a championship season, that would probably be the pinnacle of my Penn State career."

Todd lettered in 1995, and today is counseling Penn State football players with the academic support program.

✳ ✳ ✳

John Kulka, currently president of HRI, a highway construction company in State College, holds on to one lasting memory from his playing days at Penn State. "As the scores kind of get fuzzy with time, I think the relationships and the friendships that are made through the process, the training and the playing on the team, are life lasting," he says.

His brother, George, now retired after a career in construction management and living in Ivor, Virginia, agrees with that assessment, adding, "playing for Penn State certainly is a source of pride."

For the Kulkas, the "Grand Experiment" is more than football. It's friendships, it's family, and a set of values imparted by a distinguished football coach that flows through the generations at Penn State. As the Kulkas learned first hand, you just can't beat it.

nineteen

THE
PATERNOS

IF YOU EVER HAPPEN TO PASS BY Jay Paterno's office, pause a moment and stick your head in the door. Find the framed black and white photo with a message scrawled across it. Lean in close and you might be able to make out the inscription: "Jay, Thanks for all your letters. Be good, study hard. John Cappelletti."

The photo, bundled in a brown envelope, arrived at the Paterno household in 1973. Delivered by John Morris, Penn State's sports information director at the time, it might as well have been signed, "Jay, welcome to the Penn State football family." For in many ways, that was the beginning of Jay's love affair with Penn State football.

He had attended his first game earlier that same fall, sitting with his mother and siblings in the stand-alone bleachers that used to rise behind the south end zone in Beaver Stadium. He had picked out his idol, No. 22, who always seemed to be busting through a hole in the defense, dragging would-be tacklers on a relentless ride to the end zone. Then he struck up a personal correspondence with Cappy.

"I couldn't spell Cappelletti," Jay says, "but I would put 22 on a piece of paper and I'd draw a picture of him. Then my dad would take it to him. I can still remember [Morris] coming to the house with the brown envelope. . . . That's really my first memory of Penn State football."

Jay's forgotten more about Penn State football than most of us will ever recall. You would too if you hadn't missed a home game between your fifth and 22nd birthdays. But what he does remember, from Cappelletti's Heisman trophy-winning season in '73 to the 2005 Nittany Lions' magical ride, forms a highlight reel of blue and white beauty that no 10-disc collector's DVD could ever fully contain.

But do not be fooled. Jay's words and thoughts are not those of a simple superfan or Nittany Lion historian extraordinaire. They are the words and thoughts of Joe Paterno Jr., the only one of Joe and Sue's kids who took a deep breath of the Nittany Lions when he was in elementary school and decided this was going to be part of his being from that breath forward. He is the son who would follow his father through wins and losses, boos and victory rides. He is the one who always would be first to defend Dad, Dad's team, and the family they call Penn State football.

✳ ✳ ✳

This is a good one. Penn State was undefeated. Alabama was, too. The year was 1985. Jay Paterno was in high school then, spending his fall weekends in the Beaver Stadium press box charting stats and scores for Penn State's sports information department. On that early October day, Penn State was driving deep in Alabama territory, when, on a second down, Lions quarterback John Shaffer scrambled upfield and took a punishing pop from a Crimson Tide defender. Shaffer got up slowly—too slowly to stay in the game for third down. The crowd of 85,444 fell silent as Shaffer, one of the team's leaders, was helped to the home sideline. Shaffer's run set up a third-and-short for backup quarterback Matt Knizner.

At that moment, Jay's attention was diverted by several newspaper reporters talking to each other about the upcoming play call. "Oh, he's gonna run it right up the middle," said one reporter. That's all it took—Jay couldn't help himself. It wasn't that a reporter would question Joe Paterno's creativity and risk-taking on third down. Rather, Jay knew Knizner was a good athlete who could do more than just tuck it and dive into the muck.

"I said, 'You guys don't know what you're talking about. He's gonna run a bootleg,'" Jay says. "And they go, 'He'll never run a bootleg,' kind of arguing with me."

But the kid was right. Seconds later Knizner took the snap, faked a handoff, bootlegged toward the sideline, and completed a pass to his tight end. Penn State went on to score on the drive. Jay was beaming.

"I said, 'I told ya,'" he says, "and one of the writers—I'm not gonna tell you his name because he still covers us—went to the sports information director and complained. 'Hey, you'd better tell him to keep his mouth shut. We're here doing a job.' He was insulted because I said, 'I told ya so.' A 17-year-old kid had showed him up. Well, it wasn't that I'd showed him up. It's just I knew how Joe thought."

Getting inside Joe's mind isn't easy to do, but Jay was there. It was an accomplishment that took time to pull off. Throughout his childhood, Jay would wake up in the morning and wander into his dad's home office, where Joe would be watching film or scribbling down notes about new schemes, plays, or wrinkles. He would look over Joe's shoulder and ask questions: "What are you watching?" "Why are you watching?" "How does this help you?" "Can I watch, too?" Jay wanted to learn.

When Dad wasn't around, Jay would take his wooden Lincoln Logs and write jersey numbers on them. The Logs were his players. (Naturally, he always etched 22 on one of them.) Across the floor he'd arrange chess pieces representing the opposing team. "I was always Penn State," he says of his Lincoln Logs lineup. "Something about football just clicked in my mind. I took an interest in it more than anybody else in the family, and it's just something that happened."

Playing for JoePa

He's clear to point out that Joe never encouraged any of his kids to follow him into the profession. In fact, Joe always felt strongly that his family life remain separate from his football life. Jay didn't grow up in the Penn State locker room, and he certainly wasn't invited to practice. Heck, Joe wouldn't even score free tickets for his kids, insisting instead that Sue plunk down the $1 per head to get them seats in those south end zone bleachers. If Joe mentioned football at all in his home, it was usually to downplay the significance of the sport and his own status within it.

"He said to me on a bunch of occasions, 'Just because your father coaches football, doesn't make you any different or any better or any worse than anybody else,'" Jay says. "'If we win a lot of games, it doesn't make you any better. If we lose a lot of games, it doesn't make you any worse.'"

Joe took the same approach to his kids' activities. As they'd do years later when Jay announced his intention to coach football, Joe and Sue supported whatever Jay tried as a kid. But Joe was also very sensitive to the weight his own celebrity carried in Jay's life. He refused to use his name to question authority or pave an easier path for his son. Case in point: Jay played middle school basketball, and during a timeout in one of his games, his coach took Jay and his teammates out onto the floor to demonstrate how they were going to run a specific play.

Again, Jay couldn't help himself. Innocently enough, he said, "Coach, they're watching us," referring to the opposing team. Jay says the comment wasn't meant to disrespect anyone, but Sue was there watching her son, and when they got home, she told Joe what had happened. Joe forced Jay to call the coach and apologize.

The lesson? Respect your elders; speak when spoken to; and most important, being a Paterno doesn't give you special privileges to question authority, be it in State College or Joe's native borough of Brooklyn. That theme has appeared and reappeared throughout Jay's life. It's the humble nature of his father shining through, a core characteristic of the man whose teams have never worn names on jerseys. Especially when that name is Paterno.

The Paternos

Jay Paterno.

✳ ✳ ✳

When Jay was considering colleges, his father suggested that he consider Brown, where Joe had been a quarterback and defensive back in the late 1940s. But Jay wasn't focused on playing college football. He wanted to *learn* college football. And he wanted his father to be his professor.

In many ways, Joe had already filled Jay's head with football knowledge, despite his own efforts to maintain separate work-family existences. Jay started playing the game formally as a seventh-grader in a State College rec league, absorbing every detail, imagining how he might do things differently. When he was tired of lining up Lincoln Logs, he moved on to pen and paper. By high school he was drawing up his own offensive playbooks, inventing his own schemes. And when his dad did occasionally talk shop at home, Jay found a way to be in the room. "He would sit around and talk in his den," Jay says, "and I would always listen. Whether he knew I was listening or not, I would listen."

Jay never tossed out those old notebooks of his. In fact, he only grew more dedicated to the task once he enrolled at Penn State in 1986. By then he knew better than to question a coach—unless he felt like calling him to apologize—so he kept suggestions to himself. Except on one occasion in 1987. Jay recalls telling Joe that he ought to let Darren Roberts, a speedy backup quarterback at the time, throw a halfback pass. Jay's rationale was that opposing teams had no idea Roberts could throw a nice pass. They didn't even know what position he played.

So it was that against Clemson in the 1988 Citrus Bowl, Joe sent Roberts into the game at halfback, and Roberts completed a 50-yard pass on a halfback option. Joe didn't thank his son; rather, he pointed toward the field and said, "Hey, did you see that?" But Jay wasn't looking for a high-five or a hug. That Dad had listened to and acted on his suggestion was rewarding enough, especially considering the lengths Joe went to make sure his son was just another Penn State football player like everyone else.

Some of it was standard protocol for being the son of a head coach. Joe would yell at a defensive assistant coach about this detail or that, and later in the same practice, Jay would find himself under a furious blitz, or worse, beneath a pile of tacklers. Teammates loved to take a shot at the kid. Keith Goganious once had a little fun at Jay's expense, tackling the quarterback and flipping him end over end, laughing while he was delivering the punishment. Other guys would pop Jay, then say something to the effect of, "Tell Joe to stop yelling at me." And Jay would play along, quipping, "All you do when you hit me is encourage him."

"You had to be tough," Jay says, "because they'd come get ya. They wanted to see if you really belonged."

To a degree, Joe was testing his son as well. He certainly never instructed a guy like Goganious or Shane Conlan to have fun at

The Paternos

Left to right: Jay Paterno, Joe Paterno, and Sue Paterno.

Jay's expense, but he also wasn't going to protect the kid from a clean blow. Jay thinks back to many a time when he'd emerge from a pocket-collapsing pileup to see his dad and other coaches chuckling. "The more I got it," Jay says, "the more he'd laugh."

Beneath the good times, a relationship began to develop that was more professional than familial. It sounds odd at first, but for as long as Jay can remember now, he's called his dad "Coach" in public and professional settings. It started as a way to reaffirm that Jay was just like any other Nittany Lion on the team. It became more important when Jay joined the coaching staff.

He had never planned to stay on as a Penn State assistant after graduation. Long before he served as a grad assistant for the Lions in the spring of 1990, he'd spoken with Virginia head coach George Welsh, a longtime Penn State assistant, about an opening with the Cavaliers. The Welshes were like family to the Paternos; George wanted him to come to Charlottesville, and that was that. Jay bit at the chance to see how another school ran its program, and he wound up spending three years coaching the secondary, offensive line, and quarterbacks. He learned new plays, new terminology, new operating procedures. All the while, he'd talk to his father on the phone about the ways Virginia did things differently than Penn State.

It was a key period in Jay's life, because the space allowed him to shape his own coaching philosophy beyond the shadows of Mount Nittany. Those three years at Virginia, followed by single seasons as an assistant at Connecticut (he coached wide receivers and tight ends) and James Madison (quarterbacks) allow him to say today, "My dad and I are different on a lot of things, and a lot of it's because I left and went to other places."

He almost didn't come back. After the 1994 season, James Madison coach Rip Scherer left the Dukes to become head coach at the University of Memphis. He wanted Jay to come with him. James Madison also didn't want to lose him. The athletic director there went so far as to say, "Jay's a guy you gotta keep." Jay also got a call from Craig Cirbus, an outgoing Penn State assistant set to become head coach at the University of Buffalo. Was Jay interested in joining him?

Meanwhile, back in Happy Valley, Joe gathered his coaches to ask about whom to hire as a replacement for Cirbus, who'd been on staff for 11 years. That's when Bill Kenney and Kenny Jackson mentioned Jay's name. Their logic? No one's going to be more enthusiastic about selling Penn State football than Jay Paterno. Joe called Jay to feel him out about coming home to coach.

"It's one of those things," Jay says. "When you're a graduate assistant, you can never get a job offer. Then all of a sudden you get three or four."

Jay didn't hesitate. He told Joe he'd take the post.

✳ ✳ ✳

It's been 12 years now since Jay returned to State College to coach the team he loves for the man he's studied since he was five. What's clear, though, is that Jay is not Joe. They have much in common, but their jobs and their roles in the Penn State football family demand differences. "We're both detail-oriented," Jay says. "The one thing is, I think I'm probably the eternal optimist. Not that Joe's a pessimist. But there's a part of me, if I walked into a barn and it was covered in horse manure, I'm the little boy who's going to go in, look around, and say, 'Hey, there's gotta be a pony in here somewhere.' I'm always looking for that silver lining. And I think I'm more laid back than Joe in that sense."

Jay, who coaches quarterbacks for Penn State, qualifies that statement by adding that Joe, with more responsibility on him than any assistant, cannot afford to be laid back. He must be demanding, he must ride players and coaches and push for more than the average effort. Jay, with fewer players to work with, is more in touch with the criticism his quarterbacks hear and the pressure they feel.

"[Quarterbacks] have to be able to come into a room and feel like somebody's got their back," he says. "When they don't have a good game, when they come in on Monday, I can't bludgeon them to death. I've gotta say, 'Here's what you did well. Here's what you didn't do well. Here's where we move on.'

"When people have criticized the quarterbacks, I've always been one to try to step in front of it and take it. Sometimes it was my fault, sometimes they make a bad read. Doesn't matter. I take all that criticism because I get paid to do a job, and I want those guys to understand I have their back."

He has Joe's back as well. Several years ago when the program struggled as it never had before, swallowing four losing seasons in five years, Jay received several e-mails saying things such as, "Your father's an embarrassment to this university." Jay let a lot of the remarks go, but the embarrassment thing ate at him—and not because it slammed his father. Rather, because the comment made no sense to him as someone who'd grown up in the program.

Thus, to one or two of the senders, Jay wrote back: "Why is he an embarrassment to the university—because we lost some football games? He wasn't found with a 16-year-old girl. He doesn't have a DUI. He's not smoking dope. He's not hitting his players. He's donated $4 million of his own money for scholarships, for endowed professorships, to the library. So you better get your perspectives in order as to what an embarrassment to the university is."

"Some people," Jay says, "e-mailed me back and said, 'Hey, thanks for putting it that way.' Others said, 'Well, he's hired to win games.' And I said, 'No, he's hired to educate people. I had a guy say to me, 'You know what your problem is? You guys graduate too many kids.' I responded, 'What are you talking about?' He says, 'You should do what other schools do and run 'em off.' I said, 'Okay, what if your son was here and he wasn't quite good enough? You want us to graduate 50 percent of our kids instead of 80?' So every 20 kids we bring in, we gotta pick six kids in that class every year and say, 'Sorry, you don't get to graduate from Penn State because you're not quite as good as we thought you were.'"

This sentiment is key. It's key to who Jay is as a person. It's the crux of Joe Paterno's "Grand Experiment." And in Jay's eyes, if his father ever did what that fan suggested and put football ahead of all else, he'd sacrifice the beliefs and themes upon which the Penn State football family has thrived for decades: unity, sacrifice, brotherhood, respect, hard work.

"Joe has never forgotten that these kids were raised by their parents or grandparents," Jay says. "Somebody brought that child from the time he was born to the time they were ready to hand him off to us. We have that responsibility. That is the core basis of this program. That is what has guided Joe, and that is why so many family members come back. Because Joe has taken that trust and he has not broken it. The program has not broken it."

✳ ✳ ✳

Jay Paterno loves a lot of things about his living situation. His commute to work from Toftrees Resort consists of seven minutes and two red lights. Sundays he can take his kids to Mass on Penn State's campus and then hit the art museum, followed by a trip to

The Paternos

the Creamery for ice cream (Peachy Paterno, anyone?). His proximity to campus allows him to get to a player quickly in times of need; it also allows them to come to him for the rare NCAA-allowed summer barbecue at Jay's house.

Many former players have referred to Joe as the father they appreciated much more after they'd left the nest; Jay, on the other hand, is much more the brotherly type to many Nittany Lions past and present. Perhaps no recent Penn Stater better embodies that connection than Michael Robinson, now with the San Francisco 49ers. Robinson was the soul of the 2005 PSU team that won the Big Ten championship and came within a last-second Michigan touchdown pass of running the table. Robinson's credited with helping to revive a once-struggling PSU offense and rejuvenating a program and fan base that had grown painfully numb to losing seasons.

Oh yeah, and he was also Joe Paterno's favorite player. Not *that* Joe Paterno, although the 80-year-old coach loved Robinson like everyone else in Happy Valley. And not Joe "Jay" Paterno, Jr. No, we're talking about Joe Paterno III, Jay's son. In the fall of 2005, Joey, then five years old, began following Penn State football with a passion. Eerily, it was the same age at which Jay had fallen in love with the Lions. And much like his dad had done for Cappelletti, Joey began drawing pictures of Robinson that were later given to the quarterback. He also began playing with a football game on the floor that has a felt field and little players to position.

In January 2006, after Jay, Joey, and family returned from Penn State's trip to Florida for the Orange Bowl against Florida State, Joey said to Jay, "Hey dad, is my skin dark?"

"What do you mean?" Jay asked.

"Well," Joey continued, "you know, do I have darker skin than [Joey's sister] Caroline?"

"Yeah, you guys got a tan in Florida," Jay told him.

"Will it get darker?" Joey asked.

"Yeah," Jay answered, "the longer you stay out in the sun, the darker it gets."

"Well I want brown skin like Michael," Joey said innocently. "I think that would be cool."

"I thought, 'What a neat thing,'" Jay says. "It made me feel good as a parent that he would think, 'Hey, that's cool.' I told Michael Robinson's mom about it and she started laughing. She goes, 'That is so cool!' . . . It's neat that when I was a kid it was Cappelletti, Cappelletti, Cappelletti. And for my son it was Michael this and Michael that. Just idolizing him. It's been such a neat thing for me to come full circle."

The way Jay treats his profession has also come full circle. He catches himself downplaying the significance of coaching compared to military personnel or doctors—just like Dad used to do. Jay applies that humility to his vision for the future as well. He wants to complete the circle and become head coach somewhere someday, but he isn't hung up on it, and he wouldn't jump at something and move his family just to say he was a head coach once.

"If it never happens for me, so what?" he says. "It doesn't keep me from impacting people, guys I coach, and helping them grow and learn. I don't spend a lot of time worrying about two years from now, five years from now. The minute you start to transcend what your next challenge is, you lose focus on that challenge.

"There's not a lot of time to daydream or chart some career course, because you never know. If Joe coached another five years and I was an assistant coach with him for five years, and a new guy got the job and got rid of us all, so be it. If that happens, I'll react to it. If it doesn't, I'll react to that. I love coaching. But I also love my family and their happiness."

Spoken like a true Penn Stater. A family man.

✳ ✳ ✳

In 1962, Suzanne Pohland graduated from Penn State with a bachelor's degree in arts and letters. In May of that year she married Joe Paterno, the dark-haired, longtime assistant football coach with a Brooklyn accent and a trip to law school on

The Paternos

Sue Paterno with Joe Paterno in 1972.

permanent hold. Then, later that same year, Sue received a call from J.T. White, a fellow Penn State assistant under Rip Engle. White, who had come from Michigan State in 1954, told Sue about his next-door neighbor's son, a kid who was having difficulties writing his English papers. White wondered if Sue would be willing to tutor the boy. Never one to turn down an opportunity to aid another, Sue agreed.

Word traveled quickly. White must have raved about Sue's teaching skills to someone on staff, because it wasn't long before another assistant called looking for help, this time to tutor a member of the football team. Sue, then pregnant with her first child, agreed once more. The requests kept coming.

"When they found out I could help somebody, the freshman coach started saying, 'Would you help so and so?'" Sue says. "We lived in an apartment then, so they would come to the apartment and I would work with them. Then when I started having two, three, four, five kids, I couldn't leave because Joe was not home a

Playing for JoePa

lot. So coaches would bring them out to the house, then I'd call and say, 'We're done. You can come pick them up.'"

Forty-five years later, Sue's still fielding the same calls. And what's most impressive isn't the number of Nittany Lions she's enlightened in five decades—she can't even muster a ballpark guess at the total—or the fact that she hasn't taken a break from it despite raising five kids of her own and becoming a community volunteer and philanthropist on a level equal to (if not greater than) Joe. It's the reasoning behind it all.

✳ ✳ ✳

We all have our war stories, and Sue has hers. She isn't trying to gripe. Her stories are simply examples of everyday life as she's lived it in the Penn State football program. There's one she likes to tell of an offensive lineman who played for Penn State in the 1990s. (Sue prefers not to mention names of specific players she's tutored.) He'd spent his childhood years in the Caribbean, and even after attending a Philadelphia-area high school, he arrived in Happy Valley with poor language skills. Specifically, he'd often leave endings off words, a product of his native dialect.

Sue, as is her routine, had the player start with free writing, meaning write whatever you want in any style with any conjugation or punctuation you want. When you're done, roll up the paper and toss it in the trash. She's not reading it. It's a solid technique, in part because it increases the comfort level between pupil and instructor. But in the offensive lineman's case, Sue not only had to engage her student. She had to erase years of misuse and poor habits, working to convert what was essentially pigeon English to mainstream English.

"Some nights," she says, "I'd leave him and I'd say, 'Oh God, I'm dying! I can't take much more of this!' Then some nights I'd go, 'He got it!' I would drive home thrilled, walk in the house, and couldn't fall asleep. So it has its ups and downs."

Count birthdays with the downs. There was a time when Sue was working with four different players in a semester, all in one-on-one sessions at different times during the week. She'd sometimes arrive at the team's study hall late in the morning for the first session and wouldn't wrap her final sit-down until quarter to five. "I'm thinking, 'Why go home?'" she says. "'Why don't I just stay here?'"

That semester, when she already had four students on her roster, she got a visit from a walk-on who had been recruited by Penn State's minority office. The student asked if she'd take him on as her fifth student.

"I can't add anymore," Sue told the player. "Why are you asking me?"

"Well, my teammate told me that you're really helping him," he said, "and I really need help."

"I have to go home and sleep on it," she said.

It wasn't a restless sleep. Sue wasted little time in getting back to the player to say yes, she would help him. The teen was not practicing with the team at the time, so they arranged a schedule that fit for both parties, and the sessions began. Soon enough, mid-February rolled around—Valentine's Day, or as Sue prefers to call it, her birthday. She and Joe had plans; at least, they planned on having plans, seeing as how it would be the first time in 15 years that Joe, usually tied up with the all-consuming recruiting world, would be home on her birthday.

Then the walk-on called. He needed help, and he needed it that night, on Sue's birthday. At first, Sue told the student it wasn't doable. Then her internal sense of citizenship and morality—that personal guilt trip—kicked in. She waffled. She wavered. She caved. The date with Joe would have to wait.

"Anyhow," Sue says, tying the tale into a blue and white bow, "[the student] bought me a birthday card. And I thought, really, this is more important than my birthday dinner. So when I got home we ordered pizza. Whatever. At least I didn't have to cook."

Want another one? How about the kid who used to show up five, then 10, then 15 minutes late to tutoring appointments with Sue. The sessions would be scheduled for just after the dinner hour. On one occasion, Joe got home from practice, Sue and Joe scarfed down dinner, Sue quickly rinsed the dishes and dumped them in the sink. ("Joe does not do dishes," she says with a hearty chuckle.) She gassed it over to the study hall, only to find the player was his usual late self.

"I'm over here waiting, thinking, 'I could have gotten the dishes done. I had 45 people coming for dinner Saturday night, where are you?'" Sue says. "When he showed up, everything he said was, 'Yes, ma'am, Yes, ma'am,' because he was from the South. I got really mad. I got so mad I went out in the hall, closed the door, and said, 'Yes ma'am my eye!'

"Well one of the coaches was walking by and it happened to be [the player's] position coach. He went in and reamed him, and he was never late again. But I found out why he'd been coming late. He was a big star at his small high school, and if he had a headache in the morning, he didn't go to school 'til 10, 10:30, whenever he felt like it. Now, did they help him? No. But we got him straightened out."

And therein lies one reason why Sue's so passionate about her role in the program: She genuinely cares about these kids. And not necessarily as football players. She tells new students she doesn't talk to Joe about what goes on in study hall, and conversely, she doesn't ask about what takes place in practice. She's even rebuffed assistant coaches in the past who have implored her to pay particularly close attention to a certain kid or to a specific recruit's mother. Her take? "Everyone we have up here is our guest. Everyone that we have, his parents think he's the best. I treat them all alike. So don't try to tell me whom to pay attention to."

Sue wants these kids, her kids, to graduate, because if that happens, she says, "We did what we were supposed to do." Sound like Joe? Actually, it's more than that. Sue isn't here to brag about Penn State football's graduation rates over the years versus the national average, proud of the numbers as she is. She's not here to police the kids who leave State College without a degree, though there are countless stories of her reaching out to ex-Lions to give them her "Why'd you waste all those years?" talk. Simply put, she does what she does to make an impact. She's sacrificed personal time and time with her husband and kids over the years to be with the other kids in her other family—the Penn State family.

"My feeling always was, listen, if we lose this kid, we're going to lose his kids," she says. "If they feel they can't compete in college, they're going to tell their kids not to go. So you want to break some patterns and have them succeed. And that's been very rewarding. Not financially—I've never been paid, though people think I have—but internally."

✳ ✳ ✳

There's a lot more to Sue Paterno's presence in the last 45 years of Penn State football than most fans might recognize. The tutoring is certainly part of it. Then there's playing host to mothers, fathers, potential donors, former players, recruits, siblings, and more on any given weekend. If she had a penny for every appetizer she's served up over the years to guests—some announced, some unannounced—in her home, she could cover THON's annual target donation goal by herself.

And let's not overlook raising five kids in the process. Even when daughters Diana and Mary Kathryn and sons David, Jay, and Scott were babies, she'd have guests in the house for this fundraiser or that reunion. As the kids grew, she taught them a signal. They were not to barrel into the room and scream "Mom!" when they needed something. Instead they learned to quietly pull her skirt or slacks to get her attention. "It was hard for the kids to go to bed," she says, "because their bedrooms were right off the living room where all the people were. But they all survived."

The one place Sue and Joe drew the line was with the media. When it came to reporters and photographers, the kids were off limits. That rule became particularly important in the mid-1970s, when Sue says she and her family began receiving periodic threats during a football season. It was always the same man—he threatened players, too—and it eventually prompted the FBI to get involved. Those years (she lists 1975, '76, and '77) were perhaps Sue's most difficult as the matriarch of Penn State football. She began walking her kids to the bus stop, even though it was only half a block away. She suffered what she calls "raging headaches" from the stress. The FBI put a tap on their home phone, so Sue told her kids only she could answer the phone. "It was not a fun time," she says, "but hey, we got through it."

In the tough times, she's been a rock. In the good times, she's been the one who takes recruits' mothers shopping and for coffee in downtown State College. She's also the one who humanizes Joe Paterno for those who have never met the couple.

"You have to put yourself in a family that has a kid being recruited," Jay says. "Fathers, sometimes they've seen Joe on television for 25, 30 years. They have this expectation that he's going to be a larger-than-life figure. But when they get around him, when my mom's around and they get to see the whole dynamic, it really puts everybody at ease. This is a guy like you and I. Here is a husband and wife who, through all the media attention and all the money they've made, they still live in the same modest house two or three blocks from campus that they've been in for 38 years. They're just regular people. That's the thing Mom brings to the table."

✳ ✳ ✳

Sue's résumé of giving back reads like a politician's election-day home stretch:

- The Latrobe, Pennsylvania, native has held numerous volunteer positions on behalf of the Penn State libraries, including a term as chair of the Libraries Development Advisory Board, as a founding member of the Liberal Arts Alumni Society, and as honorary chair of the Penn State Alumni Association's National Service Week.

The Paternos

- She's received the Lion's Paw medal, an honor reserved for those who have given the highest level of service to the University.

- She's served as honorary chair of the Centre County United Way.

- She's pitched in on Project AIDS.

- In 2004 she was given a Distinguished Alumni Award by Penn State for her service and commitment to the university.

- She's worked with Joe to allocate millions (yes, millions) to Penn State scholarships, fellowships, and high-profile university projects like the library addition that bears her last name.

- She's been a longtime member of the board of the Pennsylvania Special Olympics, recruiting Penn State student-athletes to serve as athlete escorts for the delegations that descend on State College every summer for the Special Olympics Summer Games held there.

All of those are just examples. There's a lot more goodwill here, more awards of recognition to tick off, too, but we'd run out of paper. Sue credits some of her generosity of time and spirit to lessons learned from her mother, Alma Heinz Pohland, who was a secretary of the board for the Red Cross. Granted, one could argue Sue's been able to take advantage of her exposure as Joe Paterno's wife to do good in State College and beyond. But in the end, the person Sue Paterno is has more to do with who she set out to be in life than anything handed to her or instilled in her by a relative or friend. It has a lot to do with her mentality that Penn State— the university, the football team, the fans, and the community—

is her family. It's an approachable warmth that can comfort the soul no matter who you are or your link to PSU.

"The most important thing in your life is to be happy," she says confidently, referring to advice she bestowed upon her own children, advice that is timeless for any child of Nittany Nation. "Joe's always been happy in his job. When he's happy, that makes things better for everybody. And I'm happy in my job. . . . I think it's not what you do, it's how you do it and if you're happy doing it. If you're not happy doing it, don't do it. I mean, I can't exactly say I was always thrilled washing diapers and doing dishes at 1:30 in the morning. But it's part of life.

"Basically, I was always happy about life, period. That has to come from self-fulfillment. And I don't mean on a 'me basis.' I mean if you think you're doing what's good for other people. We've always told our kids, 'You have to help others. God has given you brains, you have to help other people. No matter how you can. Doesn't have to be financially. You can do it in other ways. Serve somebody, go visit somebody who's sick. Do what needs to be done. And don't wait. If you see a need, go fill it.'

"And when you give, you do get some reward from that."

In that sense, Sue's a multimillionaire whose made the lives of countless people throughout the years all the more valuable.

twenty

THE HAMILTONS

AT FIRST BLUSH, HARRY HAMILTON'S defining moment as a Penn State football player does not sound like anything inspirational or life-altering. After all, how much impact can four words have? Thing is, to understand what Harry means, to really get it, you need to know Harry. You also need to know his brother, Lance, his father, Dr. Stan Hamilton, and the rest of the immediate Hamilton family, which to a degree includes Joe Paterno.

It began with 1981 spring football practice at Penn State. Harry was 18 years old. He'd played sparingly as a freshman in 1980, mostly on special teams. He met with Paterno just after the season to discuss his role with the team, specifically where he would be playing in the remaining three years of his eligibility. Harry remembers Paterno saying that he wasn't sure of the position, only that he would find a spot for him because the coaching staff was determined to get its best players on the field.

A cornerback in the fall of 1980, Harry started the ensuing spring practice at free safety. Then, 10 days into the three-week practice session, Harry was moved to the Hero position, a quasi-defensive back role—the name is unique to Penn State—whose responsibilities often have more to do with stuffing the run than covering pass routes. Harry was sent to practice with the linebackers rather than the defensive backs. His new position coach was Jerry Sandusky.

Harry quickly took to his new role. It suited his approach to the physical nature of his sport: "Football's a violent game," he says, "and if you aren't coming with a vengeance, go play tennis."

When late summer arrived and Penn State broke camp in preparation for the 1981 season, Harry was still at Hero, and he was beginning to thrive. One day in preseason practice, the linebackers, Harry included, were executing a nasty little activity called the "blood drill," where guys bang helmets and pads to refine their skill of taking on blockers. In the middle of that day's blood drill, Sandusky, who basically built, grew, and sustained "Linebacker U" at Penn State, called out to Harry.

"There's a technique involved when you take on blockers," Harry explains. "Jerry was correcting my technique." But before Sandusky could finish, he was interrupted by Paterno, who had been roaming the practice field and had stopped to watch the linebackers.

"Harry," Paterno hollered, "just make the tackle."

Silence.

Harry paused. Paterno turned and walked away. When the drill resumed, Harry put technique on hold for that moment and decided to just play on instinct. "Not everybody can do it," Harry says. "It's a savvy you have to see and know. But Coach Paterno had the confidence in me to know I could take on blockers when necessary—that in the end, I would make the play. 'Just make the tackle.'

"When Coach Paterno, a man of his stature, reinforces what you've believed all along, that doesn't just stay with you for three years. It stays with you throughout your playing days. Throughout life. It's not something that's lost on a person like me."

Something happened that hot August day on a practice field in Happy Valley. It was more than just a coach pressing a player's buttons to elicit optimum effort and production. And it had

The Hamiltons

nothing to do with Coach Sandusky, whom Harry respected as a coach and a person. It was Paterno proving he knew exactly who Harry Hamilton was. Paterno knew all about the kid's background: born in Queens, New York, raised in Wapwallopen, Pennsylvania, by a strong, independent father, the product of a fully white school system and community that never appreciated nor accepted the black Hamilton family living within its borders.

Paterno knew that Harry—and Harry's younger brother, Lance, who arrived at Penn State in 1982—was different. These were smart kids, probably the hardest working set of brothers Penn State will ever see. Their backgrounds were unique. Their relationships amongst one another were unique. Their goals were unique. Paterno wouldn't be able to get by treating Harry and Lance like regular scholarship student-athletes. No. To coach them, he needed to understand them completely, which meant fostering the continuity of care they had received as kids from their father, Stan. It meant Joe Paterno had to be more than a football coach for the Hamiltons.

He needed to teach them about life.

✳ ✳ ✳

Think you have interesting childhood stories? Talk to the Hamiltons. Stan Hamilton was born in Inwood, New York, an area of Long Island known as the Five Towns. He was the seventh of 10 children born to parents Harry and Rebecca—two boys and eight girls in all.

Stan's father, Harry Edwin Hamilton, after whom Stan's eldest son is named, was a brilliant man who spoke seven languages and could read and write Chinese. A U.S. immigrant from the Dutch West Indies, Stan's father felt a strong duty to help his fellow man, but some of his other views clashed with employers, and he often had trouble holding down jobs. Still, employed or unemployed, he would take people in off the streets and feed them, even though his own family was tight on space and money for groceries.

Playing for JoePa

Stan recalls sometimes waking up in the morning and basically tripping over sleeping men and women his father had taken in the previous night. "I was confused by it at first," Stan says, "but then when I got older, I saw how people would come to him and ask him to give them food or guidance. I think that's what impressed me the most. He always found time for them. That never left me as a kid."

Listening to Stan's path from high school on, it sounds as if he lived the lives of 10 different people. He was a good athlete at Lawrence High School; in fact, he's quick to point out that he once beat Manhasset High's Jim Brown in a high-jump competition during a prep track and field meet.

But athletics did not define Stan's young life. His parents needed him to work and earn money after he graduated high school, but they allowed him to take classes at Hofstra University, a funnel for many Five Towns kids. College and Stan, however, did not fit. "I was fast but I wasn't smart," he says. He was also scared to tell his parents when he flunked out of Hofstra, especially since he had no job and his dad had warned him to focus on something else in life other than sports. So Stan, just 17, joined the Army and became a paratrooper.

That too didn't take. He hurt himself, medically retired from the service, and returned to his family in Queens. He began bouncing from school to school, City College to Hunter to Columbia. No dice. He tried business. He entered the Civil Rights Movement, and to a certain degree, that consumed him (in many respects, it still does). However, of Martin Luther King Jr., whom Stan knew fairly well, Stan says, "He was a peace advocate, and I was not going to turn any cheeks. Brilliant man, I loved the guy, nice guy. I just couldn't go along with his philosophy of life."

Stan had writing talent, too. He landed a job with the Children's TV Workshop (CTW), writing into a script bank for shows like *Sesame Street*. Someone else would always take credit for the scripts when they got picked up, but Stan didn't care. It was a steady paycheck. (He says when he left CTW, it was because Bill Cosby fired him, though he laughs and says he doubts Cosby would ever admit to it.)

The Hamiltons

Along his journey, Stan married wife Betty and had four sons. The older two, Harry and Lance, are separated by only a year and 11 months; Damon and Glenn were born nearly a decade later and raised primarily by Betty.

Along his journey, Stan also began to practice the philosophies of his own father, at least when it came to making time for those people forgotten by society. Stan refers to them as the so-called misfits or derelicts or the uneducable—the people who fall through the cracks.

Along his journey, Stan began to teach Harry and Lance about what he finally decided to dedicate the rest of his life to doing. On Christmas Eve 1966, after a bank had foreclosed on the interracial Interfaith Hospital in Queens and negotiations with the bank had broken off to the point that police were summoned, Stan took Harry, then four, and Lance, two, and stood them in the hospital doorway, daring cops to go through them. The police captain eventually backed down, and the hospital was given an extension to come up with the necessary funding.

"All I remember was trying to be brave like my dad," Harry says. "I was a little child standing there looking at police cars and everything, but I did have a sense of empowerment. Even though there was fear, there was also a feeling of strength. I am here, my dad put me here, and nobody's coming in. Not the police, not anybody."

There are other anecdotes that mirror this same theme, like a trip south to join impoverished people marching on Washington, D.C. Or Stan teaching his sons the phrase "by the bullet" so that they might better understand his death if there ever was a successful assassination attempt on Stan's life. Or the tale of Lance and Harry deciding to sell Nikki, one of their pet dogs, to save money on dog food so that they could send that money to Mississippi to feed hungry residents there.

Yet nothing embodies Stan's mission to raise strong black men better than the hospital story. Ironically, that same incident represents much of what Betty, Stan's wife, did not want for her family. And in 1969, after discussing it with Stan, Betty took

Playing for JoePa

Harry and Lance and left New York to live with her parents in Wilkes-Barre, Pennsylvania. Stan eventually came out to Pennsylvania for what he thought would be a visit of three or four weeks. He's been living in northeast Pennsylvania now for more than 30 years.

※ ※ ※

Lance and Harry might prefer that we skip right to their playing days at Penn State, for fear that their story be clouded by the trying circumstances of their youth. But actually, it's what happened before they arrived in State College that makes you appreciate even more the relationship their family forged with Paterno when they did arrive.

Both Harry and Lance acknowledge now that their parents' marriage had begun to deteriorate long before Betty moved them to Pennsylvania. It didn't make things any easier for the brothers then. Lance has referred to the period in which his parents were going through their divorce as "the nightmare months." An already difficult situation was made more intense by the fact that both Harry and Lance had already begun migrating toward the strong, positive role model set by their father. Stan had taught them to "see the world for what it is," Harry says. And though he acknowledges it surely broke Betty's heart then—and perhaps still today to hear about it—Harry says he and Lance eventually ran away to live with Stan.

If there's any silver lining to the divorce proceedings, in which Betty capitulated and Stan prevailed in gaining custody of Harry and Lance, it's that it brought the two brothers closer together. "There developed such a bond during that time, that it made us almost inseparable," Harry says. "Because we were going through something very traumatic. We were old enough to know what was going on in and out of the courts system. And we had each other."

That unity became important in each brother's development as adults and as athletes. It was crucial especially after the three Hamilton men left Wilkes-Barre in 1972, abandoning most of

The Hamiltons

their possessions and fleeing to higher ground when tropical storm Agnes blew through the Northeast and flooded the city. They later moved to a farm owned by Betty's father, Stan's ex-father-in-law, with whom Stan remained close for years after the divorce. The farm was on 150 acres in Wapwallopen, a world away from Queens.

"We were learning how to bale hay, how to stack hay on trucks, how to muck stalls, and take care of horses," Lance says. "There was a lot of snow and nice weather up there, so we did a lot of sleigh riding, a lot of little skis on your feet, just skiing and having fun. When we had a snow day, it was a chance to go have a lot of fun. I remember we would go out in the morning, play through lunch and come back for dinner. And you stayed in great shape, because when you go down a hill that's almost a quarter-mile long, you gotta walk back up that thing to sleigh ride again."

The Hamiltons took care of 42 horses on the farm, and both Lance and Harry became accomplished riders, bagging trophies and ribbons at regional equestrian events. They jokingly called themselves the "Black Cowboys." Reflecting on that time, both brothers say the farm life wasn't exactly easy. On top of chores, they were so isolated in Wapwallopen that commuting to school sometimes required three separate bus rides and some long waits in the cold. The house itself was small for the three of them, and grew even smaller when Darren Hamilton—Harry and Lance's second cousin, who had run into some trouble in his native Bronx, New York—moved in.

Harry recalls splitting a closet with Darren and Stan that was located in an unheated anteroom. The closet might as well have been outside. In the winter, he'd put a coat on to pick out his clothes. The guys wore coats into the unheated bathroom, too.

"I look back and I don't remember being deprived of anything," Lance says. "I look at some old pictures and I see the back of the farmhouse, and the different types of metals and woods holding the back of the house together because of the way the wind came from the back of the house. It does look like a

Playing for JoePa

dilapidated shack. But, nevertheless, on the inside there was a lot of love, a lot of warmth and respect."

On the outside, though, there was very little love in that area of Pennsylvania. When Harry began attending Nanticoke Area High School in 1976, he was the only black student in the school. In fact, many area residents had never seen a black man before— not in that area, but in their lives. All three Hamiltons heard more than their share of racial slurs spewed in their direction. Stan says a cross was burned on farm property. Family dinners would be interrupted by the firecracker-loud bang of glass bottles being hurled against the house.

There's more. In much the same way Lance heard, "Look, there goes the new nigger" at a Nanticoke school, locals took to calling the farm in Wapwallopen "Nigger Hill." When Lance joined Harry at Nanticoke High School in 1979, he had "Go back to Africa" and other racial slurs written inside his locker after someone had kicked off the lock. Harry said his likeness was once hung in effigy at a school pep rally. (Harry adds that there were a select few students and coaches who were not racists, but they were outnumbered by the nameless and faceless who refused to accept the Hamiltons.)

Here's where it gets truly amazing. The Hamiltons didn't run. Matter of fact, both Lance and Harry became standout prep athletes. Harry, for one, switched to quarterback of the Nanticoke High football team, his reason being that if he took the direct snap, no one could keep the football out of his hands because of color. Lance, having heard his father preach about taking time to remember those less fortunate, began counseling kids of alcoholic or abusive parents, some of whom were his own age. Even informally he would talk to people if they needed guidance or just a nonjudgmental ear, something he does to this day.

"My father said there are a lot of small-minded, ignorant people out there," Lance says. "He'd tell us, 'Of course defend yourself, protect yourself, but by the same token, there are a lot of people out there still in need. So you'll go and help them.'"

The Hamiltons

Long before reaching Wapwallopen, Stan had started an outreach program called Hands of Hope ministries. In the late 1970s, the Hamiltons—Stan, Harry, Lance, Darren, and others who essentially grew up with the family—continued working to help people in the same community that hardly tolerated them. Through Hands of Hope, they collected food for the hungry and gifts for kids who would otherwise go without at Christmastime. Stan would take his kids out on cold nights to deliver blankets to homeless people sleeping under bridges or in abandoned railroad cars, homeless people most of the greater Wilkes-Barre region thought didn't exist in their towns.

"You had an appreciation for those who were not as fortunate as you," Harry says, "because you had a roof over your head and blankets to put on in a warm house—even if parts of it were cold."

* * *

Joe Paterno made two trips to Wapwallopen to recruit Harry Hamilton. And as the story goes, when he made his first trip east from State College, he didn't know Harry was black until he actually met the Hamiltons. Paterno first came out in 1979 with assistant coach Jim Williams in tow. The Hamiltons met them just off Route 81 to make sure the coaches wouldn't get lost on the drive to Wapwallopen.

"I'd heard of Joe Paterno," Stan says, "but I'd never met him. As a matter of fact, I didn't like the way he wore his socks on the football field. But I'd heard about him and I'd heard about Penn State. I heard it was very racist out there in Happy Valley. But Joe kind of made the difference. He set himself apart."

After pleasantries were exchanged that day, Stan got down to business. If Harry chose Penn State, Stan began, and he ever got hurt to the point where he could no longer play football, would he remain on scholarship?

"Yes," Paterno replied.

Check.

Playing for JoePa

Okay, then if Harry chose Penn State and he ever had a change of heart and decided football was no longer for him, would he remain on scholarship for four years?

"Yes," Paterno replied.

Check.

Stan, who had always seen football as more of a means to an end than as a profession, was intrigued. The men talked about the importance of education, Paterno at one point turning to Williams to have the assistant read off the current graduation rate for Penn State football players (it was around 90 percent). Stan asked about an opportunity for Lance to someday play at Penn State too, should Lance continue to excel on the football field and in the classroom.

"Yes," Paterno said, Lance would receive consideration for a scholarship as well when the time came.

Check.

Then, toward the end of the visit, Stan and Joe stood in the farmhouse kitchen, eyeball to eyeball, and they shook hands. Nothing was signed or decided that day, but from where we now sit nearly 30 years later, everything was decided that day. The relationship between Stan and Joe, struck with a handshake in Wapwallopen, set the stage for everything else. Says Stan quite succinctly, "It was a beautiful day for all of us."

Harry still had to actually settle on Penn State. And he had options. He'd run for more than 1,000 yards as a high school senior, and it earned him invites to places like Virginia and Florida State, where he sat one-on-one with Bobby Bowden. He visited West Point and even thought about San Diego State, in part because of its track and field program. (Harry, like Stan, excelled in the jumps, as he competed in the long, triple, and high jump at Nanticoke High, where some of his records still stand.)

Harry used his official visits to see some of the country, but when it came down to it, no one did a better sales job—both of his school and of himself—than Joe Paterno. So much so, in fact, that race and racism and the dearth of black athletes in State College never really became a factor in Harry eventually picking

The Hamiltons

Harry Hamilton.

Penn State. Instead, Joe promised the Hamiltons that Harry would get his education, promised that his best players would play, and promised that he was committed to Harry whether Harry was healthy enough or committed enough to play four years of ball at Penn State. And Penn State was close, just two and a half hours west of Wapwallopen. That would allow Stan to get to home games.

It also meant the relationship between the Hamiltons and Paternos could thrive. See, by the time Joe and Sue Paterno invited recruits' parents to come to their house in 1979, Stan Hamilton had already heard everything he needed to hear from Joe. Their handshake, that eyeball-to-eyeball session, that was his deal-sealer. So when Stan arrived at the Paternos' place on McKee Street in State College for parents' night, he passed on most of the hobnobbing in the living room and instead wound up playing games with Joe's youngest sons, Jay and Scott. From that trip forward, when Stan—Jay and Scott took to calling him Uncle Stan, a nickname that sticks today—would come to town, he'd find time to hang with the Paterno kids, starting water gun fights or building tents or playing arcade games.

"Jay and Scotty and I, we'd have a ball," Stan says. "We'd go play pinball and Pac-Man. That was the rage at that time. . . . The relationship has been a very, very good one with the Paterno family and myself."

✳ ✳ ✳

While Harry was playing football at Penn State and witnessing the "Just make the tackle" side of Joe Paterno, Lance was back in the Wilkes-Barre area without his older brother to lean on for immediate support. He had first planned to stay at Nanticoke High, where he'd emerged as a football talent, starting in the secondary as a sophomore. Sure, he'd seen the rage and jealousy come to life as locals learned that Penn State was recruiting Harry. He'd heard the slurs, seen the ugliness. Yet part of him figured he could handle that treatment from the overall Nanticoke student body, so long as he had a tighter community of student-athletes around him who checked their hate at the door.

That all changed when he had his football locker smashed in by a 45-pound plate. That locker room was for teammates only. Someone he thought he trusted had violated the circle of athletes. The animosity was getting too close, and it simply wasn't safe for Lance at Nanticoke anymore.

It may never have been safe; after all, when Harry was still there and would stay home sick for a day, Lance would often call out sick, too, so as not to have to go it alone in the halls. It made

Lance Hamilton.

sense that Lance would transfer to Meyers High in Wilkes-Barre for his junior and senior years of high school. When his son transferred, Stan moved out of the farmhouse in Wapwallopen back to Wilkes-Barre to be closer to Lance's new school. The Wilkes-Barre community didn't exactly embrace Stan: He recalls opening his front door to dead cats hanging on his porch, and, in 1991, someone set fire to his house. But if there was a plus, it was that Stan was at least back in more of his element in the city, an activist who could put his Hands of Hope ministries into action with some help from media outlets and supporters who would listen.

"I was not going to be intimidated, and I was not going to be run out of town," says Stan, who remains in the area today. "I'm still raising the same kind of hell. I'm still championing the cause of the underdog."

He also remains a close friend of Joe Paterno's, and there are many reasons for that. First, to back up, the 1980s might as well have been called the Decade of the Hamiltons at Penn State. Harry, all 5-foot-11, 188 pounds of him, became a tackling machine from his Hero position, at which he began earning starts in 1981 and remained the starter in 1982 and '83, when he led the team in tackles and made third-team All-America. He had 10 tackles as part of Jerry Sandusky's swarming defensive unit that held down Georgia running back Herschel Walker in Penn State's national championship win to cap the '82 season. After that game, Paterno said Harry had been the best defensive player on the field that day, a quote Harry says later boosted his draft stock.

Also in New Orleans for that Sugar Bowl victory were Lance and Darren. Lance played on special teams in the game while Darren was there but didn't get to see action. Lance and Darren remained in Happy Valley as undergrads through 1985, Lance fondly recalling the joy he felt getting to start alongside Harry, his big brother, in the 1983 Aloha Bowl. That game marked their first start together since high school and, it being Harry's last game as a Nittany Lion, their last.

"It was as if we had come full circle in our athletic careers up to that point, from starting mini-football games together in the Wapwallopen area to starting that bowl game together in Hawaii," says Lance, a cornerback at Penn State. "By then, Harry had passed along Joe's 'Just make the tackle' philosophy, and it was finally working for me, too."

It certainly worked for him two seasons later, when Lance delivered a punishing hit on Maryland running back Alvin Blount, which caused a fumble that Penn State recovered to squelch what looked like a sure game-winning drive deep in PSU territory. The Nittany Lions held on, 20-18, against the No. 1-ranked Terps.

The family legacy didn't stop there. Dan Skrip, who had lived with the Hamiltons on their farm and was a sort of quasi-brother

The Hamiltons

to Lance and Harry, was another Nanticoke Area grad who played for Paterno, lettering one year in 1991. Stan's nephew, Neil Hamilton, also joined the Penn State program, though he didn't letter until 1988. More than a decade later Stan even sent his youngest child, daughter Sheila, to Penn State.

Of course, if you think the Hamilton-Paterno relationship has survived through the years because of football, you'd be wrong. It started with consistency of messages. As Lance and Harry witnessed as undergrads, Joe Paterno and Stan Hamilton were becoming nearly interchangeable, their values and teachings were so similar. In particular, both men preached education first, and Harry and Lance benefited from such emphasis, each earning first-team Academic All-America status twice. In fact, Harry and Lance are two of only five players in the history of Penn State football to earn Academic All-America honors two times. (John Runnells, Jeff Hartings, and Paul Posluszny are the others.)

In the past 28 years, Joe Paterno has also become one of the biggest personal supporters of Stan's efforts to aid those in need. When Paterno's mug was put on special-edition regional Wheaties cereal boxes in 2003, he picked Hamilton's Hands of Hope ministries as the charity to appear on the side of every box. Unprompted, Paterno has sent additional dollars and food to back Stan's efforts. When Stan has asked for favors, like the times he's called on Paterno to make speaking appearances in northeast Pennsylvania, Joe's come through. Paterno created an endowed scholarship in Stan's name that exists to this day at the PSU satellite campus in Wilkes-Barre. Even Scott and Jay Paterno have gotten in on it, occasionally dropping off food donations with Stan.

"There's more to life than sports and football, and you must weave them into making the world a better place for all of us," Stan says. "I think that's what Joe Paterno has attempted to do by still being my largest donor.

"See, there's another side to Joe Paterno. Every night he's feeding hungry children. Every day he's feeding displaced families and battered women through his efforts with me. He's made an impression on [my kids] and had an impact on their lives. You talk about Joe Paterno winning games, becoming the winningest coach. I think that's unfair and unfortunate. Will the real Joe Paterno please stand up?"

Harry and Lance have seen the real Joe Paterno. And time and time again, he's reminded them an awful lot of their father. Harry talks about the time he was getting set to leave Penn State and follow a lifelong dream of becoming a pro football player. Paterno didn't tell him not to pursue that goal, but he did try to convince him to use his smarts for professional pursuits off the field, too. Even earlier in his career at Penn State, whenever Harry would leave practice with a headache or feel the aches and pains of game day Saturdays, Paterno would jump in, applaud Harry's academic acumen, and say, "Go do something else."

"He placed the dream into perspective, that it's not the end all be all, that you have so much more going for you, and your greatest impact will be beyond the football field," Harry says.

On the lighter side, Lance talks about the time during his freshman year when he jokingly brushed a part in his hair that made it look like he'd shaved a deeper part into his hair—except he forgot to brush it out before going to practice. Lance says that when he got to the field, Paterno stopped him and said, "Whoa, you changed your hair?"

Lance tried to play it off.

"Does your dad know?" Paterno asked.

"Coach," Lance responded, "it's not real, it's fake."

"I was about to say, because that doesn't look like you," Paterno said.

"My dad would have said the same thing," says Lance, now 42, laughing at the memory. "We basically went from being raised under Stan to being raised under Joe, because there wasn't a big gap as far as the things that were expected of you. He cared about us as people, and I think that parental father image carried over, because it was more than just football. It was you and your total development as a person."

That helps explain why Joe always treated the Hamilton kids like adults. It's why when Harry asked that the team's training table menu

The Hamiltons

be amended to include foods he and other black players had grown up eating, Joe happily obliged, opening the door to greens, yams, pigs feet, and more to stream from the Penn State cafeteria kitchen. It's why when Harry went to Paterno about donning green wristbands as tribute to the well-known Atlanta child murders case, Paterno not only okayed it, he wore one himself. It's why Paterno called Harry on NFL Draft day in 1984 to see how he was holding up when his name wasn't called in the early rounds. (The Jets eventually took Harry in the seventh round, and he went on to play four years in New York and four more in Tampa Bay, retiring after the 1992 season.) It's why when Lance was cut by the New York Giants as a rookie in 1986 and told he might have a future in coaching with the Giants if he gained some experience, Paterno called then Giants coach Bill Parcells to confirm that Parcells wasn't just throwing Lance a compliment because he didn't know how else to cut him. It's also why, after Parcells confirmed that Lance had the makeup of a coach, Paterno offered Lance an opportunity to gain experience by working with Penn State's defensive backs.

The scenario ultimately led to Lance suing the Giants, league commissioner Pete Rozelle, and the other 27 NFL teams at the time. The suit claimed breach of contract and racial discrimination as the reason the Giants wouldn't hire him after his apprenticeship at Penn State. The Giants said age and experience were the reasons they would not hire Lance. That reasoning didn't fly with Lance then, and it doesn't fly now, especially when Lance thinks about the example of Mike Shula, son of legendary Miami Dolphins coach Don, who was cut by the Tampa Bay Bucs in 1987 and landed an assistant coaching gig with the Bucs before the 1988 season, despite lacking the same experience the Giants had cited in not hiring Lance. Moreover, Lance proudly points to the coincidence that the league began to see an influx of black coaches around the same time his case went to trial.

"This is what I call continuity of care," explains Stan, now 72, who still talks to Joe, who's 80, on a regular basis about everything from their health to their grandkids. "You care for my sons, you care for my family, I will care for you and I will care for yours.

Playing for JoePa

And we will care for each other as human beings until you cease to be and I cease to be, and hope to God that we bequeath to our heirs that attitude to continue caring for each other."

And, in case you missed it, everything that exists between the Paternos and Hamiltons now and then—the donations, the Wheaties box, the Stan Hamilton Scholarship, the memories—has nothing, zero, to do with football.

"That's Joe," Stan says, "and that's what we've gotten, and that's what we're giving, and that's what we're trying to pay back."

And that's why despite everything Lance and Harry have going today in their busy lives—their own kids and friends; their own careers (Harry is a lawyer and Lance a law professor); their fist-tight relationships with one another and with Stan; their own charitable programs—there will always be time to work at being part of Joe Paterno's team.

Says Harry, now 44: "If you ask Coach what his best team is, it would be that group of athletes who played and have gone on to make an indelible impact in or contribute to their communities for the betterment of people. His best team is not defined by tackles, interceptions, touchdowns, or passing efficiency. He defines his best team in a way that lends itself to the core values instilled in me by my dad long before I got to Penn State. And in a very unique way, the continuity of care that must concern every parent including my dad remained intact during that critical pathway from childhood to adulthood. In my mind, that is the greatest compliment to Coach Paterno. That is why I am still hitting life's practice field, I am still honing my efforts, I am still doing what I can to make a positive impact and passing along those values to my children and the people I touch. So that when life's whistle blows, I am on Coach Paterno's best team."

Funny. All Joe ever asked in return was that Harry just make the tackle.

PHOTO CREDITS

INDEX

Index

Playing for JoePa

Index

Index

Celebrate the Heroes of Pennsylvania Sports in These Other Releases from Sports Publishing!

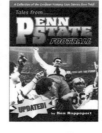
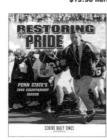